SOCIAL JUSTICE AND PUBLIC POLICY

Seeking fairness in diverse societies

Edited by Gary Craig, Tania Burchardt and
David Gordon

D0557950

This edition published in Great Britain in 2008 by

The Policy Press
University of Bristol
Fourth Floor
Beacon House
Queen's Road
Bristol BS8 1QU
UK

Tel +44 (0)117 331 4054
Fax +44 (0)117 331 4093
e-mail tpp-info@bristol.ac.uk
www.policypress.org.uk

British Library Cataloguing in Publication Data
A catalogue record for this book is available from the British Library.

Library of Congress Cataloging-in-Publication Data
A catalog record for this book has been requested.

ISBN 978 1 86134 933 0 paperback
ISBN 978 1 86134 934 7 hardcover

Cover design by Robin Hawes.
Front cover: image kindly supplied by www.reportdigital.co.uk
Printed and bound in Great Britain by Hobbs the Printers, Southampton.

In memory of Robina Goodlad
and Iris Marion Young

Contents

List of tables, figures and boxes

Tables

Figures

Boxes

Acknowledgements

This book is dedicated to the memories of Robina Goodlad of Glasgow and Iris Marion Young of Chicago. The idea for the book emerged from a seminar series, funded by the Economic and Social Research Council, for which Robina was the early inspiration and organising force. Sadly, she died at a tragically early age before the seminar series was completed. Iris, a leading US social justice scholar and activist, agreed to allow us to include her chapter in a shortened form but died, again at an unexpectedly early age, before the book was completed.

We would also like to thank Anna Tamas who meticulously undertook much of the very detailed and careful work of preparing the disparate texts for publication; and contributors to and participants at the seminar series, many of whose ideas are reflected in the contents of this book. In this sense, as readers might expect, the book has been a truly collaborative project.

Notes on contributors

Maria Adebowale is the Founder-Director of Capacity Global, the only non-governmental organisation and social enterprise in the UK focusing specifically on environmental justice. She is the co-founder of the UK Environmental Justice Network and also the author of the Third Sector Climate Change Declaration. She has a Masters in Public International Law (human rights and environmental law) and has written a number of publications on environmental justice, social inclusion and regeneration.

Christopher Bertram is Professor of Social and Political Philosophy at the University of Bristol, UK. He is the author of *Rousseau and the social contract* (Routledge, 2004) and numerous papers on political philosophy and the history of political thought.

Harry Brighouse is Professor of Philosophy and Affiliate Professor of Educational Policy Studies at the University of Wisconsin, Madison, USA. He is author of *On education* (Routledge, 2006) and is currently working with Adam Swift on a book about the place of the family in egalitarian liberal theory.

Tania Burchardt is Senior Research Fellow at the Centre for Analysis of Social Exclusion, London School of Economics and Political Science, UK. Her research interests include theories of social justice, definitions and measurement of inequality and social exclusion, and welfare and employment policy. She is Editor of *Benefits: The Journal of Poverty and Social Justice*.

Gary Craig is Professor of Social Justice and Associate Director of the Wilberforce Institute for the study of Slavery and Emancipation at the University of Hull, UK. His research focuses on 'race' and ethnicity, including modern slavery, community development, poverty and deprivation, children and young people and local governance.

David Gordon is Director of the Townsend Centre for International Poverty Research and Professor of Social Justice in the School for Policy Studies at the University of Bristol, UK. He is currently working with UNICEF (United Nations Children's Fund) on their first ever *Global study of child poverty and disparities*.

Will Kymlicka is the Canada Research Chair in Political Philosophy at Queen's University in Kingston, Canada. He works on issues of the accommodation of minority ethnic groups within the theory and practice of liberal democracies. His most recent book is *Multicultural odysseys* (Oxford University Press, 2007).

Ruth Lister is Professor of Social Policy at Loughborough University. She is a former Director of the Child Poverty Action Group. She has served on various Commissions, including the Commission on Social Justice. Her main research areas are citizenship, poverty and gender. Her publications include *Citizenship: Feminist perspectives* (2nd edition, Palgrave, 2003), *Poverty* (Polity Press, 2004) and (with others) *Gendering citizenship in Western Europe* (The Policy Press, 2007).

David Piachaud is Professor of Social Policy at the London School of Economics and Political Science and an Associate of the Centre for Analysis of Social Exclusion, London School of Economics and Political Science, UK. He was Social Policy Adviser in the Prime Minister's Policy Unit (1974-79) and has been Consultant to the European Commission, the International Labour Organisation (ILO), the Organisation for Economic Co-operation and Development (OECD) and the World Health Organization (WHO). He has written books and papers on children, poverty, social security, social exclusion and social policy.

Katie Schmuecker is a Research Fellow at ippr north, the Newcastle office of the Institute of Public Policy Research, UK. She specialises in devolution and public policy, governance and regional development. She has published work on the UK devolution settlement and policy divergence and convergence since devolution, co-editing the publication *Devolution in practice 2006: Public policy differences within the UK* (IPPR, 2005) as well as co-authoring two chapters. Other recent publications include 'The end of the Union?' (with Guy Lodge) in *Public policy research* (IPPR, 2007). Before joining ippr north she worked for the campaign for regional government in the North East of England.

Adam Swift is Fellow in Politics and Sociology at Balliol College and Director of the Centre for the Study of Social Justice at the University of Oxford, UK. He is co-author of *Liberals and communitarians* (2nd edition, Blackwell, 1996) and *Against the odds? Social class and social justice in industrial societies* (Oxford University Press, 1997) and author of *How* *not to be a hypocrite: School choice for the morally perplexed parent* (Routledge, 2003) and *Political philosophy: A beginner's guide for students and politicians* (2nd edition, Polity Press, 2006). He is currently working, with Harry Brighouse, to develop a liberal egalitarian theory of the family.

Jonathan Wolff is Professor of Philosophy at University College London, UK. His books include *An introduction to political philosophy* (Oxford University Press, 1996), *Why read Marx today?* (Oxford University Press, 2002) and, with Avner de-Shalit, *Disadvantage* (Oxford University Press, 2007). His current work concentrates on the relation between political philosophy and public policy. He was a member of the Gambling Review Body, the Nuffield Council Working Party on the Ethics of Research Involving Animals, and the Academy of Medical Sciences Working Group on Brain Science and Addiction.

Sadly, **Iris Marion Young** died as this book was in preparation. She was Professor of Political Philosophy at the University of Chicago, USA, and had previously taught at Pittsburgh, Worcester and Miami. Her most influential book was *Justice and the politics of difference* (Princeton University Press, 1990) and her work has been translated into more than 20 languages. She was a committed political activist around issues such as women's rights, debt relief for Africa and workers' rights.

Introduction

Tania Burchardt and Gary Craig

Social justice rhetoric

Everybody is in favour of social justice, almost by definition. But what they mean by social justice, the priority they accord to it relative to other objectives, and the public policies they believe follow from it, vary widely. In the UK in 2007, for example, the recommendations of the right-wing Conservative Party's Social Justice Policy Group, chaired by ex-leader Iain Duncan-Smith, while attempting to distance itself from laissez-faire approaches, nevertheless focused on reinforcing the 'welfare society' rather than the welfare state.[1] Tackling 'an underclass, where life is characterised by dependency, addiction, debt and family breakdown' (SJPG, 2007, p 5), was to be achieved largely by means of charitable and family help, including support specifically for the institution of marriage, because, 'Government action [...] can often exacerbate existing problems or create new ones' (p 4). The approach was described as based on the belief that 'people must take responsibility for their own choices but that government has a responsibility to help people make the right choices' (p 7). Just over a decade previously, the Labour Party's Commission on Social Justice (CSJ), instigated by its then-leader John Smith, came to radically different conclusions (CSJ, 1994). For that Commission, social justice meant the:

- equal worth of all citizens;
- equal right to be able to meet basic needs;
- need to spread opportunities and life chances as widely as possible; and
- requirement to reduce and where possible eliminate unjustified inequalities.

A number of key differences are apparent. The CSJ approach is based on rights, rather than charity, on society as whole, rather than on an underclass, and the recommendations identify government action as central to tackling structural inequalities. Of the several options examined by the Commission, its preferred approach was described as 'Investor's Britain'.

In office, (New) Labour's approach has been somewhat different from that propounded by the CSJ. Although some elements of Investor's Britain have been apparent, for example in the emphasis given to education, other policy initiatives appear to have been based on quite different conceptions of social justice. The Social Exclusion Unit, established almost immediately by Tony Blair on election in 1997, initially tackled street homelessness, teenage pregnancy and pupils excluded from school – rather closer to the Conservative's notion of an underclass than to the CSJ's emphasis on the equal right of all to meet their basic needs. Social policies more generally have extended beyond these groups in extreme circumstances, including tax and benefit reforms to 'end child poverty within a generation', and welfare-to-work programmes not just for the unemployed as conventionally defined, but also for lone parents and disabled people. However, these policies remain focused on 'the poor', rather than the Commission's aspiration of eliminating unjustified inequality. Labour has not fundamentally tackled inequality: neither the stretching of the upper half of the income distribution, nor the runaway accumulation of wealth at the very top (Hills and Stewart, 2005). Moreover, New Labour policies reflect a somewhat narrow interpretation of 'opportunities and life chances' – reduced in the main to the chance to engage in paid employment. This is summed up in the Department for Work and Pensions' statement of principles of welfare reform: 'The Government is committed to achieving a fairer, more inclusive society where nobody is held back by disadvantage or lack of opportunity. To achieve this, we are tackling child poverty and extending employment opportunity to all' (DWP, 2007). Neither the quality of employment, nor aspects of inclusion other than being part of the process of production, are considered.

Conservative, Liberal (the main UK centrist party), traditional Labour and New Labour 'third way' approaches are all advocated in the name of social justice. Internationally, too, the rhetoric of social justice and tempering the pursuit of economic growth with concern for the less fortunate has gained ground. The Millennium Declaration of the United Nations affirmed: 'we have a collective responsibility to uphold the principles of human dignity, equality and equity at the global level. [...] We are determined to establish a just and lasting peace all over the world' (United Nations General Assembly, 2000, paras I.2 and I.4). Even the World Trade Organization, not generally associated with a social justice agenda, explains that it promotes free trade, '*because* this is important for economic development and well-being' (WTO,

2007; emphasis added), and asserts that one of its principles is to make the trading system 'more beneficial for less developed countries'.

When governments and organisations implementing such a diverse range of actual policies, including some that manifestly fail to advance social justice according to any reasonable criteria, all nevertheless claim to be promoting 'social justice' (or, in some cases, the benefit of the least well-off), there is an urgent need to be more explicit in political debate, nationally and internationally, about the different conceptions of social justice being employed, to identify the tensions between them, and provide a sharper analysis of the demands of justice, however conceived.

The principal aim of this book, then, is to promote engagement between theories of social justice and real-world policy problems. Political philosophers tend to start with coherent and sophisticated theories and — occasionally — consider their application to practical problems, although often these applications are limited by unrealistic assumptions about the state of the world. On the other hand, social policy commentators tend to start with in-depth understanding of social problems, but rarely relate their analysis and recommendations to specific theories of justice. This lack of effective cross-disciplinary connection allows the claims of politicians of all colours and stripes to be champions of social justice to go unchallenged, and the quality of public debate suffers as a result.

Many of the contributors to this volume participated in an Economic and Social Research Council (ESRC) seminar series on social justice and public policy.[2] Early meetings in the series were characterised by mutual incomprehension between the different disciplines (economics, social policy, philosophy) and representatives of the different interests (academics, policy makers and practitioners), prompting baffled questions ('But what does that mean in the real world?', 'Why should it matter what *the public* think?'), and not infrequently a degree of amusement about the naive assumptions, with respect to theory or practice, that others were apparently making. However, considerable progress had been made by the time of the final conference, which included, for example, analyses of the pressing problem of the appropriate role for 'family values' in contemporary society by a political philosopher (see Chapter Seven), of new inequalities drawing on theories of human rights (Phillips, 2006) and of intergenerational justice (Willetts, 2006) by practitioners and policy makers (see special issue of *Benefits: The Journal of Poverty and Social Justice*, 2006, vol 15, no 2). Our intention is that this book continues the process of mutual education that began with the seminar series, and to share our new understandings with a wider audience.

Theories of social justice

John Rawls' *A theory of justice*, published in 1971, has defined academic debates about social justice ever since. Rawls argued that justice meant 'the way in which the major social institutions distribute fundamental rights and duties and determine the division of advantages from social co-operation' (1971, p 6). A 'well-ordered society' was one in which 'everyone is presumed to act justly' (p 8), where vested interests are put aside. Specifically, Rawls derived a number of principles of justice: first, each person is entitled to the most extensive set of basic liberties compatible with the same liberty for all; second, any positions of public responsibility or private advantage should be open to all on the basis of fair (not merely formal) equality of opportunity; and third, any inequality in the distribution of 'primary goods' is permissible only in so far as it is to the advantage of the worst-off group in society. Primary goods include income, wealth and the social bases of self-respect, among other things – a set of resources that everyone can be presumed to need, whatever their individual conception of the good life. Rawls accorded the first principle priority over the second, and the second over the third.

The third principle, often referred to as the 'difference principle', is potentially a strong requirement. Those who wish to justify a deviation from total equality in key social and economic outcomes must demonstrate that such an arrangement will be of benefit to the least well-off in society. One such justification might be that unless socially necessary occupations that require long periods of training – such as doctors and lawyers – are rewarded with higher salaries, these roles would not be filled and the worst-off (along with others) would suffer. This is relatively uncontroversial – even though in practice the same logic is not applied to other equally socially necessary occupations that involve exposure to significant risks such as firefighters and miners – but other potential justifications for inequalities are more debatable. For example, some have sought to argue that the six- and seven-figure salaries currently enjoyed by top executives benefit the least well-off in society through a 'trickle-down' effect (Brummer, 2006), even though this theory of economic development (supported by, among others, Margaret Thatcher), has now been thoroughly discredited. Thus, the strength of the difference principle depends on the range of justifications for inequality that are admitted, and their admissibility according to Rawls' criteria in turn depends on questions that can be resolved only empirically. This interdependence of theory and application is one of the themes that runs through this book.

The reach of the difference principle may also be limited by its position as the last in Rawls' order of priority. For example, an early and influential critic of Rawls, Robert Nozick (1974), argued that compulsory (state-mandated) redistribution was incompatible with taking liberty seriously. Nozick's conception of justice instead emphasises the fairness or otherwise of the *process* by which material goods and other benefits are acquired. More recently, Iris Marion Young (1990; see also Chapter Four) has argued that distributional issues are only one part of social justice; other dimensions such as the relations between people also need to be considered, in particular the elimination of institutionalised domination and oppression. Similarly, Fraser (2001) and Lister (2004; see also Chapter Five) draw attention to culturally and socially constructed differences based on gender, ethnicity, sexuality and disability. As well as thinking about how benefits are distributed among the club, we need to consider who is counted as a member of the club – to whom respect and recognition are afforded.

Even those who follow Rawls in focusing mainly on distributional justice have challenged aspects of his theory. Dworkin (2000) argues that it pays insufficient attention to individual responsibility. A theory of justice must, in his view, distinguish between inequalities that arise because people have different preferences and hence make different choices, and inequalities that arise from characteristics or circumstances beyond individual control. Although both types of inequality may need to be addressed, the extent to which there are obligations on others to do so, and the mechanisms by which they should be addressed, differ. It is important, Dworkin argues, to allow individual choice and responsibility to have some real consequences. In a crude form, the distinction between disadvantage arising from circumstance and disadvantage arising from choice is often mapped onto the deserving and undeserving poor – a categorisation that has had strong resonance in political discourses about the provision of welfare since at least the time of the Victorian Poor Law, and which both current Conservative and Labour Party statements emphasise (see previous section). Other challenges to Rawls have taken issue with his definition of primary goods as the 'distributend' (that is, that which is to be distributed). Equality should be evaluated not in terms of the resources you have, according to Sen (1985, 1999), but according to the substantive freedom you have to achieve outcomes you value or have reason to value (see Chapter Ten).

As will be apparent, theories of social justice make use of a number of other concepts that have perhaps more familiar currency in social policy debate, such as inequality, rights and citizenship. The kinds and degrees of inequality that are regarded as unacceptable vary between different theories: there are important distinctions between equality of opportunity (or access), equality of outcome and equality of status. Similarly, rights and citizenship merit further specification and analysis (Roche, 1992). Marshall's (1950) groundbreaking work advanced a taxonomy of rights by which one could identify the characteristics of citizenship. These incorporated: civil rights (property rights, legal guarantees and freedoms); political rights (right to vote, rights of association, constitutional participation); and social rights (entitlements to basic standards of education, health and social care, housing and income maintenance). Many present-day commentators (Dean and Melrose, 1999; Lister, 2003) do not regard these rights as of equal weight. Dean and Melrose (1999, p 180) argue that 'Civil rights underwrite the operation of the market economy and are entirely consistent with class inequality', whereas, 'political rights and social rights tend to challenge such inequality'. From this perspective, there remains a major political question about the degree to which social justice is compatible at all with the operation of a market economy (Doyal and Gough, 1991; Donnison, 1998).

The chapters that follow draw on many of these theories and concepts. We have not attempted to impose a single theory of social justice on the contributors, but rather have sought to encourage engagement and debate between a range of different conceptions.

Outline of the book

The first two chapters address head-on the gap between theories of social justice and policy applications. Chapter One, by Jonathan Wolff, offers the perspective of a political philosopher, while Chapter Two, by David Piachaud, provides insights from a social policy viewpoint. Wolff canvasses a range of egalitarian positions, including those advocated by Rawls, Dworkin and Sen, drawing particular attention to discussions of the appropriate metric of equality (in response to the question, 'equality of what?') and the related issue of how – or whether – to take account of individual responsibility for tastes and circumstances. Wolff also reminds us that not all interpretations of justice require equality, strictly speaking: some are based on sufficiency (for example, meeting basic needs), or on priority (paying particular attention to the worst-off). In the final section of the chapter, Wolff offers a case study, analysing the kinds of policy that would be derived by application of Dworkin's and Sen's ideas to the question of support for disabled people. Crudely, Dworkin would offer financial 'compensation' while Sen would advocate 'changing the world, not the person'. Wolff concludes that because Sen's capability approach provides a more plausible account of well-being, the policies it implies are more likely to address the needs of disabled people, one of the groups characteristically most overlooked by social policy. But the flipside of this strength of the capability approach is also a weakness: identifying priorities within or across policy areas based on a multidimensional measure of well-being is much more problematic than identifying priorities using a single index, such as income or subjective well-being.

Piachaud adds Nozick to the range of theorists under consideration, and emphasises what three of the most prominent approaches have in common, as well as examining where they differ. There are similarities between apparently competing approaches: for example, all of the main contenders accept the importance of securing the basic civil and political liberties for everyone. (This has been a presumption of social democratic politics too – at least until it came under attack as part of the so-called 'war on terror'.) Piachaud analyses differences between the approaches by examining their attitudes to the past, present and future, and draws out some of the implications for social policy, particularly with respect to public/private boundaries, children (see also Chapters Seven and Eight) and global justice (see also Chapter Six). Nozick regards most activity in the private sphere as outside the scope of considerations of justice, and Rawls, while acknowledging the significance of an individual's characteristics, beliefs and choices, also regards justice as an essentially public affair. Piachaud highlights the difficulties that arise in practice if public policy declines to get involved in influencing personal behaviour, because so many types of personal behaviour have social consequences – parents failing to engage with their children's education, for example, or citizens opting out of civic duties. In practice, social policies require decisions about the past – what account should be taken of past history; about the present – what is a fair distribution; and about the future – what regard should be paid to the longer-term consequences of policies, including how they will affect social justice in the future.

Chapters Three, Four and Five address issues of cultural (or other) diversity and distributional justice. In Chapter Three, Will Kymlicka dissects the widespread belief, popularised among the chattering classes by Goodhart (2004) that increasing ethnic diversity within societies will erode the sense of national solidarity that is thought to underpin the welfare state. Kymlicka identifies that this belief rests on two assumptions: a 'heterogeneity/redistribution trade-off hypothesis', which states that it is difficult to sustain national solidarity in the form of welfare spending across increasingly diverse ethnic or racial groups, and a 'recognition/redistribution trade-off hypothesis', which states that the more a country adopts multicultural policies, recognising its minority ethnic groups, the harder it is to maintain (national) economic redistribution. Existing evidence in support of the first hypothesis comes from sub-Saharan Africa and the US; both areas with quite distinctive racial histories. Kymlicka tests the hypothesis in the context of other forms of ethnic diversity – indigenous peoples (such as American Indians) and national minorities (for example the Quebecois) – and finds that there is no correlation between the size of the minority and change in welfare spending over the past 30 years (although the *rate of change* in the size of immigrant minorities may have some impact). Evidence to support the second hypothesis is also lacking: Kymlicka finds no correlation between an index of the strength of multicultural policies in 21 established democracies and change in welfare spending. In short, once empirical evidence is brought to bear, anxiety about a possible trade-off between ethnic diversity and multiculturalism on the one hand, and the welfare state on the other, is shown to be misplaced.

Sadly, Iris Marion Young, author of Chapter Four, died while this volume was in preparation. We are extremely fortunate that she had written a (slightly longer) version of the chapter before her untimely death and we are honoured to be able to include it in this collection. Young makes a powerful case for not allowing the politics of cultural difference – important though they may be – to obscure the significance of *positional* difference, that is, structural inequalities deriving from the operation of public and private institutions, including, for example, the labour market and the family. She illustrates the differences with reference to disability – an analysis which strongly echoes Wolff's critique of luck egalitarian approaches in Chapter One – and with reference to ethnicity, engaging explicitly with Kylmicka's defence of multiculturalism.

The theme of identity politics is continued in Chapter Five, in which Ruth Lister argues that the recognition paradigm can usefully be applied to understanding contemporary debates about poverty, despite the fact that poverty is more usually thought to be an issue of distributive justice. Drawing on her experience as part of the Commission on Poverty, Participation and Power, among other sources, Lister identifies misrecognition and being treated with disrespect as acutely harmful and painful aspects of the experience of being poor. Moreover, by distancing 'Us' – the non-poor – from 'Them', this kind of language and behaviour towards people in poverty undermines the solidarity that might otherwise support more radical and effective measures to eliminate poverty, and denies the people with the most relevant experience a voice at the negotiating table. Lister concludes that the attack on poverty must draw on both the recognition and redistribution paradigms of social justice.

Each of the next group of Chapters, Six to Nine, considers a specific policy problem or area, mainly focusing on distributional issues. In Chapter Six, Christopher Bertram invites us to raise our sights to the global level. Traditionally, theories of justice have concerned themselves with redistribution within a nation state, but Rawls' later work (1999) and other more recent contributions have sought to address what responsibilities we have cross-nationally, if any. Bertram comes down decisively on the side of those arguing that there is no justification for thinking that redistributive principles hold only within national boundaries, because the system of economic cooperation that social contractarians hold to be the foundation of our duties towards each other extend well beyond the nation state. Moreover, the country one happens to be born in is morally arbitrary and is tied to welfare and other entitlements only through a coercive system of attribution of nationality and border control, which is itself global in its reach. Bertram goes on to consider the measures likely to be necessary to deliver global justice and identifies significant limitations in current (and likely future) supranational institutions.

Harry Brighouse and Adam Swift's attention, in Chapter Seven, is focused closer to home, indeed in the home: their chapter examines the tension between egalitarian objectives and respect for 'family values', where 'family values' is understood to mean the special commitment people have to providing the best for their nearest and dearest. The family is both an obstacle to achieving social justice, because so many formal and informal advantages are passed on within families, and a necessary component of a just society, because of people's entitlement to respect and privacy for their nurturing and intimate relationships. Brighouse and Swift delineate a legitimate sphere for partiality, based on activities whose value is inextricably bound up with the relationship in question, such as reading bedtime stories, as distinct from forms of transmission of advantage that have no necessary or intrinsic link to the relationship, such as providing a leg-up on the housing ladder. Public policies should be designed, they argue, to support intrinsically valuable 'relationship goods', while decoupling this form of advantage from the distribution of other goods (such as education or standard of living).

In Chapter Eight, David Gordon discusses distributional justice for children. He laments the paucity of philosophical and economic theories taking children seriously as human beings in their own right; Brighouse and Swift's approach in the preceding chapter is unfortunately the exception rather than the rule. Many theories treat children merely as a manifestation of the consumption preferences of their parents, as the property of their parents, or, at best, as future citizens.

In Chapter Nine, Katie Schmuecker charts differences between social justice policies adopted in Scotland, Wales and England since devolution, particularly in relation to anti-poverty strategies and healthcare. As she notes, the real test of the devolution settlement is only just beginning, with different parties in power in the three countries. At present, attitudinal survey evidence suggests some tension between the continuing popularity of devolution and local control, and a strong preference for common standards for welfare provision across the whole of the UK (and a dislike of a 'postcode lottery' of services). Moreover, since the majority of revenue is raised and distributed centrally, the scope for divergence among devolved administrations remains constrained. However, Schmuecker argues that devolution has brought greater transparency in service provision at a country level and that this in turn has the potential to lead to convergence on best practice.

Chapters Ten and Eleven explore the application of some of the theories discussed earlier in the book to inequality in the UK. In Chapter Ten, Tania Burchardt offers a case study of the application of the capability approach, as discussed by both Wolff and Piachaud in their opening chapters. The context is the creation in Britain – as elsewhere in Europe – of a unified Equality and Human Rights Commission, with responsibility for promoting human rights and monitoring and reducing inequality by gender, ethnicity, disability, sexual orientation, age, and religion or belief. The measurement framework proposed by Burchardt and Vizard (2007) for the Commission derives a set of 10 domains of central and valuable capabilities by subjecting an initial list based on international human rights conventions to a (small-scale) deliberative consultation with the general public and with groups at particular risk of discrimination and disadvantage. Limitations of both the process and the outcome are discussed, including the difficulty of identifying priorities using a multidimensional measure, as alluded to by Wolff. Nevertheless, Burchardt argues that the framework has potential advantages over some of the alternatives, in that it focuses on intrinsically valuable ends (rather than the means), has greater democratic legitimacy and offers a common basis for evaluation and monitoring across strands of inequality previously treated largely separately.

In Chapter Eleven, Gary Craig picks up the thread of the politics of multiculturalism introduced by Kymlicka and Young. He outlines policies towards accommodating diverse cultures in different societies and historically in the UK, distinguishing assimilationist, integrationist and downright hostile tendencies. He establishes that whatever forms of multicultural (or plural monocultural) policies have been pursued by the British state since the 1950s, from when large-scale immigration into the UK can be dated, social justice for the UK's minority ethnic groups has not been achieved – in terms of equality of outcome, equality of status or even meeting basic needs. Craig concludes that a concerted effort to root out racism is required, not only as it manifests itself in interactions between individuals but also in the design and operation of public and private institutions and in the effective implementation of legislation. In line with Kymlicka, he argues that there is, contrary to much current thinking, no necessary tension between diversity and solidarity. It is not that multiculturalism has failed but that it has never properly been implemented.

Finally, Chapter Twelve, by Maria Adebowale, explores the connections between sustainable development and social justice. She surveys international law, policy and practice, highlighting areas where the interdependence of environmental protection and enforcement of human rights has been recognised. The second part of her chapter turns to the UK and examines the reasons why separate environmental policies and social deprivation and regeneration policies have not yet been joined together in a comprehensive environmental justice policy. She argues that the failure of the environmental movement, until recently, to address social justice and equality issues, combined with a common misperception in government and elsewhere that communities are interested only in specific local social and economic issues, are key causes of the lack of joined-up policy. However, there are a number of new policy frameworks that show promise, which are beginning to address the difficult issue of the distribution of environmental goods and 'bads'.

Common themes

Theories of social justice help to identify and classify different aspects of a person's life with which we should be concerned: the extent to which their basic needs are met, the resources available to them relative to others, their negative and positive freedoms, their status, and the degree of recognition they receive, to name just a few. To gain a foothold, theories must distinguish themselves from each other, and this tends to exaggerate the differences between them, such that one comes to be associated with championing distributive concerns (for example Dworkin's luck egalitarianism), while another becomes identified with the politics of recognition (Fraser), even if the original texts are more nuanced. But when we consider individual lives as they are lived, the experience of injustice is not so neatly compartmentalised. Different aspects of justice are not just interrelated at an individual level, they may be inseparable. A Somali refugee in Scotland does not separately experience the injustice of a global system that fails to redistribute between nations and which defines her individual entitlements according to her nationality, the lack of respect she receives as a minority ethnic person in a rapidly-diversifying community, her poverty as someone outside the labour force and the constraints imposed on her freedom of movement and right to a family life.

At a societal level too, as several of the chapters in this volume demonstrate, different dimensions of justice are interconnected. Justice considered in terms of distribution and recognition (Wolff, Young, Lister), recognition and voice (Lister, Craig), and justice in public and private spheres (Brighouse and Swift, Piachaud) is − or should be − mutually reinforcing.

Acknowledging this interdependence indicates that we cannot afford to be reductionist in our approach to theories of social justice. This applies to the broad dimensions of justice described above, and also, in the case of distributional concerns, to the metric of equality. No one indicator, whether of resources or subjective well-being, is likely to be sufficient to capture the aspects of life that are important and relevant to the evaluation of justice (Wolff, Burchardt).

On the other hand, embracing pluralism is not the same as saying 'anything goes'. Theories do conflict with each other over which principles should take priority, and public policies developed in ignorance of these differences are likely to lead to inconsistencies in practice. For example, Nozick's account emphasising negative liberty and fair process gives free rein to intergenerational transmission of material and other advantages within families. But Brighouse and Swift, starting from a more egalitarian perspective, derive a formula that distinguishes impersonal benefits (including financial resources) from intrinsically intra-familial ones. Actual social policy in this area is hopelessly confused within the UK − with tax breaks for privately funded education but very limited support for parents to spend time with their children – no doubt partly as a result of political compromise, but also, plausibly, as a result of muddled thinking about the true nature of 'family values'.

Finally, recognising the interrelatedness of different aspects of social injustice in theory and in everyday life implies developing joined-up and pluralistic policies. As Kymlicka demonstrates, the choice between policies that promote redistribution and policies that promote recognition is a false one. Diversity need not undermine solidarity. Likewise, Bertram explores ways in which (moving towards) meeting our global responsibilities need not exclude the possibility of continuing to support effective intranational institutions. Environmental concerns can only be addressed, in the long run, by examining them in combination with social justice and human rights issues. What appear at first sight to be threats to the attainment of social justice, need not be, once we are freed from a unidimensional understanding of what it is we are trying to achieve.

In the context of a globalising world and diversifying societies, social justice is becoming more complex both theoretically and in practice, but we can and must rise to the challenge. To do so, we need more sophisticated engagement between different academic disciplines, and between academia and policy makers and practitioners, to ensure that the proposals that emerge are both coherent and realistic, and so that they can attract widespread political and public support. It is hoped that this book contributes, in however small a way, to meeting that need.

Notes

[1] Lister (2007) argues that this represents a significant distinction between the present-day Conservative Party and its predecessors, signifying a break with Hayekian neoliberalism.

[2] The series was initiated, and inspired, by Robina Goodlad of Glasgow. Sadly, Robina died before the seminar series ended. We are grateful to the ESRC for funding the series (grant number RES-451-26-0305).

References

Brummer, A. (2006) 'Do City workers earn their mega-money?', thisismoney.co.uk (published by The Daily Mail), www.thisismoney.co.uk/news/special-report/article.html?in_article_id=414105&in_page_id=108 (accessed 24/08/2007).

Burchardt, T. and Vizard, P. (2007) *Definition of equality and framework for measurement: Final recommendations of the Equalities Review Steering Group on Measurement, paper 1*, http://sticerd.lse.ac.uk/dps/case/cp/CASEpaper120.pdf (accessed 24/08/2007).

CSJ (Commission on Social Justice) (Chair: Sir Gordon Borrie) (1994) *Social justice: Strategies for national renewal*, London: Verso.

Dean, H. and Melrose, M. (1999) *Poverty, riches and social citizenship*, London: Routledge.

Donnison, D. (1998) *Policies for a just society*, Basingstoke: Macmillan.

Doyal, I. and Gough, R. (1991) *A theory of human need*, Basingstoke: Macmillan.

Dworkin, R. (2000) *Sovereign virtue: The theory and practice of equality*, Cambridge, MA: Harvard University Press.

DWP (Department for Work and Pensions) (2007) 'Welfare reform', www.dwp.gov.uk/welfarereform/ (accessed 24/08/2007).

Fraser, N. (2001) 'Recognition without ethics?', *Theory, Culture and Society*, vol 18, no 2-3, pp 21-42.

Goodhart, D. (2004) 'Is Britain becoming too diverse to sustain the mutual obligations behind a good society and the welfare state?', *Prospect*, February.

Hills, J. and Stewart, K. (2005) *A more equal society? New Labour, poverty, inequality and exclusion*, Bristol: The Policy Press.

Lister, R. (2003) *Citizenship: Feminist perspectives* (2nd edition), Basingstoke: Palgrave.

Lister, R. (2004) *Poverty*, Cambridge: Polity Press.

Lister, R. (2007) 'Social justice: meanings and politics', *Benefits: The Journal of Poverty and Social Justice*, vol 15, no 2, pp 113-26.

Marshall, T. (1950) *Citizenship and social class, and other essays*, Cambridge: Cambridge University Press.

Nozick, R. (1974) *Anarchy, state and utopia*, Oxford: Blackwell.

Phillips, T. (2006) 'Equality and human rights: siblings or just rivals?', *Benefits: The Journal of Poverty and Social Justice*, vol 15, no 2, pp 127-38.

Rawls, J. (1971) *A theory of justice*, Oxford: Oxford University Press.

Rawls, J. (1999) *The law of peoples*, Cambridge, MA: Harvard University Press.

Roche, M. (1992) *Rethinking citizenship: Welfare, ideology and change in modern society*, Cambridge: Polity Press.

Sen, A. (1985) *Commodities and capabilities*, Oxford: North-Holland.

Sen, A. (1999) *Development as freedom*, Oxford: Oxford University Press.

SJPG (Social Justice Policy Group) (2007) *Breakthrough Britain: Ending the costs of social breakdown. Policy recommendations to the Conservative Party*, www.centreforsocialjustice.org.uk/default.asp?pageRef=182 (accessed 23/08/2007).

United Nations General Assembly (2000) *United Nations Millennium Declaration*, Resolution 55/2, www.un.org/millennium/ (accessed 23/08/2007).

Willetts, D. (2006) 'Social justice across the generations', *Benefits: The Journal of Poverty and Social Justice*, vol 15, no 2, pp 163-70.

WTO (World Trade Organization) (2007) 'What is the World Trade Organization?', www.wto.org/english/thewto_e/whatis_e/tif_e/fact1_e.htm (accessed 23/08/2007).

Young, I. (1990) *Justice and the politics of difference*, Princeton, NJ: Princeton University Press.

ONE

Social justice and public policy: a view from political philosophy

Jonathan Wolff

Introduction

Many of those active within social policy, either as theorists or practitioners, became interested in the field in which they work at least in part through their perception of what they believe to be the profound social injustices they see around them. Hence they conceive of their work as part of a movement for social justice. Despite this, the positive requirements of social justice, in detail, are contested. Of course, some gross social injustices are easily recognisable even without an explicit theory of justice. In other cases there can be serious disagreements about what social justice requires. Commonly it is assumed that social justice is in some way connected with ideas of equality, but how an ideal of equality is to be formulated, and the relation between social justice and equality, remain disputed.

The difficulties theorists in social policy have in identifying a clear theory of social justice reflect a series of disagreements within political philosophy. These disagreements arise at more than one level, and this is clearly an impediment for those who wish to take a definitive notion of social justice from political philosophy and use it to assess, or even generate, social policy. Hence, this is an obstacle for those in social policy who wish to see their work informed by greater theoretical engagement. Yet it is also a problem for political philosophers who can find themselves sidelined and ignored when their theories cannot be brought into contact with real-life policy issues.

The remainder of this chapter falls into four sections. The next section surveys the existing state of debate on equality and social justice within political philosophy. The second section explores some topics within social policy, looking particularly at the issue of disability to explore the connections with theoretical approaches to social justice. A way forward is suggested in the third section, by a combination of suspending some philosophical disputes that currently have little practical bearing, and enriching philosophical conceptual vocabulary in the light of social policy. The final section concludes by reviewing the advantages for both political philosophy and social policy of taking such an approach.

Contemporary theories of social justice

Contemporary philosophical discussion of social justice – although this was not a term he much used – must take as its starting point John Rawls' *A theory of justice*, first published in 1971 and dominating the scene ever since. In *A theory of justice*, Rawls sets out his famous two principles of justice. First, each person is to have an equal right to the most extensive basic liberty compatible with a similar liberty for all. Second, social and economic equalities (i) are to be arranged so that they are to the greatest benefit of the least advantaged and (ii) should be attached to offices open to all.

The first principle, the 'liberty principle', Rawls argues, has 'lexical priority' over the second. In cases of conflict between the principles, where, for example, we could advance the economic interests of the worst-off by restricting individual liberties, the liberty principle takes priority. By this Rawls means that at least when society has reached a certain level of material wealth, protection of the basic liberties always takes priority over economic interest. Furthermore, the second part of the second principle – the 'fair opportunity' principle – takes priority over the first part, which is known as the 'difference principle'. The two principles – which are really three – all require further explanation, but here we will concentrate on the difference principle as this is closest to the focus of traditional concerns of social justice.

The difference principle is Rawls' most distinctive contribution. Rawls argues that even if we initially suppose that justice requires equal division of resources there is a sense in which this is likely to be inefficient. A system with incentives for people to work hard may well create a much larger stock of goods than a system of flat equality. Indeed, the extra stock created could, in certain circumstances, be redistributed to make everyone better off. If this is so – if even the worst-off would benefit from inequality in income and wealth – who could object to those inequalities? Hence, Rawls derives his principle that we should judge the justice of society by how well it treats the worst-off. A society is just only if the worst-off in that society are better off than the worst-off would be under any alternative arrangement.

Rawls' theory has, of course, been the subject of huge debate, intensified by the influential criticisms of Ronald Dworkin (1981a, reprinted 2000) and Amartya Sen (1992). Dworkin can be read as raising two central challenges to Rawls (see also Kymlicka, 2002; Chapter Three). The first can be put like this: before devoting social resources to improving the position of those with the least income and wealth, should we not, at the very least, first investigate how they came to be in that position? Some may be badly off because they are unable to work, or unable to find work. But others may have chosen to do no work. Are they equally deserving or entitled to benefit from the work of others? Can it be fair to tax the hardworking for the benefit of those who are equally capable of hard work, and equally talented, but choose to laze around instead? The difference principle, however, does not require answers to these questions. Hence, to put Dworkin's first argument in a nutshell, it subsidises scroungers, or to put it less tendentiously, the deliberately underproductive. In Dworkin's view, this is contrary to equality. Equality should, other things being equal, allow those who work hard to reap the rewards, while those who choose to do less should bear the consequences of their choices.

A second objection raises a new difficulty. The index of primary goods, and in particular the focus on income and wealth, ignores the fact that some people have much more expensive needs than others. In particular, people who are severely disabled, or have expensive medical requirements, may have a reasonable income, but this could be wholly inadequate to pay the expenses needed to achieve a reasonable level of well-being.

The natural response to the problem of expensive needs, such as those of disabled people, would be to abandon income and wealth as a currency of justice, and move to assessment of well-being in terms of some form of welfare, such as happiness or preference satisfaction. However, Dworkin argues that this would be a mistake. First he unleashes a battery of objections against the coherence of a welfare measure – essentially the difficulty of determining when two different people are at the same level, which, of course, is central to any theory of equality. But the argument that is most distinctive and has had the greatest impact is the problem of expensive tastes. Imagine two people who have the same ordinary tastes, talents and resources, and the same ability to convert resources into welfare, however that is construed. Now one of them – Louis – decides that he wants to change his tastes, and manages to develop a taste for pre-phylloxera claret and plovers' eggs, and is consequently unsatisfied with beer and hens' eggs. According to Dworkin, the theory of equality of welfare would require a transfer of resources from the person with ordinary tastes to the person with expensive tastes, in order to equalise their welfare. This, he plausibly argues, is deeply counterintuitive (Dworkin, 1981b, reprinted 2000).

Dworkin addresses the difficulties he identifies in Rawls' theory in a way which avoids the problem of subsidising expensive tastes. The key insight is that a notion of responsibility can be incorporated within the theory of equality. It is possible to make people responsible for matters within some domains, but not within others. Dworkin makes a distinction between one's ambitions – including the realm of the voluntary choices one makes – and endowments, which we can think of as including inborn talents, genetic predispositions and so on. In brief, Dworkin's theory is that while equality requires government to take steps to compensate for the bad 'brute luck' of being born with poor endowments, or unforeseeable poor luck in other aspects of life, it does not require compensation for poor 'option luck', which typically includes the results of freely made choices. Hence, on Dworkin's view there is no reason to subsidise Louis, who has made his own choice to develop expensive tastes. Similarly, those who choose not to work, if they are able to, will not be subsidised either, and this, in principle, overcomes the 'problem of responsibility' identified with Rawls' difference principle.

This, however, leaves us with the question of how to determine the appropriate level of compensation or subsidy. Here Dworkin makes the brilliant move of appealing to the idea first of insurance, and then of hypothetical insurance. His initial observation is that real-life insurance converts brute luck into option luck. It may be a matter of pure chance whether lightning strikes my house. But it is not a matter of pure chance if I have declined to take out an easily available insurance policy to protect myself from loss. Dworkin's argument is that if insurance is available against a hazard, and I decline the opportunity to take it, then, against a background of equality, there is no case in justice for subsidising the uninsured by taxing others who beforehand were no better off. If it were possible to insure against all brute luck then it appears that Dworkin's theory would simply require an equal distribution of resources and then allow people to make their own choices and run whichever risks they wished.

Life, however, is not so simple. Brute lucks affect us from the moment we are born. Some people are born with low talents or, as already discussed, with disabilities: this was one of the problems Dworkin identifies for Rawls. But it is not possible to take out insurance against bad brute luck that has already happened. However, it is possible to imagine what insurance one would take out, hypothetically, behind a veil of ignorance in which you knew the preponderance of, and disadvantage caused by, different types of disability, but did not know whether or not you personally were affected. Knowing this information should allow one to decide whether to insure, and if so at what level. Averaging the decisions gives a standard hypothetical premium and payout, and these can be used to model a just tax and transfer scheme. A similar move is available to model appropriate compensation payments for those of low talent.

Dworkin, we saw, considers and rejects equality of welfare as a possible response to the problem presented by the fact that disabled people may need more resources than other people in order to achieve an acceptable standard of living. The rejection is based on the argument from Louis' expensive tastes. Richard Arneson (1989), however, suggests that this argument is confused. The problem with Louis is that he has deliberately cultivated expensive tastes. He could have achieved the same level of welfare as other people by remaining content with hens' eggs and beer, but for whatever reason he decided to cultivate expensive tastes. Arneson's response is that we need to understand that there is a distinction not only between theories of resources and theories of welfare, but also between what we could call 'outcome' and 'opportunity' theories. It is true, Arneson accepts, that equality of welfare outcomes would require subsidising Louis' deliberately cultivated expenses tastes. However, Louis does have equality of *opportunity* for welfare, but he squanders this by deliberately cultivating expensive tastes. If he was born with expensive tastes then the case for subsidising is more compelling, for he would then lack equality of opportunity for welfare. Hence, Arneson argues, Dworkin has drawn the wrong conclusion from his example. In effect, Arneson suggests, Dworkin has compared equality of welfare outcomes with equality of opportunity for resources. The expensive tastes argument shows that equality of welfare outcomes is unacceptable, but this is a reason for moving to an opportunity conception, not a resources conception.

G. A. Cohen (1989) argues in a similar way, although, unlike Arneson, he claims that an adequate theory of equality must use the currency of 'advantage', which incorporates both welfare and resources. Cohen endorses one of Dworkin's arguments against pure welfarism; that it would have the bizarre consequence that it would require transfers from the very cheerful poor – such as Dickens' Tiny Tim – to the wealthy but miserable, such as Scrooge. But equally, Cohen argues, it would be wrong to follow Dworkin and endorse a pure resource-based metric in which people were not compensated for pain and suffering, for example.

The issues between Dworkin, Cohen and Arneson remain unresolved (see Burley, 2004). Nevertheless, they all agree that Rawls' theory needs to be modified to incorporate a notion of responsibility. A different dispute within those sympathetic to the general idea of equality focuses on the question of whether equality is really the goal that those interested in social justice should seek. A traditional argument against equality is that it requires levelling down: that if there is a choice between equality at a lower level and inequality at a higher level for all, then the theory demands equality, even if it makes literally every individual worse off. Although familiar with this argument, few egalitarians took it seriously, brushing it aside one way or another, until Rawls presented the difference principle, in which inequalities are tolerated when they are to the advantage of the worst-off. This prevents levelling down, of course, which is its aim.

It was, however, unclear whether Rawls' theory should be treated as one of equality or not. On the one hand, theorists such as Nagel (1979) treated Rawls as a paradigm example of a theorist of equality, and critics of equality take Rawls as their target. On the other hand, it cannot be denied that Rawls' theory permits inequality, and so some more radical theorists criticised Rawls as a theorist of inequality (Daniels, 1975). The situation, however, has been clarified by two papers, by Harry Frankfurt (1987) and Derek Parfit (1998), which generate distinctions between a range of theories of different strength and commitment.[1]

First, Frankfurt (1987) argues that egalitarians are not, or at least should not be, concerned with equality as such, but with whether individuals are leading sufficiently good lives, where this is to be understood non-comparatively. What matters, argues Frankfurt, is whether people have enough to flourish. Comparisons with others are alienating, and deflect oneself from the value of one's own life. Whatever we think of this further point, it cannot be denied that there is a certain attraction to such a 'sufficiency' view, as distinct from equality.

However, there are further options. Parfit (1998) describes a Rawlsian-style view as one of 'priority to the worst-off', which again is distinct from equality. Indeed, this view comes in various strengths. Rawls' own view is one of absolute priority, where the claims of the worst-off must always be given priority. Parfit's view is one of a form of 'weighted priority' in which the claims of the worst-off have greater weight than the claims of others, but can, at least in theory, be outweighed. On this view there is such a thing as 'asking too much' even if you are the worst-off in society.

The contributions of Frankfurt and Parfit have been immensely valuable, allowing theorists better to understand their own intuitions and theoretical commitments. For example, Arneson (1999) has moved from an equality view to one of weighted priority. We will see further applications of these distinctions shortly.

In parallel to Dworkin, Amartya Sen was also developing an egalitarian response to Rawls. Sen was particularly exercised by Rawls' index of well-being in terms of goods such as income and wealth, and by the fact that this ignored the plight of disabled people, or those with other special needs. Sen's (1992) suggestion is that evaluation of how well an individual's life is going, from the point of view of whether they should be offered state support, should measure neither the resources someone has, nor the welfare they are able to derive, but their 'capability to function'. A functioning is what a person can 'do or be': achieve nourishment, health, a decent life span, self-respect and so on. A capability is the freedom to achieve a functioning, and a person's 'capability set' is the alternative sets of functionings they are able to achieve with their resources and opportunities.

This pluralist view of well-being is often regarded as a more realistic account than any theory of welfare or resources. Sen's theory has become extremely important in development economics, influencing policy within organisations such as the United Nations Development Programme (2005), encouraging a move away from income measures of poverty, to 'lack of basic functioning'. This has been among the contributions that won him the Nobel Prize in Economics in 1998. However, political philosophy has found it harder to incorporate Sen's theory, for two main reasons. First, Sen has always refrained from setting out a definitive list of human functionings, suggesting that different societies can engage in the democratic exercise of specifying their own account of functioning. Second, on a pluralist view it is very hard to understand what equality means. Equality seems to require a way of measuring functionings against each other, but the essence of a pluralist view is that this is not, in general, possible. Suggesting a solution to the first problem, as Martha Nussbaum (2000) has attempted to do in laying out an account of essential human functionings,[2] simply brings out the difficulty of the second.

Nevertheless, the contributions of Frankfurt and Parfit have allowed political philosophers to make better use of Sen's approach, in that a 'sufficiency view' of capabilities has appeared a more promising approach in which the goal of social policy is to bring each person to a threshold level of sufficiency in each capability (Anderson, 1999; Nussbaum, 2006). There are, however, severe difficulties when resource constraints make this impossible (Arneson, 2005). The theory will need to be supplemented in some way to deal with priority setting between competing claims, and many of the initial difficulties reassert themselves. However, the position may not be completely hopeless, and it has been argued that it is possible to combine a prioritarian position with a (modified) capability view (Wolff and de-Shalit, 2007).

Alongside the revival of Sen's approach, a set of criticisms has been levelled against the way in which responsibility is incorporated into the theories of Dworkin, Cohen and Arneson. Together, in a phrase coined by Anderson (1999), those theories are collectively referred to as 'luck egalitarianism' as their goal is to 'neutralise' the effects of luck on individual lives. Pursuit of this goal, however, appears to have a number of unfortunate effects. For example, it will have to split claimants into those who are responsible for their plight and those who are not, which in some circumstances can be humiliating even for those who are entitled to help, who, for example, might have to argue that they are untalented in order to qualify for state support (Wolff, 1998; Anderson, 1999). Furthermore, many of the policies strictly entailed by the theory seem deeply inhumane, for example discriminating between disabled people. Those who are responsible for their own disability, on the luck egalitarian view, should not be entitled to any state help. By contrast, Anderson suggests that the 'negative aim' of egalitarianism should not be to eliminate the effects of bad luck, but to end oppression, domination and exploitation. An equal society is not one that has eliminated the effects of luck, but that has achieved relations of equality between individuals. Such a view has also been defended in writing by Samuel Scheffler (2003).

This move towards 'relational' or 'social' equality picks up a concern running from a older tradition in thinking of equality, exemplified in the works of such thinkers as R. H. Tawney (1931), and carried forward by Bernard Williams (1973), Michael Walzer (1983), Richard Norman (1998) and David Miller (1999). The central idea is that a society of equals has to create conditions of mutual respect, and self-respect, and thereby overcome hierarchical divisions. This type of view has strong affinities with the work of the 'difference' theorist Iris Marion Young (1990; Chapter Four, this volume) and 'recognition' theorist Nancy Fraser (Fraser and Honneth, 1998). There are numerous variations on this theme, but the basic idea is that an equal society is one that has the right quality of relations between individuals, rather than one that distributes the 'currency' of justice the right way. Even though there appears to be increasing sympathy for the idea that social equality is an indispensable part of an equal society, it is also noted that distributive elements cannot be ignored either (Phillips, 1999), as indeed was emphasised by earlier writers such as Tawney (1931).

Disability and social policy

One of the merits of Dworkin's work is taking the issue of disability seriously, and specifying a mechanism by which we can measure appropriate 'compensation' for disability. Nevertheless, there are reasons to be concerned about Dworkin's treatment of disability. As has been pointed out by Shelley Tremain (1996), Dworkin implicitly assumes a 'medical' model of disability, in which disability is thought of as a 'lack of internal resources' and for which financial compensation is an appropriate remedy. Yet when we consider successful and enlightened social policy aimed at improving the lives of disabled people there is a far more complex picture. Society changes building codes; it changes the configuration of public spaces; it attempts to change social attitudes. Disabled individuals are provided with resources to help them live relatively independently, as well as being provided with medical services of numerous kinds. Although there is a transfer of resources in favour of disabled people away from others, only a proportion takes the form of cash transfers, and very rarely in the name of 'compensation'.

To see this in more detail, we can split factors that affect people's opportunities in life into three. The first is people's 'internal resources', such as strength and skill. The second is their 'external resources', including wealth and income, but also such things as family support. The third is the social and material structure in which they operate: laws, customs, conventions, the configuration of the material environment and so on. The idea is that your resources – internal and external – provide you with the 'pieces to play with' while the social structure determines the 'rules of the game'. It follows that we can alter someone's opportunities by adjusting any of these factors. This, then, provides a fairly rich range of possible strategies for addressing disability or indeed any form of disadvantage or injustice.

One thing we can do to improve such a person's life or opportunities is to attempt to provide a medical cure. This would be to act on their internal resources; a policy of what can be called 'personal enhancement'. This can include surgery, medicine and physiotherapy, but in other cases education and skills-training. A second 'space' in which society can act is on an individual's external resources, by the provision of extra resources. However, this can come in two fundamentally different forms. The first is to provide money as a free asset, which can then be used however the person wishes. This, in other words, is to offer cash compensation. However, in social policy, cash compensation of this form is rather limited in application. Of course, societies do provide disabled people with cash to spend as they like, although typically it is spent on bare necessities, in order to compensate for the special expenses and loss of income generation that disabled people face. Beyond this, societies often provide disabled people with forms of equipment and personal care, but not as a freely disposable asset. For example, a disabled person provided with a wheelchair is not normally at liberty to sell the wheelchair and use the cash for something else. Hence, resources are provided for their use and not as individual private property. A similar example is that there are cases where disabled people are provided with a significant sum of money, over which they have great discretion, but not the complete discretion one would have if it was private property. For example, they would not be permitted to take it to Las Vegas and spend it on slot machines. Where people are provided with either resources to use, or money with strings attached, it can be called a 'targeted resource enhancement'.

Finally, it is possible to improve a person's opportunities without changing their internal or external resources. The clearest type of example would be a law ending legal discrimination; for example a law which abolished a racial bar to employment. In the case of disability the most obvious move in this direction is to try to refigure the material environment, including the work environment, to allow disabled people the same level of access as others. It is, of course, examples like this that inspire the social model of disability. This type of change – changing the world, not the person – can be called 'status enhancement'.

Note that all of the strategies we use in real life are followed in pursuit of a broad range of goals, each designed to improve disabled people's opportunities to lead a fulfilling life. But how can we connect these social policies with theories of social justice? At this point we see what could be the central dilemma for philosophical theories of social justice. To explain, steps taken to improve people's lives aim to improve what we can call their well-being. Looking at issues in social policy, we can see that well-being is a highly complex notion. Even in the sphere of disability there are many indicators of well-being: independence, control over the environment, a sense of belonging, to say nothing of mental and physical functioning, freedom from pain and life expectancy. When we consider other policy areas these indicators will multiply. A realistic theory of well-being must be multifaceted. Realism requires pluralism. However, theories of social justice require comparisons between different people, and therefore it must be possible to index people's levels of well-being against each other. This is why income measures, for example, are so appealing. But a complex theory of well-being makes indexing problematic.

Looking back at the theories of Sen and Dworkin, we can see that Sen's capability theory is a very attractive one in order to achieve a realistic account of well-being, and accordingly capability theory has been thought to be very helpful in understanding disability. Yet Dworkin's theory is far better at meeting the need to index well-being. Understanding everything in terms of resources, which can be converted into cash through a hypothetical insurance market, allows a great degree of comparison, and allows one to be able to state, for example, when the position of two people is equal or unequal. On capability theory this is a huge barrier. It will often be very hard to say when one person is better off than another. Yet Dworkin's theory of well-being fits very badly with existing social policy.

A way forward?

In the second section of this chapter, we looked at a number of varieties of accounts of social justice, and points of disagreement within a broadly egalitarian theory. The third section, I hope, brought out the problem of how to connect philosophical theory with social policy: the dilemma of realism versus indexing. Here I want to suggest a way of overcoming this problem.

Although there are, as we have seen, many disputes within egalitarian theory, how important they are for social policy varies. We have seen that the question of 'currency' is indeed vitally important. The issue of when people are responsible for their own plight is also of great practical importance, although I am not able to discuss it further here. However, the question 'equality, sufficiency or priority' is of a different order. Whatever our currency of justice – whether resources, welfare or capability – the question of, say, whether society should aim at equality, priority to the worst-off, or a high level of sufficiency is one that will leave rather less trace on policy. Now, of course, people are worried about inequalities in particular areas, with health and education being prominent examples, but when we look at what we can call 'overall well-being' the decision between equality and high sufficiency is less central. Of course, those who argue for equality might oppose high incomes and bonuses that are much less objectionable to sufficiency theorists. Nevertheless, whichever theory one adopts, the immediate injunction for government is to take steps so that the lives of the people who are currently worst-off are improved. That is to say, all these theories converge on the short- to medium-term strategy of some sort of priority to the worst-off, whether or not that is their ultimate goal.

Now it may be thought that this is little help in answering the 'indexing/realism dilemma'. After all, we still need to be able to identify the worst-off, and how is this to be done with the sort of pluralistic view that realism apparently demands? However, this may be more of a philosophical problem than a practical one, and arguably overstates the difficulty. First, by a combination of democratic consultation and expert reflection society needs to identify the most important social functionings, and explore how individuals, or perhaps groups, perform on these selected dimensions. If it turns out that some people are disadvantaged according to a number of the selected dimensions – if disadvantage clusters, as we can put it – then there is no need to come up with a unique weighting function for different disadvantages in order to determine who is towards the bottom of the social ordering. However the dimensions are weighted, at least within reason, the same individuals will very often turn up towards the bottom of the ordering, even if their precise places in the ordering will change somewhat. That is to say, the ordering will be relatively robust under different weightings of the chosen dimensions. On the other hand, if disadvantage does not cluster, and who the least advantaged are changes each time we change the weightings of different functionings, then there is a sense in which society is not in too bad a shape from the point of view of inequality. In other words, it would be very good to live in a society where the philosophical problem is a practical one; where there is no non-arbitrary way of determining who is the least advantaged. That, we might even say, is a society that has achieved social justice; a 'declustering' of disadvantage. However, in the actual world there is compelling evidence that disadvantage does cluster, and so the least advantaged are reasonably easily identified.

The consequences for social policy of this analysis are not difficult to see. What we can call a 'corrosive disadvantage' is a disadvantage that causes further disadvantages while a 'fertile functioning' boosts other functionings. In order to decluster disadvantage social science needs to do more to uncover these types of causal relations – not, of course, that it is easy to do so – and governments need to shift resources and incentivise agencies so that they pay special attention to corrosive disadvantages and fertile functionings. So, for example, if social science reveals that the best way of improving general success in life is through employment, then this should become a government priority. Other claims, of course, are made for such things as early years education and mental health. Each of these claims should be investigated, and any success built upon. This may well be the best way of helping the least advantaged and ultimately declustering disadvantage. At the same time, and again resuming an earlier theme, governments need to be very careful how they act. Attempts to address distributional problems in a clumsy way can increase stigma and division in society and thereby undercut social equality. Consequently, where possible and appropriate, governments should use what was called above 'status enhancements' by changing laws, public services, social attitudes and the material environment. This can address disadvantage without identifying, and thereby stigmatising, individuals. Furthermore, it can boost affiliation and reduce risk for all, thereby having much wider social advantages. It is not always possible, but where it is, it will often be the best available strategy.

Concluding reflections

What, then, can political philosophy and social policy do for each other? The traditional picture is that political philosophers design theories of social justice, and then social policy activists apply them. The reality is that political philosophers design theories of social justice, and then social policy activists find them useless for their own purposes and so devise their own theories for the fragment of society that concerns them most. Here I am proposing a different model. First, political philosophers must attend to social policy in order to develop a theoretical vocabulary that is rich enough to conceptualise the various policy areas under discussion. Having done this they can develop richer and more detailed theories which will connect with policy issues. But the benefits will also be felt in social policy. Once philosophers have developed their theories they will be able to assist social policy theorists and practitioners not only in helping them devise a theoretical framework to explore the issues which concern them, but also to help set priorities for action, taking and bringing together a diverse set of inputs from political philosophy, social policy and the values and concerns revealed through the democratic process. Importantly, in some cases, this will be a matter of helping to determine priorities between different 'spheres' of social policy, and hence overall patterns of budget setting. This, it seems, is a fruitful model of future cooperation, for mutual benefit.

Notes

[1] See also Temkin (1993).

[2] See also Alkire (2002); Robeyns (2006).

References

Alkire, S. (2002) *Valuing freedoms*, Oxford: Oxford University Press.

Anderson, E. (1999) 'What is the point of equality?', *Ethics*, vol 109, pp 287-337.

Arneson, R. (1989) 'Equality and equal opportunity for welfare', *Philosophical Studies*, vol 56, pp 77-93.

Arneson, R. (1999) 'Equality of opportunity for welfare defended and recanted', *Journal of Political Philosophy*, vol 7, pp 488-97.

Arneson, R. (2005) 'Distributive justice and basic capability equality: "good enough" is not good enough', in A. Kaufman (ed) *Capabilities equality: Basic issues and problems*, London: Routledge.

Burley, J. (ed) (2004) *Dworkin and his critics*, Oxford: Basil Blackwell.

Cohen, G. A. (1989) 'On the currency of egalitarian justice', *Ethics*, vol 99, pp 906-44.

Daniels, N. (1975) 'Equal liberty and unequal worth of liberty', in N. Daniels (ed) *Reading Rawls*, New York: Basic Books.

Dworkin, R. (1981a) 'What is equality? Part 2: equality of resources', *Philosophy and Public Affairs*, vol 10, pp 283-345.

Dworkin, R. (1981b) 'What is equality? Part 1: equality of welfare', *Philosophy and Public Affairs*, vol 10, pp 185-246.

Dworkin, R. (2000) *Sovereign virtue*, Cambridge, MA: Harvard University Press.

Frankfurt, H. G. (1987) 'Equality as a moral ideal', *Ethics*, vol 98, pp 21-43.

Fraser, N. and Honneth, A. (1998) *Recognition or redistribution?*, London: Verso.

Kymlicka, W. (2002) *Contemporary political philosophy: An introduction* (2nd edition), Oxford: Oxford University Press.

Miller, D. (1999) *Principles of social justice*, Cambridge, MA: Harvard University Press.

Nagel, T. (1979) 'Equality', in *Mortal questions*, Cambridge: Cambridge University Press.

Norman, R. (1998) 'The social basis of equality', in A. Mason (ed) *Ideals of equality*, Oxford: Basil Blackwell.

Nussbaum, M. (2000) *Women and human development*, Cambridge: Cambridge University Press.

Nussbaum, M. (2006) *Frontiers of justice*, Cambridge, MA: Harvard University Press.

Parfit, D. (1998) 'Equality and priority', in A. Mason (ed) *Ideals of equality*, Oxford: Blackwell.

Phillips, A. (1999) *Which equalities matter?*, Cambridge: Polity Press.

Rawls, J. (1971) *A theory of justice*, Oxford: Oxford University Press.

Robeyns, I. (2006) 'The capability approach in practice', *Journal of Political Philosophy*, vol 17, no 3, pp 351-76.

Scheffler, S. (2003) 'What is egalitarianism?', *Philosophy and Public Affairs*, vol 31, no 4, pp 5-39.

Sen, A. (1992) *Inequality re-examined*, Oxford: Clarendon Press.

Tawney, R. H. (1931) *Equality*, London: George Allen and Unwin.

Temkin, L. (1993) *Inequality*, New York: Oxford University Press.

Tremain, S. (1996) 'Dworkin on disablement and resources', *Canadian Journal of Law and Jurisprudence*, vol 9, no 2, pp 343-59.

United Nations Development Programme (2005) *Human development report*, http://hdr.undp.org

Walzer, M. (1983) *Spheres of justice*, Oxford: Blackwell.

Williams, B. (1973) 'The idea of equality', in *Problems of the self*, Cambridge: Cambridge University Press.

Wolff, J. (1998) 'Fairness, respect and the egalitarian ethos', *Philosophy and Public Affairs*, vol 27, no 2, pp 97-122.

Wolff, J. and de-Shalit, A. (2007) *Disadvantage*, Oxford: Oxford University Press.

Young, I. M. (1990) *Justice and the politics of difference*, Princeton, NJ: Princeton University Press.

TWO

Social justice and public policy: a social policy perspective

David Piachaud

Introduction

From a small child protesting that 'It's not fair', to a former Enron employee, commenting on a senior executive who had been urging employees to invest their savings in Enron stock at the same time as he was unloading his, saying 'It was unjust', a concern for social justice dominates much of everyone's lives. 'Social justice' is a term that is both normative and prescriptive: situations are assessed in terms of their social justice and actions are guided by concepts of social justice.

Social policy is to a large extent concerned with social justice. For example, in Britain, politicians commonly espouse social justice: the leader of the Labour Party set up a Commission on Social Justice in 1992 and a former leader of the Conservative Party set up a Social Justice Policy Review in 2005. For many social democratic politicians the pursuit of social justice is a genuine and central political objective; certainly, few politicians espouse social injustice. Whether social justice requires some degree of equality of outcomes or requires equality of opportunities has been a continuing debate. Gordon Brown stated that 'real equality in life chances is what government seeks' (Leonard, 1999, p 46).

The very ambiguity of the term 'social justice' – a 'feel good' term that almost all can subscribe to – may of course be one reason why it is useful for many engaged in persuasion, the manipulation of public opinion and the solicitation of electoral support. For practitioners of social policy, concerned with practical policies reflecting many motivations, social justice is often a remote reference point, as abstruse as a lecture on thermodynamics to someone on the footplate of a steam engine. But if what is meant by social justice is unclear, the destination seen but darkly, then there is little chance of it being achieved.

Social justice tends to be discussed at an abstract, perhaps refined, level by political and economic philosophers. Many political philosophers have attempted to clarify what social justice is or should be. On this, there has not been unanimity of views. The purpose here is not to join in this very extensive debate (Chapter One); shelf-loads of books have been devoted to this task. Rather, the objective is to consider three of the most important theories in the past half-century – those of Nozick, of Rawls, and that associated jointly with Sen and Nussbaum – and discuss what they contribute to thinking about social policy. To a considerable extent, each of these theories can be seen as a different paradigm with its own intellectual faction or claque that defends the chosen approach and criticises or ignores other approaches. (Factional disputes characterise much intellectual activity and there is little doubt that professional superstar status comes with a personalised paradigm.) Certainly the stakes are high – a philosophic approach that may underlie the thinking and action of governments around the globe is not insignificant. Yet this factionalism and product differentiation is not wholly illuminating.

The chapter proceeds as follows. First, key features of the three theories are briefly outlined. Then what they share in common and what are their principal differences are examined. Some implications of the three theories for social policy are then considered. Three particular issues are then discussed: first, the relationship between public policy and private behaviour in so far as it affects social justice; second, children and the issues they pose for social justice; third, global inequality and justice in the world. Finally, the key questions that any conception of social justice and any practical social policies must answer are summarised.

The three approaches

Nozick

Robert Nozick's 'entitlement theory' in *Anarchy, state and utopia* (1974) sets out three components for a 'wholly just' world:

1. A person who acquires a holding in accordance with the principle of justice in acquisition is entitled to that holding.
2. A person who acquires a holding in accordance with the principle of justice in transfer, from someone who is entitled to a holding, is entitled to the holding.
3. No one is entitled to a holding except by repeated applications of (1) and (2).

> The complete principle of distributive justice would say
> simply that a distribution is just if everyone is entitled to
> the holdings they possess under the distribution. (Nozick,
> 1974, p 151)

Justice in transfer requires fair contracts without stealing, fraud,
enslavement or forcibly excluding others from competing in exchanges.
Justice in acquisition involves exclusive property rights over the material
world. Nozick follows Locke's notion that mixing one's labour with
the world can generate ownership providing the position of others
was not worsened compared to when the acquisition was unowned
or held in common.

If past acquisitions or transfers did not satisfy the conditions for
justice of acquisition, Nozick argues that a principle of rectification for
past injustices is necessary. But he does not explain with any precision
the circumstances in which acquisition could be judged unjust. Some
have argued that such a rectification principle is in practice impossible.
Nozick (1974, p 231) has acknowledged that without it no system of
transfers can be condoned.

Nozick describes his entitlement theory as 'historical' in that the
justice, or not, of the distribution depends on how it came about. In
a just society:

> What each person gets, he gets from others who give to
> him in exchange for something, or as a gift. In a free society,
> diverse persons control different resources, and new holdings
> arise out of the voluntary exchanges and actions of persons.
> (Nozick, 1974, pp 149-50)

Nozick's approach has been widely interpreted as a libertarian position
in which any taxation is effectively theft, depriving individuals of
property they are entitled to on the assumption that past acquisitions
have been freely contracted and justly obtained. As he put it, 'the
minimal state is the most extensive state that can be justified. Any state
more extensive violates people's rights' (Nozick, 1974, p 149).

Rawls

John Rawls' *A theory of justice* (1971) is a monumental work that has
influenced virtually all recent discussions of social justice. He set out
to examine the principles that should underlie a just society.

Rawls (1971, p 303) summarised his general conception of justice as follows:

> All social primary goods –liberty and opportunity, income and wealth, and the social bases of self-respect – are to be distributed equally unless an unequal distribution of any, or all, of these goods is to the advantage of the least favoured.

Rawls proposed the principle of fair equality of opportunity according to which 'those with similar abilities and skills should have similar life chances' (Rawls, 1971, p 73). But he does not spell out the meaning of 'similar life chances'.

He considered what principles we would choose if we did not know what position we would have in the society – the 'veil of ignorance'. His conclusion was to propose two principles of justice:

1. Each person is to have an equal right to the most extensive total system of liberties, with a similar system of liberty for all.
2. Social and economic inequalities are to be arranged so that they are both:
   a. to the greatest benefit of the least advantaged, consistent with the just savings principle; and
   b. attached to positions and offices open to all under conditions of fair equality of opportunity.' (Rawls, 1971, p 302)

Principle 2a is referred to as the difference principle.

To promote distributive justice the state requires a number of institutions, described as follows:

> I assume that the basic structure is regulated by a just constitution that secures the liberties of equal citizenship.... I assume also that there is fair (as opposed to formal) equality of opportunity.... Finally the government guarantees a social minimum either by family allowances and special payments for sickness and unemployment, or more systematically by such devices as a graded income supplement (a so-called negative income tax). (Rawls, 1971, p 275)

To achieve this, the government requires four branches:

---

(1) the allocation branch 'to keep the price system workably competitive and to prevent the formation of unreasonable market power';
(2) the stabilisation branch 'to bring about reasonably full employment';
(3) the transfer branch 'to ensure the social minimum';
(4) the distribution branch 'to preserve approximate justice in distributive shares by means of taxation and the necessary adjustments in the rights of property' (Rawls, 1971, pp 276-7).

Sen and Nussbaum

Amartya Sen (1992, 1999) rejected utilitarian and resource-based concepts of justice. Instead, he saw the requirement of a just society as being that all should have certain capabilities – what people are actually able to do and to be. Sen's thinking on capabilities has evolved over a considerable period and he has been reluctant to specify what these capabilities should be. Martha Nussbaum (2003) has supported Sen's general approach and has proposed a set of 10 capabilities, comprised of the following:

(1) To live to the end of a human life of a normal length.
(2) To have good health, to be adequately nourished and to have adequate shelter.
(3) To move freely from place to place, to be secure against violent assault, to have opportunities for sexual satisfaction and for choice in matters of reproduction.
(4) To use the senses to imagine, think and reason – and to do these things in a 'truly human way' – including political activities and religious freedom.
(5) To experience emotions – love, grief, anger, etc. – unblighted by fear and anxiety.
(6) To form a conception of the good and to reflect on one's life.
(7) To live with concern for other human beings and be treated as a dignified being whose worth is equal to that of others.
(8) To live with concern for and in relation to animals, plants, and the world of nature.
(9) To laugh, play and enjoy recreational activities.

(10) Politically, to participate in choices that govern one's life. Materially, to hold property and to seek employment on an equal basis with others, and to work as a human being. (Nussbaum, 2003, pp 41–42)

Sen distinguished the capability perspective as follows:

> The capability perspective ... differs from various concepts of 'equality of opportunities' which have been championed for a long time. In a very basic sense, a person's capability to achieve does indeed stand for the opportunity to pursue his or her objectives. But the concept of 'equality of opportunities' is standardly used in the policy literature in more restrictive ways, defined in terms of equal availability of some particular means, or with reference to equal applicability (or equal non-applicability) of some specific barriers or constraints. Thus characterised, 'equality of opportunities' does not amount to anything like equality of overall freedoms. (Sen, 1992, p 7)

Sen stresses the importance not only of personal characteristics – sex, health, intelligence and so on – but also of social characteristics – public policies, social norms, roles and hierarchies and so on and environmental characteristics – infrastructure, institutions, climate and so on.

For example, for a disabled wheelchair user, substantive freedom to move from place to place depends on more than income; it also depends on whether buildings and buses are designed in a way that allows access. If income is defined as command over resources in terms of purely private purchases, then money income is an appropriate measure. If it is defined as command over *all* resources then accessibility to public and private facilities is also important. For money to be exchanged for resources and, ultimately, improve an individual's welfare, requires the ability to engage in exchange, as well as something that can be exchanged.

Similarities and differences

Similarities

All three approaches emphasise the importance of basic political liberties and the importance of fair process. The advantages of free, voluntary exchange are recognised and treated as desirable in all three theories.

Markets should be open to all without discrimination. None should be excluded on any basis from access to free and open exchange. It is a common feature that social justice requires a liberal, open system in which all have access to all markets, be they for labour or for goods.

This area of common, shared views may seem rather limited but basic political liberties and fair exchange are not enjoyed by most of the world's population. The political and social institutions necessary for these aspects of social justice are not set out by any of the writers in any detail but it must be recognised that achieving them is something only recently achieved in only some countries. Unless active steps have been taken to fight oppression and end discrimination on the basis of gender, colour or creed, then discrimination persists. It can be argued, following T. H. Marshall, that without social rights – literacy, shelter, an end to destitution – then open access to fair exchange is not possible. Thus, in the specification of even a minimal state with equality of process put forward by Nozick, there is already an extensive, if unacknowledged, role for social policy. Yet, in contrast to Rawls and Sen and Nussbaum, this is almost the limit of Nozick's concern with social justice.

Differences

The principal differences between the three theories may conveniently be considered in relation to time – time past, time present and time future. What does each theory have to say about the past, what aspects of the present are relevant to social justice, and what relevance does the future have?

Time past – what is a fair starting point?

In what way is an assessment of social justice dependent on what has happened in the past? Is the starting point fair?

Nozick presumes that the past has been just, providing fair process has been followed. The starting point for different individuals may not be the same but it is not so different that it renders future social and economic exchanges unjust. However, holdings may have been acquired by means not sanctioned by the principle of justice in acquisition. 'Rectification' is required to deal with such injustices but Nozick does not spell out clearly what he considers to be past injustices. Slavery, seizure of lands used for grazing or habitation from native Americans and racial discrimination have all featured significantly in the history of the US. Given that history, one might conclude that Nozick should say nothing about social justice. Nozick has, nevertheless, been generally interpreted to assume that the past has been just and that there has been justice in acquisition. As a consequence, on this Nozickian approach, providing the principle of justice in transfer has been adhered to, the current distribution of income or wealth is just, however unequal it may be.

If one goes back in time far enough, something very unjust could be found in the past antecedents of everyone, either boosting or depleting their inheritance. Thus, the past has an overwhelming, inescapable and incalculable bearing on the justice of the present situation. In a sense, we are all products of our history, and all our histories involve injustices that might justify rectification. For example, Owen John Thomas told of a Welshman accused of trespassing:

> 'Your land, is it? Where did you get it from?' said the Welshman. 'Why, I got it from my father, and my father's father's father,' replied the landowner indignantly. 'Well, where did your father's father's father get the land in the first place,' asked the Welshman. 'He fought for it, my man,' answered the angry landowner. 'Well', said the Welshman, 'take your coat off and I will fight you for it now.' (National Assembly for Wales, Official Record 11/7/2002, p 103)

Central to Rawls' theory of justice is the 'veil of ignorance'. A new society is to be constructed in which you will not know which place you will be in – the Original Position. People decide on the rules to adopt without knowing who they are going to be. In so far as people are who they are because of their history, then this, in effect, neutralises any individual's history. Another way of thinking about this exercise is that you would not bring to this new society your own, actual past. Yet, it is difficult to think of being allocated the past of another member of society, for example the least advantaged person in the 'old society'. Therefore, Rawls seems to imply the elimination of the past as a consideration in determining a just society.

Sen and Nussbaum are concerned that all have a set of capabilities. This requires both personal resources and the appropriate economic and social context. They do not elaborate on inequality or social justice as such but rather talk in terms of a minimum necessary to ensure each of a set of capabilities. If people lack the skills or other resources to achieve that set of capabilities then the implication is that they should be brought up to the necessary level, offsetting past inequalities. Similarly, if the economic and social context restricts capabilities then it must be brought up to the necessary level – for example by ensuring wheelchair access into public buildings. They in effect imply that achieving a fair starting point for all is a prerequisite for substantive freedoms and social justice. Whether that fair starting point requires some minimum level of capabilities or requires equal capabilities is not made clear.

Thus, all three theories make different assumptions about the past and how it should be taken into account. Both Rawls and Sen and Nussbaum treat some degree of equal opportunity as essential for social justice.

Time present – what is the measure of inequality?

In what way should present circumstance be assessed in judging the justice of society? There is a tendency to treat any inequality as synonymous with inequity. This is clearly nonsense. Hours of sunshine in Barbados and Bradford are unequal but scarcely unjust.

The most commonly used measure of social inequality is income inequality. Yet, many inequalities in income are entirely just in most people's reckoning. For example, income may be higher because of years invested in training on a low income, because of longer hours put in, or because of worse working conditions. It would not be just if such differences were ignored although how large the differences such factors warrant is contentious. Some justifications for differences in incomes are, however, less widely agreed. Often the very highly paid justify their incomes on the basis of the responsibilities they bear. Yet, responsibility, even great responsibility, is for many an added advantage of a job, not a burden that must be compensated; certainly there are many willing to serve as government ministers, although how many of these are suitably qualified is open to question.

What is clear is that none of the three theories discussed here treats income as a good measure by which to assess social justice. On the other hand, none of them gives an entirely clear answer to the question of 'inequality of what?'. Nor do they answer the related and crucial question of 'what degree of inequality is just?'. If the top decile has on average twice the income of the bottom decile then most would agree that this was a more just society than one where the top has 20 times the bottom.

For Nozick, there is no point in even posing these questions. There is no purpose or need to assess the degree of inequality and consider its justice, providing his principles of justice have been followed. All are entitled to the full fruits of their labour. They may exchange freely with others and give to and receive from others. Providing this has taken place without coercion, the result may be deemed just or fair – although Nozick rarely uses these terms. Private decisions reflect abilities, effort, tastes and preferences and are no concern of others. Individuals may choose to work overtime hours with more income and less leisure – or not. They may choose a job with a higher wage that has worse working conditions, that is less geographically convenient or that has worse prospects – or not. Nozick, following Adam Smith's (1776, Book I, Ch X, Part I) discussion of equalising net advantages and disadvantages, clearly regards many inequalities as 'equalising differences'. Incentive payments designed to boost output may result in more income inequality but the extra income may be compensation for loss of leisure, comfort, convenience or prospects. This income inequality may in turn affect future levels of living.

For Rawls, the distribution of primary goods should be equal except in so far as any inequality benefits the least advantaged – the difference principle. Instead of a social welfare function that gives extra weight to those less advantaged (assuming diminishing marginal utility of income), Rawls in effect puts *all* the weight on the least advantaged. Regardless of whether this weighting is just, the more practical limitation of this approach is that it could in principle justify almost any inequality. While individual exchanges may be a private matter, social events are not. For example, if 10,000 of the least advantaged people thought it worthwhile to pay at least £100 to hear Pavarotti, then if the singer had been paid £1 million the resulting distributional impact, however unequal, would, in Rawls' terms, have been socially just. What is clear is that the effects of how income is distributed on what is produced – and in turn the resources available for the least advantaged – are important. Efficiency and equity cannot be separated.

Sen and Nussbaum argue that, providing all have a requisite set of capabilities, it is not an issue that the diversity of values and preferences may result in unequal outcomes. Sen also suggests that account may be taken of variation in needs, but he does not specify which needs are to be considered.

Both Rawls and Sen and Nussbaum are, then, concerned with the present distribution in assessing social justice but the parameters of the present that are judged relevant may differ. It is only possible to say that they 'may differ' because none of them are precise about which dimensions of the present should appropriately be considered. Certainly, the language and examples used suggest different sets of parameters but these are not intrinsic to the different approaches.

Time future – what is the relevance of the future?

What are the consequences of inequality for the future and should these be taken into account in deciding what is socially just? Is the future of any relevance in deciding what is now socially just?

For Nozick, future consequences have no relevance at all. What will be, will be. Certainly, individual decisions have consequences for the future but it is not for 'society' or the government to try to shape the future, nor should it consider the future in assessing what is just – except that contracts involving future commitments should be enforced not just now, in the present, but also in the future.

Rawls only refers to benefiting the least advantaged without making clear the timeframe involved. Do the disadvantaged need to benefit just at the present time or do they need to benefit evermore? Could a distribution that is just in Rawls' sense fail to provide equal starting points for future generations? Rawls does not make it clear whether the difference principle only justifies inequality if it is of immediate, rather than long-term benefit to the least advantaged. (Some, such as the Communist Party of the Soviet Union, justified elite treatment of senior Party apparatchiks on the grounds – however dubious – that they were building a more equal society for the future.)

Sen and Nussbaum acknowledge that some advantages and some disadvantages accumulate over a person's lifetime and across generations. Some capabilities and choices have more implications than others for the future. Neuberger and Fraser (1993, pp 58-9) propose that there should be:

> an explicit identification of functionings which are ordered
> thus in descending order of significance:
> a. life;
> b. physical functioning, the avoidance of acute suffering;
> c. the basis for citizenship including civil liberties.

One method of taking account of the future to a greater (or lesser) extent could be to give higher (or lower) priority to those capabilities such as bodily health that are most crucial for future prospects of individuals and future generations. But Neuberger and Fraser do not discuss doing this because the capabilities are a set rather than a checklist to be achieved one by one.

Just as the past affects the present, the present affects the future. Current income inequality affects future income inequality. This is most obvious if current privilege is used to purchase education or property that ensures future inequality. A wider question is, then, how far the concern should be focused on inequality now and how far account should be taken of future inequality.

An illustration of the relevance that the future may have to thinking about social justice is to compare those who believe that death marks the end of existence with those who expect something more. Some Hindus – but certainly not all in such a diverse and unorganised faith – believe in reincarnation and that those rich in their current life will be poor or even non-human in a future life; by contrast, many poor will be reincarnated in a wealthy household. Some Christians profess to believe that the poor are blessed because they will inherit the earth. Anticipated afterlife futures clearly affect the level of concern about inequalities in the current life.

Some implications of the three theories for social policy

Fair process

The requirements to achieve an open, free society with fair competition, no discrimination and no controlling monopolies are, as stated above, extensive. All three theories share the implication that this openness is fundamental to a just society. These requirements have not, until recently, been given high priority in most nations' social policies.

Fair starting points

Our genetic inheritance is beyond our control. Only eugenic prescriptions with most far-reaching, indeed chilling, dangers would seek to alter genetic inheritance. By contrast, inheritance of wealth in the form of physical and financial resources is subject to social and economic systems. While wealth is often mentioned in passing in discussions of social policy, it has been given little attention (Atkinson, 1972, and Rowlingson and McKay, 2005, are distinguished exceptions). Yet the policies affecting rights to own and bequeath property and to inherit, the distribution of bequest and gifts, and the taxation of inheritance and gifts are crucial to the inequality of starting points, and thus to social justice. How far social justice is possible given the degree of inequality in starting points is a serious question that is highlighted by the work of both Rawls and Sen.

A much wider issue is raised by Nozick's rectification principle. The present life of all African Americans in the US has been fundamentally influenced by slavery. No clearer example of unjust acquisition can be found than the seizure and enslavement of millions of Africans. The rectification principle thus raises the entire issue of reparations. It certainly casts doubt on the justice of a distribution in which the proportion living in poverty is over twice as high among the black as among the white population and life expectancy is five years less (US Census Bureau, *2007 Statistical Abstract*, Tables 694 and 100).

Income and social policy

Income is used as a crucial metric – in determining ability to pay tax, in deciding on need for means-tested benefits, indeed throughout social policy. Income may be defined in many ways (gross, net, original, final, equivalised, earned and so on) for many different units (individual, family, household and so on) over many different time periods (hour, day, week, month, year, lifetime). But, whatever the definition, income is an ever-present measure. In large part this is because money income is one thing that can be conveniently counted, being measured in the unit of the currency.

Yet, from the perspective of social justice, income is a very poor measure. First, money income is not a true measure of command over resources. Second, income is in effect the outcome of the choices made given the available opportunities. What Rawls and Sen emphasise is the importance of primary goods and of capabilities. Both these are much more about opportunities than about outcomes.

The implication of this for social policy is that efforts to alter opportunities and capabilities may be more equitable than efforts to alter outcomes. This is complicated by the fact that opportunities and capabilities often depend crucially on income, itself the outcome of opportunities. In practice in most industrialised nations far more government spending is devoted to altering outcomes, by means of redistribution through the tax and benefit systems, than is devoted to extending or, more crucially, equalising opportunities.

Income remains highly relevant and important but more because it influences the opportunities and capabilities of a person and their dependants than as a direct indicator of level of living.

Inequality and inequity

In thinking about social justice in actual social policies and systems, Rawls and Sen show that it is necessary to distinguish between equitable and inequitable inequalities. The practical problem is that every inequality is justified by someone. Yet, it is surely absurd to justify an income one hundred times another's on the grounds of, say, extra work when extra work consists of working 60 instead of 50 hours a week. There are no limits to human inventiveness in the justifications offered for extravagant greed. Yet, treating all inequalities as socially unjust is clearly wrong. One way of recognising that inequity and inequality are not synonymous is to concentrate on opportunities and capabilities. If these are not too unequal, then inequalities in income are likely to be much less in extent and of much less concern.

Future consequences

Do possible future reductions in injustice justify present injustice? How far should it be an objective of social policy to prevent future injustice? Or should its role be limited to alleviating current injustices?

This can be illustrated with a simplified but real example. Maths teachers are employed earning an average of, say, £30,000 per year; at this rate of pay most are satisfied with their job. But at this rate of pay the number of new maths teachers being recruited is inadequate. The British government has therefore decided that all maths teachers should receive a premium (which it cannot offer only to new teachers since this would create resentment among the 'old' maths teachers). Does this premium add to or reduce social justice? It could be said to be fair since the premium is needed to compensate for the costs and benefits of being a maths teacher and the loss of other earnings for the new recruits into maths teaching. The premium could be said to be unfair in that the 'old' maths teachers receive a windfall for social reasons unrelated to them individually.

The prevention of future social injustices is a concern of many preventive social policies, in health, education, housing and so on. If social policy were confined to present and revealed injustices, it would be hard to justify policies concerned with lifetime redistribution or human capital formation. By highlighting choices between present and future social justice, it is possible to think more clearly about the balance between immediate and long-term concerns.

Three issues

The relation of public and private actions

Many phenomena are the result of a complex interplay of public and private behaviour.

The determinants of an individual's health include water supply and sanitation, diet, exercise, smoking, drinking, stress, the prevalence of communicable diseases, genetic inheritance, and availability and quality of health services. Educational achievement depends on genetics, early years' experience in the home, parental support at school, peer group composition, and, of course, the school system.

There are, then, many influences on health and education in addition to the social services. Yet, public actions, in the form of government policy, only directly determine the quantity and quality of social service provision. The problem for a government concerned with social justice is that many of the determinants of social outcomes are essentially private.

One response – that of Nozick – is to treat inequality as something reflecting inherent human differences, as being unavoidable, and not being a concern of justice. Rawls is deeply concerned with social justice, but tends to treat it as something that can be delivered through public policy, largely ignoring the effects of actions in the private sphere on social justice. Sen and Nussbaum are, by contrast, much concerned with the role of agency and the importance of individuals being able to make real choices, an issue discussed in relation to caring for children in the next section.

How far private behaviour can and should be altered is clearly a pressing issue in many areas of social policy – in relation to reproduction, parenting, health-related activities and self-provision for old age, for example. Such issues do raise major problems for political philosophy, yet up to now they have been little considered.

There is an old saying that economics is about how people make choices and sociology is about how people do not have choices to make. In so far as people can choose personal behaviour, many types of personal behaviour have social consequences – it is not wholly private behaviour. This is obvious if a person chooses to drive recklessly. It is also true if someone encourages their child to read. Social policy, until recently, has been largely concerned with complementing or responding to private behaviour – often literally picking up the pieces. In the future there may be much more of an attempt to alter private behaviour for social reasons.

Children

What are outcomes for one generation are crucial determinants of opportunities for the next generation. The British government has set the aim of providing equal opportunity for all. As Blair, when Prime Minister, put it:

> [L]ife chances should depend on talent and effort, not the chance of birth; and that talent and effort should be handsomely rewarded. The child born on a run-down housing estate should have the same chance to be healthy and well educated as the child born in the leafy suburbs. (Blair, cited in Walker, 1999, pp 8-9)

The issue of how far children can and should be given an equal start in life underlies much social policy thinking and policy (see also Chapters Seven and Eight, this volume). Equal opportunity has for the most part been discussed in terms of educational provision. Yet, there is much evidence that inequalities in life chances to a substantial extent reflect the inequalities that have developed by the time small children enter the educational system. The factors affecting the start that children get in life – their genetic and material inheritance, their home environment, early years' parenting, living in poverty or material comfort – are crucial to their prospects. Whether such factors can or should be treated as 'primary goods' in Rawls' terms or treated as essential for developing capabilities, they cannot be neglected when assessing social justice from a child's perspective.

Social policy has largely neglected many of the factors which undoubtedly affect life chances of children, such as inheritance of wealth, preparation for parenthood, preschool provision, social policy on space and time for children to play, and commercial pressures on childhood. Concentration on educational targets, such as GCSE pass rates, is no route to developing wide-ranging capabilities. These capabilities require the nurturing of mind, body, emotions and spirit – the development, in Nussbaum's (2003, p 40) phrase, of young people who are truly human.

As Nussbaum discusses, the need for social care of children poses the problem of restricting the freedom of parents, particularly of mothers. Lewis and Giullari (2005) discuss this and argue that:

> Both employment and care are necessary for human flourishing.... From the point of view of human welfare, it is impossible to choose not to care or not to work. In this sense, to choose between them has the hallmarks of tragedy as much or more than opportunity, which makes it all the more important seriously to address the policies

that play a part in structuring people's choices. (Lewis and Giullari, 2005, pp 97-8)

Global injustice

Abstract political philosophy frequently transcends boundaries of thought or jurisdiction. That is both its fascination and its limitation. There is certainly in all three theories discussed here a lack of clarity about which territory is under discussion (see also Chapter Six, this volume). By contrast, social policy is much concerned about eligibilities and entitlements based on nationality or residence as well as with issues that are directly concerned with nationality, such as migration controls. Whereas in the past, many concerns were seen in purely national terms, now there is increasing acknowledgement of the extent of cross-boundary influences.

HIV/AIDS, with its devastating social consequences and massive challenges to social policy, is not confined within national borders. Similarly, climate change, with its potentially vast social impact, is a global phenomenon. Both these phenomena have major consequences for social justice at a global level.

In the past, the concern within richer nations for poorer nations was largely confined to the most extreme poverty, such as fundraising for disaster relief. Overseas aid is to some extent concerned with broader economic development but it is also often used as an instrument of foreign policy and arms sales. Its impact is limited and haphazard, even when well intentioned.

Now there is more attention devoted by governments, non-governmental organisations and people generally – and particularly young people – to international development, the achievement of millennium development goals for water supply and primary schools, and the promotion of fair trade. All these issues are basically concerned with global social justice.

Neither Nozick nor Rawls in their main works were concerned with issues of global justice. (In Rawls' later work *The law of peoples*, 1999, he discussed issues of international relations but not specifically global justice.)

Sen has argued that his approach is of global relevance: capabilities reflect common human needs, the meeting of which depends on the national context. For example, moving freely from place to place may require a boat, a bicycle or a car depending on whether the setting is Micronesia, rural Africa or Texas. In addition, Sen in his specifically economic work has been much concerned with development (for example, Sen, 1999).

Yet, for the most part, both social justice and social policy have been and continue to be thought about within national boundaries. Perhaps the greatest challenges to thinking about social justice and to the development of social policy are to transcend national boundaries and treat humans equally whatever their race, colour or creed. It seems probable that each challenge will be met only to the extent that they are both met.

Conclusion

The pursuit of social justice has been the driving force behind much, perhaps most, social change. It is not surprising, therefore, that opinions about what is fair and just have differed, and will probably always do so. No attempt is made here to suggest how social justice should be defined. Instead, it may be worth repeating the three questions posed above – questions that have to be answered by any theory of justice and by any social policies that seek to be fair. These questions relate to the past, the present and the future:

(1) What is a fair starting point? The past cannot be changed, however much aspects of it may be regretted. Much in the past seems to us now grossly unjust. What should be done to take account of the past?

(2) What is just and unjust about the present distribution of resources? Which inequalities are justified and which are downright unjust?

(3) What is the relevance of the future? In assessing social policies, should the consequences for future social justice be considered? We are only temporary stewards of the earth and it is clear that how we use the world's resources determines the future physical state of the world. How far should we also be concerned with the consequences of our actions for social justice in the future? There can be little doubt that the justice or injustice of the distribution of power and resources within communities and nations and across the world will shape the lives of future generations.

References

Atkinson, A. B. (1972) *Unequal shares: Wealth in Britain*, London: Allen Lane.

Leonard, D. (ed) (1999) *Crosland and New Labour*, London: Macmillan and Fabian Society.

Lewis, J. and Giullari, S. (2005) 'The adult worker model family, gender equality and care: the search for new policy principles and the possibilities and problems of a capabilities approach', *Economy and Society*, vol 34, no 1, pp 76-104.

Neuberger, H. and Fraser, N. (1993) *Economic policy: A rights-based approach*, Aldershot: Avebury.

Nozick, N. (1974) *Anarchy, state, and utopia*, Oxford: Blackwell.

Nussbaum, M. (2003) 'Capabilities as fundamental entitlements: Sen and social justice', *Feminist Economics*, vol 9, no 2-3, pp 33-59.

Rawls, J. (1971) *A theory of justice*, Cambridge, MA: Harvard University Press.

Rawls, J. (1999) *The law of peoples*, Cambridge, MA: Harvard University Press.

Rowlingson, K. and McKay, S. (2005) *Attitudes to inheritance in Britain*, Bristol: The Policy Press.

Sen, A. K. (1992) *Inequality re-examined*, Oxford: Oxford University Press.

Sen, A. K. (1999) *Development as freedom*, Oxford: Oxford University Press.

Smith, A. (1776) *An inquiry into the nature and causes of the wealth of nations*, Edinburgh.

Walker, R. (ed) (1999) *Ending child poverty*, Bristol: The Policy Press.

THREE

Multiculturalism, social justice and the welfare state

Will Kymlicka

Introduction

One of the major challenges facing Western societies concerns increasing ethnocultural diversity. There are three diversity-related trends that are transforming Western societies:

- the increasing ethnic and racial heterogeneity of the population;
- the increasing politicisation of ethnocultural identities, and the rise of 'identity politics'; and
- partly in response to the first two trends, the increasing adoption of 'multiculturalism' policies to accommodate ethnocultural groups.

In short, there are changes in demographic composition, political mobilisation, and public policies.

These diversity-related trends pose several challenges for the pursuit of social justice. First, there are questions about the fairness of multiculturalism policies themselves. How can society fairly accommodate differences in language, culture and religion? In a democracy, public institutions are likely to be shaped by the culture of the dominant group. When does this result in injustice against minority groups, and what forms of accommodation or recognition can remedy these injustices?

Second, these trends raise indirect challenges for the pursuit of social justice. It is widely believed that the increasing presence and politicisation of ethnic and racial diversity is jeopardising the pursuit of more traditional issues of social injustice, particularly class-based economic inequalities. There is a fear that multiculturalism will erode the sense of national solidarity and common citizenship that underpins the welfare state, and hence erode the capacity of the state to engage in economic redistribution.

In this chapter, I will explore these two challenges. What is the relationship between fairness in the accommodation of diversity (through multiculturalism policies) and fairness in the distribution of economic resources (through the welfare state)? I will start by outlining some current work on multicultural citizenship, and then examine the concern that there is a trade-off between multiculturalism and the welfare state.

Making sense of multiculturalism

Across the Western democracies, minority ethnic groups are demanding greater recognition and accommodation of their distinctive identities. In some cases, they seek only greater protection, on a non-discriminatory basis, of the familiar set of civil, political and social rights of citizenship that are protected in all constitutional liberal democracies. But in many cases, they also seek a more 'multicultural' conception of citizenship, one that includes various group-specific rights regarding their language, religion or culture in addition to the common individual rights of citizenship. How are we to evaluate these multiculturalist claims?

To understand the logic of multiculturalism, we need to understand what it is a response to, or what it is a reaction against. All struggles for multiculturalism share in common a rejection of earlier models of the unitary, homogenous nation state. In order to understand the idea of a multicultural democracy, therefore, we need first to understand this older model of a homogenous nation state, and why it has been rejected.

Until recently, most states around the world aspired to be 'nation states'. In this model, the state was implicitly (and sometimes explicitly) seen as the possession of a dominant national group, which used the state to privilege its identity, language, history, culture, literature, myths, religion and so on, and which defined the state as the expression of its nationhood. Anyone who did not belong to this dominant national group was subject to either assimilation or exclusion.

There is nothing natural about such nation states. Very few countries around the world are historically mono-national (Iceland and Portugal are the most frequently cited examples). In most countries, this ideal of national homogeneity had to be constructed by the state through a range of 'nation-building' policies that encouraged the preferred national identity while suppressing alternative identities.

The character of these nation-building policies has varied from country to country. In most Western countries, there has been a single dominant ethno-national group forming a clear majority of the population (for example, the Greeks in Greece, the Castilians in Spain and so on), and nation-building policies have been used to impose this dominant group's language and culture on the rest of the population. Some of the policies adopted to achieve this goal include:

- the adoption of official language laws, which define the dominant group's language as the sole official 'national' language, and which require this to be the only language used in the bureaucracy, courts, public services, military, higher education and so on;
- the construction of a nationalised system of compulsory education promoting a standardised curriculum, focused on teaching the dominant group's language, literature and history (which are redefined as the 'national' language, literature and history);
- the centralisation of political power, eliminating pre-existing forms of local autonomy enjoyed historically by minority groups, so that all important decisions are made in a forum where the dominant group forms a majority;
- the diffusion of the dominant group's language and culture through national cultural institutions, including national public media and public museums;
- the adoption of state symbols celebrating the dominant group's history, heroes and culture, reflected in the choice of national holidays, the naming of streets and so on;
- the construction of a unified legal and judicial system, operating in the dominant group's language and using its legal traditions, and the abolition of any pre-existing legal systems used by minority groups;
- the adoption of settlement policies that encourage members of the dominant national group to settle in areas where minority groups have historically resided, so as to swamp the minorities even in their historic homelands;
- the adoption of immigration policies that require knowledge of the 'national' language/history as a condition of gaining citizenship, and that often give a preference to immigrants who share the same language, religion or culture as the dominant group; and
- the seizure of lands, forests and fisheries that used to belong to minority groups and indigenous peoples, and declaring them to be 'national' resources, to be used for the benefit of the nation.

The intended outcome of these policies is clear:

- to centralise all political and legal power in forums dominated by the majority group;
- to privilege that group's language and culture in all public institutions, which are then diffused throughout the territory of the state; and
- to make minority languages and cultures invisible in public space.

Various justifications have been offered historically for this pursuit of national homogeneity. In some contexts, it was argued that the state needed to be more unified in order to effectively defend itself against external or internal enemies, or to build the civic solidarity needed for a welfare state. Or that a culturally unified state was easier to administer, and would have a more efficient labour market. But these justifications were also typically buttressed by racialist and ethnocentric ideologies, which asserted that the language and culture of minority groups and indigenous peoples were backward and inferior, unworthy of respect.

The pursuit of homogenising nationhood has had profound effects on sub-state ethnocultural groups. Within the territory of most states there are many groups possessing their own language, history, culture, heroes and symbols. Such groups are often excluded by the process of nation-building, or included only at the price of accepting assimilation and second-class status, stigmatised by the racialist and ethnocentric ideologies used to justify nation-building. Indeed, minorities are typically the first target of these policies, since they are the greatest obstacle to the goal (or myth) of a unified nation state, and hence most in need of 'nationalisation'. The result, over time, has been the creation of multiple and deeply-rooted forms of exclusion and subordination for minorities, often combining political marginalisation, economic disadvantage and cultural domination.

As a result, various sub-state groups have contested efforts to construct homogeneous nation states, and have advocated instead for a more multicultural state.

What does a multicultural state look like? The details vary from country to country, for reasons I discuss below. The sorts of political reforms demanded by African Americans in the US differ from those demanded by indigenous Maori in New Zealand or by Chinese immigrants in Canada. However, three general principles are common to these different struggles for a multicultural state. First, a multicultural state repudiates the older idea that the state is a possession of a single national group. Instead, the state must be seen as belonging equally to all citizens. Second, as a consequence, a multicultural state repudiates any nation-building policies that assimilate or exclude members of non-dominant groups. Instead, it accepts that individuals should be able to access state institutions, and to act as full and equal citizens in political life, without having to hide or deny their ethnocultural identity. The state accepts an obligation to accord recognition and accommodation to the history, language and culture of non-dominant groups, as it does for the dominant group. Third, a multicultural state acknowledges the historic injustice that was done to minority groups by these policies of assimilation and exclusion, and manifests a willingness to offer some sort of rectification for them.

These three ideas – repudiating the idea of the state as belonging to the dominant group; replacing assimilationist and exclusionary nation-building policies with policies of recognition and accommodation; and acknowledging historic injustice and offering amends for it – are common to all struggles for multiculturalism.

These points of commonality are very abstract, and once we look at the details of particular cases, enormous differences emerge. The precise ways in which minority groups wish to be accommodated, or to have their historic injustices amended, varies from country to country, as well as between different minorities within a single country.

I cannot provide a comprehensive overview of the different forms that multiculturalism can take, but for the purposes of illustration, let me focus on three general trends within Western democracies.

Indigenous peoples

The first trend concerns the treatment of indigenous peoples, such as the Indians and Inuit in Canada, the Aboriginal peoples of Australia, the Maori of New Zealand, the Sami of Scandinavia, the Inuit of Greenland and Indian tribes in the US. In the past, all of these countries had the goal and expectation that indigenous peoples would disappear as distinct communities, as a result of dying out, intermarriage or assimilation. A number of policies were adopted to speed up this process, such as stripping indigenous peoples of their lands, restricting the practice of their traditional cultures, languages and religions, and undermining their institutions of self-government.

However, there has been a dramatic reversal in these policies, starting in the early 1970s. Today, all of the countries I just mentioned accept, at least in principle, the idea that indigenous peoples will exist into the indefinite future as distinct societies within the larger country, and that they must have the land claims, cultural rights and self-government rights needed to sustain themselves as distinct societies.

Sub-state nationalisms

A second trend concerns the treatment of sub-state 'national' groups, such as the Québécois in Canada, Scots and Welsh in Britain, Catalans and Basques in Spain, Flemish in Belgium, the German-speaking minority in South Tyrol in Italy and Puerto Ricans in the US. These regionally concentrated groups conceive of themselves as nations within a larger state, and mobilise behind nationalist political parties to achieve recognition of their nationhood, either in the form of an independent state or through territorial autonomy within the larger state. In the past, Western countries have attempted to suppress expressions of sub-state nationalism. To have a regional group with a sense of distinct nationhood was seen as a threat to the state, putting into question the state's legitimate right to rule all of its territory and population. Various efforts were made to erode any sense of distinct nationhood, often using the same tools that were used against indigenous peoples – for example, restricting minority language rights, abolishing traditional forms of regional self-government and encouraging members of the dominant group to settle in the minority group's homeland.

However, there has been a dramatic reversal in the way Western countries deal with sub-state nationalisms. Today, all of the countries I have just mentioned have accepted the principle that sub-state national identities will endure into the indefinite future, and that their sense of nationhood and nationalist aspirations must be accommodated. This accommodation has typically taken the form of creating a federal or quasi-federal sub-unit in which the minority group form a local majority, and can thereby exercise meaningful forms of self-government.[1] Moreover, the group's language is typically recognised as an official state language, at least within its federal sub-unit, and perhaps throughout the country as a whole.

Immigrant groups

A third trend concerns the treatment of immigrant groups. Historically, the four main countries of immigration (Australia, Canada, New Zealand and the US) had an assimilationist approach to immigration. Immigrants were expected to assimilate to the pre-existing society, with the hope that over time they would become indistinguishable from native-born citizens in their speech, dress, recreation, voting patterns, and way of life generally. Any groups that were seen as incapable of this sort of cultural assimilation were prohibited from emigrating in the first place, or from becoming citizens. This was reflected in laws that excluded Africans and Asians from entering these countries of immigration for much of the 20th century, or from naturalising.

Since the late 1960s, however, there has been a dramatic change in this approach. There have been two related changes: first, the adoption of race-neutral admissions criteria, so that immigrants to these countries are increasingly from non-European (and often non-Christian) societies; and second, the adoption of a more multicultural conception of integration, one which expects that many immigrants will visibly and proudly express their ethnic identity, and which accepts an obligation on the part of public institutions (like the police, schools, media, museums and so on) to accommodate these ethnic identities.

These twofold changes have occurred in all four traditional countries of immigration, although there are important differences in how official the shift to multiculturalism was. In Australia, Canada and New Zealand the shift was marked by the declaration of an official multicultural policy by the central government. The US, by contrast, does not have an official policy of multiculturalism at the federal level. However, if we look at lower levels of American government, such as states or cities, we often find a broad range of multiculturalism policies. If we look at state-level policies regarding the education curriculum, for example, or city-level policies regarding policing or hospitals, we will often find that they are indistinguishable from the way provinces and cities in Australia or Canada deal with issues of immigrant ethnocultural diversity. As Nathan Glazer (1997) puts it in the title to his book, 'we are all multiculturalists now'.

This trend applies primarily to countries of immigration – that is, countries that legally admit immigrants as permanent residents and future citizens. It is a different story, however, in those countries that do not legally admit immigrants, such as some countries of Northern Europe. These countries may well contain large numbers of 'foreigners', in the form of illegal economic migrants, asylum seekers or 'guest-workers', but these groups were not admitted as part of a deliberate immigration policy. As it happens, even some of these countries have adopted aspects of a 'multicultural' approach (for example, the Netherlands and Sweden). But in general, the trend from assimilation to multiculturalism is one that has taken place most strongly within countries of immigration.

In all three contexts, therefore, we see a shift towards a more multicultural model of citizenship. To be sure, these trends are contested and uneven, subject to backlash and retreat.[2] But it is widely accepted that at least some forms of multiculturalism are legitimate. Given the way that public institutions have explicitly been skewed in favour of the language, culture and religion of the dominant group, and given the way that these biases have historically been justified in the name of racialist and ethnocentric ideologies, some form of multiculturalism is needed to remedy these injustices.

It is important to emphasise that the rise of multiculturalism is not a repudiation of liberal democratic values. On the contrary, human rights norms both inspire and constrain the pursuit of multiculturalism. The human rights revolution has delegitimised older ideologies of racial and ethnic hierarchy that historically justified the exclusion or assimilation of minorities, and has thereby encouraged and inspired struggles for greater recognition and accommodation. But the human rights revolution also constrains the way these claims are advanced: it requires minorities to abandon any supremacist ideologies that they may have historically embraced. After all, many minority groups have their own traditions of racism, anti-Semitism, homophobia, sexism, and discrimination against lower-caste groups. All of this must be renounced if minorities want to take advantage of the human rights revolution in order to contest their historic exclusion. Liberal democratic multiculturalism is an iterative process. For example, it allows the Québécois to challenge their historic subordination to English-Canadians, but equally allows immigrants in Quebec to challenge their historic exclusion from Québécois society.

Viewed this way, multiculturalism can be seen as a process of 'citizenisation', in sociological jargon. Historically, ethnocultural and religious diversity in the West has been characterised by a range of illiberal and undemocratic relations – including relations of conqueror and conquered; coloniser and colonised; settler and indigenous; racialised and unmarked; normalised and deviant; orthodox and heretic; civilised and backward; ally and enemy; master and slave. The task for all liberal democracies has been to turn this catalogue of uncivil relations into relationships of liberal democratic citizenship, both in terms of the vertical relationship between members of minorities and the state, and the horizontal relationships among members of different groups.

In the past, it was assumed that the only way to engage in this process of citizenisation was to impose a single undifferentiated model of citizenship on all individuals. But liberal multiculturalism starts from the assumption that this complex history inevitably and appropriately generates group-differentiated ethnopolitical claims. The key to citizenisation is not to suppress these differential claims, but rather to filter and frame them through the language of human rights, civil liberties and democratic accountability. And this is what liberal multiculturalism seeks to do.

In my view, the acceptance of multiculturalism is centrally tied to this process of citizenisation. The idea that multiculturalism can serve as an effective vehicle for consolidating relations of liberal democratic citizenship in multiethnic states is contested. Indeed, most commentators writing in the 1950s and 1960s would have rejected this idea, fearing that it would simply reproduce relations of enmity or hierarchy. But we now have close to 40 years of experience in the West with various models of liberal multiculturalism, and there is growing evidence that they can indeed help to reduce historic inequalities between groups, while strengthening practices of democratic citizenship.[3]

Multiculturalism and the welfare state

Multiculturalism, then, can be seen as an attempt to remedy the longstanding patterns of injustice that have characterised state–minority relations in the era of nation-building states. In this way, it is a contribution to social justice. But many commentators worry that the pursuit of multiculturalism makes it more difficult to achieve other dimensions of social justice. In particular, there is a concern that the increasing salience of ethnocultural diversity may erode the welfare state, and thereby undermine the redistribution of economic resources.

To understand this concern, we need to examine the link between the welfare state and ideologies of nationhood. The national welfare state is precisely a *national* institution, and its historic evolution is tied up with ideas of nationhood. In fact, the link between the welfare state and national identity runs in both directions. On the one hand, politicians appealed to ideas of common nationhood and national solidarity to legitimise the welfare state. Citizens were told that they should be willing to support the welfare state because its beneficiaries are co-nationals to whom we have special obligations: they are 'one of us'. On the other hand, the welfare state also served to spread ideas of nationhood. Access to common national educational and healthcare systems, and to other social rights, gave concrete substance to ideas of common nationhood. Participating in the institutions of a national welfare state provided a source of common experiences and loyalties that helped bind together the disparate populations of Western countries.

In short, the welfare state both presupposed and perpetuated an ideology of nationhood. This raises the worry that the trends towards increasing ethnic diversity, identity politics and multiculturalism policies are undermining the national identities and solidarities that have historically sustained the welfare state. There are actually two concerns here:

- that ethnic/racial diversity as such makes it more difficult to sustain redistributive policies, since it is difficult to generate a common sense of national identity and feelings of national solidarity across ethnic/racial lines. We can formulate this as the hypothesis that the larger the size of ethnic/racial minorities as a percentage of the population, the harder it is to sustain a robust welfare state (I will call this the heterogeneity/redistribution trade-off hypothesis); and
- that the multiculturalism policies adopted to recognise or accommodate ethnic groups tend further to undermine national solidarity, since they emphasise ethnic differences rather than national commonalities. We can formulate this as the hypothesis that the more a country embraces a multicultural 'politics of recognition', the harder it is to sustain the 'politics of redistribution' (I will call this the recognition/redistribution trade-off hypothesis).

The first hypothesis argues that the very presence of ethnic/racial diversity erodes the welfare state, regardless of what sorts of policies governments adopt to manage that diversity. The second hypothesis argues that the typical way in which Western states today attempt to manage diversity – namely, by accommodating it through multiculturalism policies, rather than ignoring or suppressing it – worsens the problem.

If either of these hypotheses were true, the very idea of a 'multicultural welfare state' – a welfare state that respects and accommodates diversity – would be almost a contradiction in terms. This worry has been labelled as the 'progressive's dilemma' (Pearce, 2004). Social democrats, it is said, are faced with a tragic trade-off between sustaining their traditional agenda of economic redistribution and embracing ethnocultural diversity and multiculturalism. The belief in such a trade-off is creating a major political realignment on these issues. In the past, most resistance to immigration and multiculturalism came from the Right, who viewed them as a threat to cherished national traditions or values. Today, however, opposition to immigration and multiculturalism is emerging within the Left, as a perceived threat to the welfare state.

But are these two hypotheses true? Let me look at the two claims in turn.

The heterogeneity/redistribution hypothesis

The idea that ethnic/racial heterogeneity can weaken the pursuit of the welfare state is an old one, dating back at least to Marx. Yet, until recently, no one has attempted systematically to test the impact of heterogeneity on welfare state spending.

Attention to heterogeneity initially emerged in two discrete geographical contexts. First, development economists pointed to ethnic and tribal diversity in attempting to explain the poor economic and social performance of countries in sub-Saharan Africa. The focus here was initially on the impact of ethnic heterogeneity on economic growth, but subsequent research has extended the focus to include the negative impact of heterogeneity on the provision of public goods, such as public education.

The second context concerns the US, where ethnic and racial heterogeneity has been invoked to explain differences in social expenditures across cities and states within the country. These studies consistently show, for example, that the higher the proportion of African Americans within a state, the more restrictive state-level welfare programmes such as Medicaid are.[4]

Based on these two experiences, several scholars have concluded that there is a universal tendency for people to resist interethnic redistribution. Explanations differ as to why this tendency exists. Some argue that ethnocentrism is a genetically determined disposition, since evolution would select for 'ethnic nepotism'. From an evolutionary perspective, it is rational to make sacrifices for those who are more likely to share one's genes, but irrational to help those who do not, and ethnicity is in effect an extended kin-group. If the increasing level of ethnic and racial heterogeneity means that citizens can no longer see the national community as essentially co-extensive with their own ethnic group, support for national-level redistribution will diminish (Salter, 2004).

Others offer more nuanced accounts. Even if people are willing in principle to make sacrifices for co-citizens who are not co-ethnics – perhaps motivated by a sense of common citizenship or patriotism – they are only likely to do so if they trust the would-be recipient to reciprocate. However, this sort of trust is difficult to generate across ethnic lines. For one thing, it is easier to sanction 'defectors' within one's own ethnic group than to sanction members of other ethnic groups (Miguel and Gugarty, 2005). Also, trust can be seen as a component of social capital that develops in associational life, and Putnam (2004) argues that the sort of associational life that generates social capital is lower in ethnically heterogeneous neighbourhoods. Other analysts emphasise electoral dynamics (Kitschelt, 1995), or the challenges ethnic cleavages raise for the formation of labour-based political parties (Alesina and Glaeser, 2004).

Whatever the explanation, there is an increasing tendency to assume that ethnic/racial heterogeneity erodes redistribution. Although the main evidence for this assumption comes from two specific contexts – namely, sub-Saharan Africa and the US – it is increasingly treated as a universal tendency. The strongly racialised dimension of US welfare politics is no longer seen as an anomaly – a pernicious legacy of the peculiar American history of slavery and segregation – but rather as a normal reaction to the simple fact of ethnic/racial heterogeneity.

Based on this assumption, scholars have drawn dire predictions about the future of the welfare state across the West. If it is the mere presence of ethnic and racial minorities that has weakened the welfare state in the US, then increasing immigration threatens to do the same in Europe. As early as 1986, Gary Freeman (1986, p 62) predicted that immigration would lead to 'the Americanization of European welfare politics', and more recent studies have reiterated this prediction. In their comparison of the US and European welfare states, Alesina and Glaeser (2004, pp 180-1) conclude that:

> As Europe has become more diverse, Europeans have increasingly been susceptible to exactly the same form of racist, anti-welfare demagoguery that worked so well in the United States. We shall see whether the generous welfare state can really survive in a heterogeneous society.

This, then, is the basic case for a heterogeneity/redistribution trade-off. It begins with strong empirical evidence from two specific contexts – Africa and the US – where negative correlations between ethnic/racial heterogeneity and public spending have been found in several studies. This evidence is then combined with some speculations about the underlying mechanisms at work, and the conclusion is drawn that there is a general tendency for heterogeneity to erode redistribution.

This basic case has some initial plausibility, but it is not watertight. The empirical evidence is drawn from two contexts that are atypical. In the sub-Saharan context, the artificiality of state boundaries, combined with the weakness of state institutions at the time of independence, meant that states had no usable traditions or institutional capacity for dealing with diversity. In the US context, racial animosity had been sedimented by centuries of slavery and segregation, whose maintenance depended on state-sponsored ideologies that dehumanised black people. One could argue that neither of these contexts provides a reliable basis for predicting the impact of, say, Turkish immigration on the German welfare state, or Philippine immigration on the Canadian welfare state. We need more research before drawing firm conclusions about the heterogeneity/redistribution trade-off.

The recognition/redistribution hypothesis

Much of the literature to date has focused on the link between levels of ethnic/racial heterogeneity and the welfare state. But in many public policy contexts, the level of heterogeneity is a historical given: a country already contains certain ethnic and racial minorities. For most policy makers, therefore, the crucial issue is not 'what level of ethnic heterogeneity is desirable', but rather 'how should we respond to the ethnic heterogeneity that already exists in our society'. And here, as I noted earlier, we see an important shift: many Western democracies have repudiated older policies of assimilation or exclusion, and moved towards a more accommodating approach to diversity. This is reflected in the widespread adoption of multiculturalism policies for immigrant groups, the acceptance of territorial autonomy and language rights for national minorities, and the recognition of land claims and self-government rights for indigenous peoples. I will refer to all such policies as 'multiculturalism policies' or MCPs.

This trend has generated the second concern noted above – namely, the fear that there is a trade-off between MCPs and the welfare state. MCPs recognise and institutionalise heterogeneity, and if we assume that heterogeneity weakens the welfare state, this negative impact may be compounded by policies that heighten its public visibility and political salience. Critics worry, therefore, that there is a conflict between multicultural recognition and economic redistribution.

These critics acknowledge that defenders of MCPs do not *intend* to weaken the welfare state.[5] On the contrary, most defenders of MCPs are also defenders of the welfare state, and view both as flowing from the same principles of social justice. The conflict between MCPs and the welfare state, therefore, is not a matter of competing ideals or principles, but of unintended sociological dynamics. MCPs, critics worry, erode the interpersonal trust, social solidarity and political coalitions that sustain the welfare state.

Why do critics assume that there is a recognition/redistribution trade-off? Unlike the case of the heterogeneity/redistribution hypothesis, there are no empirical studies that have revealed a negative correlation between the adoption of MCPs and the welfare state. No one has even attempted such an empirical test of the recognition/redistribution hypothesis.

Instead, the argument for a recognition/redistribution trade-off is entirely speculative. Critics have speculated about a range of mechanisms by which the adoption of MCPs could inadvertently erode the welfare state. We can summarise these mechanisms under three headings:

Corroding effect

One line of argument suggests that MCPs weaken redistribution because they erode the underlying collective imaginary of nationhood that sustains trust and solidarity among citizens. MCPs emphasise differences between citizens, whereas the ideology of nationhood requires emphasising commonalities. Citizens have historically been willing to make sacrifices to support their disadvantaged co-citizens because they viewed these co-citizens as 'one of us', bound together by a common national identity and common sense of belonging. However, MCPs are said to corrode this overarching common identity. MCPs tell citizens that what divides them into separate ethnocultural groups is more important than what they have in common, and that co-citizens from other groups are therefore not really 'one of us'.

According to Wolfe and Klausen, for example, in the early days of the British welfare state in the 1940s and 1950s, 'people believed they were paying the social welfare part of their taxes to people who were like themselves'. But with the adoption of MCPs, and the resulting abandonment of the 'long process of national homogenization', the outcome has been growing 'tax resistance', for 'if the ties that bind you to increasingly diverse fellow citizens are loosened, you are likely to be less inclined to share your resources with them' (Wolfe and Klausen, 2000, p 28).

Crowding-out effect

According to a second argument, MCPs weaken pro-redistribution coalitions by diverting time, energy and money from redistribution to recognition (Barry, 2001, p 325). People who would otherwise be actively involved in fighting for economic redistribution are instead spending their time on issues of multiculturalism.

Todd Gitlin gives an example of this. He discusses how left-wing students at UCLA (University of California, Los Angeles) fought obsessively for what they deemed a more 'inclusive' educational environment, through greater representation of minority groups in the faculty and curricula.

At the same time, however, they largely ignored huge budget cuts to the state educational system that were making it more difficult for minority students to even get to UCLA. As he puts it, 'much of the popular energy and commitment it would have taken to fight for the preservation – let alone the improvement – of public education was channelled into acrimony amongst potential allies' (Gitlin, 1995, p 31).

Misdiagnosis effect

A third argument suggests that MCPs lead people to misdiagnose the problems that minority groups face. It encourages people to think that the problems facing minority groups are rooted primarily in cultural 'misrecognition', and hence to think that the solution lies in greater state recognition of ethnic identities and cultural practices. In reality, however, these 'culturalist' solutions will be of little or no benefit, since the real problems lie elsewhere.[6]

This argument comes in two different forms. One version claims that the focus on cultural difference has displaced attention to *race*, and thereby ignored the distinctive problems facing groups like African Americans. The rhetoric of MCPs lumps all ethnic groups together, as equal victims of cultural misrecognition, while obscuring the distinctive problems faced by those racial groups that suffer the consequences of segregation, slavery, racism, and discrimination.

A second version claims that the focus on cultural difference has displaced attention to *class*. On this view, the real problem is economic marginalisation not cultural misrecognition, and the solution is not to adopt MCPs but rather to improve people's standing in the labour market, through better access to jobs, education and training and so on. The multiculturalist approach encourages people to think that what low-income Pakistani immigrants in Britain need most is to have their distinctive history, religion or dress given greater public status, when in fact their real need is for improved access to decent housing, education and training and gainful employment (see Craig, Chapter Eleven) – a need they share with the disadvantaged members of the larger society or other minority ethnic groups, and a need which can only be met through a pan-ethnic class alliance.

This, then, is the basic case for the recognition/redistribution trade-off. At first glance, all three arguments have some plausibility. Yet here again, the case is not watertight. For one thing, as I mentioned earlier, there is as yet no empirical evidence for the existence of such a trade-off. It remains wholly speculative. Moreover, one can imagine equally plausible (and equally speculative) arguments as to why MCPs might strengthen the welfare state. Far from corroding trust and solidarity, perhaps MCPs can help build them, by overcoming legacies of division, and thereby helping to build a new, and more truly inclusive, national identity. Here again, more research is required before we make definitive judgements.

Testing the trade-offs

Any attempt to systematically test the two hypotheses would be a massive undertaking, in part because the existing data are insufficient to test the claims. We do not have reliable cross-national data over time on many of the crucial variables, such as levels of ethnic heterogeneity, or levels of MCPs. Nonetheless, there are some preliminary ways of testing the two hypotheses.

Testing the heterogeneity/redistribution trade-off

As I noted earlier, those who believe in a heterogeneity/redistribution trade-off invoke it both to explain the historic weakness of the American welfare state, and to predict the future of European welfare states as immigration increases. Sceptics respond that the racialisation of American welfare politics is an idiosyncratic product of the history of American race relations, and need not be a harbinger of the impact of immigration on European welfare politics.

Is there a way to test this dispute? In a recent study, three of my colleagues analysed the relationship between immigration and change in the level of social spending across Organisation for Economic Co-operation and Development (OECD) countries from 1970 to 1998 (Soroka et al, 2006). In this study, immigration was measured using United Nations data on 'migrant stock' – the proportion of the population born outside the country. If a heterogeneity/redistribution trade-off existed, it would be expected that those countries with higher levels of migrant stock would exhibit either a decrease in social spending, or at least slower rates of growth compared to countries with lower levels of immigration. However, the study revealed that there is no relationship between the proportion of the population born outside the country and growth in social spending from 1970 to 1998, controlling for other factors associated with social spending. There was simply no evidence that countries with large foreign-born populations had more trouble sustaining and developing their social programmes over these three decades than countries with small immigrant communities.

This finding has been confirmed in a more recent study we conducted (Banting et al, 2006), and in a separate analysis conducted by Peter Taylor-Gooby (2005). He too finds that once the other factors that affect social spending are controlled for, the size of immigrant groups has no statistically significant effect on social spending in Western Europe. Studies of public attitudes across the West also find no evidence that the size of immigrant groups erodes support for the welfare state (Crepaz, 2006).

Our recent study also examined the impact of two other (non-immigrant) forms of ethnoracial diversity: namely, indigenous peoples (for example, American Indians, Maori, Sami) and national minorities (for example, Scots, Catalans, Québécois). Here again, in both cases, there is no correlation between the size of the minority and change in welfare spending over the past 30 years (Banting et al, 2006). In short, attempts to test the heterogeneity/redistribution trade-off beyond the US and Africa have found little support for this hypothesis.[7]

Testing the recognition/redistribution trade-off

In order to test the heterogeneity/redistribution trade-off, the studies I have just described made use of several existing databases that give the size of ethnic/racial minority groups in different countries around the world. In order to test the recognition/redistribution trade-off, we would need to find comparable databases that measure the level of MCPs in different countries. Unfortunately, there are no such databases. No one has attempted to develop a cross-national index of MCPs.

In order to test the hypothesis, therefore, Keith Banting and I have constructed such an index. This involved several steps. We first developed a representative list of multiculturalism policies; we then checked to see which countries had adopted which policies, and on that basis categorised countries as stronger or weaker in their level of MCPs. Finally, we then asked whether countries that have adopted strong MCPs over the last two decades have experienced a weakening in their welfare states compared to countries that have resisted such policies.

As an illustration, consider the case of immigrant groups. We began by selecting the following eight policies as the most common or emblematic of a 'multicultural' approach to immigrant integration:

- constitutional, legislative or parliamentary affirmation of multiculturalism;
- the explanation/celebration of multiculturalism in the school curriculum;
- the inclusion of ethnic representation/sensitivity in the mandate of public media;

- exemptions from dress codes, Sunday-closing legislation and so on;
- allowing dual citizenship;
- the funding of ethnic group organisations or activities;
- the funding of bilingual education or mother-tongue instruction; and
- affirmative action for disadvantaged immigrant groups.

The list is inevitably partial, and could be extended, but we believe it is a fair representation of the sorts of policies that have been defended by advocates of multiculturalism and attacked by their critics.

We then examined 21 Western democracies, to see which of these eight policies had been adopted. A country that had adopted six or more of these policies was classified as 'strong' in its commitment to MCPs; a country that had adopted two or less of these policies was classified as 'weak'; countries falling in between were categorised it as 'modest'. The resulting groupings of countries are reported in Table 3.1.

Table 3.1: The strength of multiculturalism policies in democratic countries

Strong	Australia, Canada
Modest	Belgium, the Netherlands, New Zealand, Sweden, UK, US
Weak	Austria, Denmark, Finland, France, Germany, Greece, Ireland, Italy, Japan, Norway, Portugal, Spain, Switzerland

The second step was to examine how the three groups of countries fared in terms of change in the strength of their welfare state between 1980 and 2000. Did countries with strong MCPs for immigrants have more difficulty in maintaining and enhancing their welfare states over the last two decades of the 20th century? Table 3.2 provides a first cut at the issues. There is no evidence here that immigrant MCPs weaken the welfare state. Countries that adopted such policies did not experience erosion of their welfare states or even slower growth in social spending than countries that resisted such policies. Indeed, on the two measures that capture social policy most directly – the level of social spending and the redistributive impact of taxes and transfers – the countries with the strongest immigrant MCPs did better than countries with weak or modest MCPs.[8]

We conducted a similar analysis for indigenous peoples and national minorities. In each case, we identified a list of representative MCPs applicable to such groups, categorised countries as strong, modest or

Table 3.2: Multiculturalism policies and change in social redistribution

Multiculturalism policies	Social spending average % change	Redistribution average % change
Strong	42.8	11.8
Modest	3.8	−9.2
Weak	18.3	10.6

Source: Banting et al (2006, Appendix 1)

weak in their level of MCPs, and tested whether strong–MCP countries experienced more difficulty sustaining their welfare state compared to other countries. Here again, there was no evidence that engaging in a strong 'politics of recognition' regarding indigenous peoples and national minorities entailed a trade-off with a politics of redistribution (Banting et al, 2006).

In short, we have found no support for the claim that there is an inherent trade-off between policies of ethnocultural recognition and economic redistribution, or that 'a politics of multiculturalism undermines a politics of redistribution' (Barry, 2001, p 8).

Conclusion

These results are preliminary, and require further testing. But if they hold up, they have implications for how we think about social justice in an era of diversity. The clearest lesson is simply that we should avoid premature judgements about the inevitability of tragic choices between recognising diversity and sustaining the welfare state. The evidence summarised here suggests that a variety of relationships between ethnic heterogeneity, multiculturalism and the welfare state are possible, and that under some circumstances robust minority rights can be combined with robust redistributive commitments. There is no inevitability at work, and policy choices count. This alone is an optimistic note in the increasingly fractious debate about the future of the multicultural welfare state.

Of course, none of this as yet provides a positive argument in favour of MCPs. The evidence here simply disputes one familiar objection to those policies – namely, that they unintentionally set in motion sociological dynamics that erode the welfare state. If we set aside that concern about the potential side-effects of MCPs, we are still left with debates about the intrinsic fairness of these policies. In previous work (Kymlicka, 1995), I have argued that most (but not all) of the MCPs adopted recently by Western democracies respond to legitimate moral claims by minority ethnic group, providing appropriate acknowledgement of historic wrongs, reducing unjustified barriers and stigmatisations, and helping to ensure greater fairness in the ways societies recognise and accommodate the diverse languages, identities and practices that exist within their borders. These are complex questions, and there are grounds for debate about how well MCPs track legitimate moral claims and grievances. But this indeed is where the debate should be: MCPs should be evaluated primarily on their own terms, as attempting to fairly accommodate ethnocultural diversity, not rejected on the basis of unsupported speculation about their side-effects on the welfare state.

The analysis in this chapter may also have a more general lesson. If ethnic heterogeneity and MCPs have not had the corrosive effect that many commentators have supposed, it is partly because the ideology of nationhood has turned out to be more adaptable than many people supposed, capable of incorporating ideas of diversity within its narratives. The evidence suggests that there is greater scope for reconciling ideas of nationhood and the recognition of diversity than is often realised. Scripts of nationhood may not be as inherently homogenising as many commentators suppose, and claims to recognition are often tied to, and nested in, larger national narratives.

It used to be assumed that the idea of nationhood could only serve as an effective focal point for people's identities and claims-making if it was a 'thick' identity, based on a dense constellation of shared values, beliefs, historical myths and other ethnic, religious and cultural similarities. In the past 40 years, we have seen a dramatic 'thinning' of national identities, as they have been stretched to accommodate demands for inclusion by a range of historically disadvantaged groups, including religious, racial, indigenous, linguistic, ethnic and regional minorities. At each step of this process, commentators have feared that the thinning of national identity to make it more inclusive would undermine its power to create meaningful solidarities. And yet it seems clear that thin national identities are still capable of sustaining the sort of solidarity that enables societies to adopt progressive social policies. Even when national identities have been redefined as 'multicultural', explicitly disavowing any pretence to ethnic purity and cultural homogeneity, they can still serve as mobilising elements.

Yet precisely how thin collective identities serve this function is less clear. An important topic for future research, therefore, is to examine in a more fine-grained way the relationship between nationhood, ethnic diversity and multiculturalism, across a wide range of contexts, to see how they interact.[9] This can help identify the potential room for creating new approaches that generate solidarity while accommodating diversity.

Notes

[1] In Belgium, Canada, Spain and Switzerland, territorial autonomy for national minorities was achieved through federalising the state, creating a federal sub-unit that was dominated by the national minority. Britain did not federalise the entire country, but created quasi-federal forms of autonomy for Scotland and Wales. Similar quasi-federal autonomy regimes exist for the Swedes in Finland, the Germans in South Tyrol and the Puerto Ricans in the US.

[2] For an attempt to measure the extent (and unevenness) of these three trends, see Banting and Kymlicka (2006).

[3] For the evidence, see Kymlicka (2007, Chapter 5).

[4] For more on these studies, see Banting and Kymlicka (2006).

[5] For canonical statements of the recognition/redistribution trade-off hypothesis, see Gitlin (1995); Wolfe and Klausen (2000); Barry (2001).

[6] For a version of this concern, see Chapter Four, this volume, by Iris Marion Young.

[7] These studies do reveal one note of caution, relating to the case of immigrants: the *pace of change* does seem to matter. When the analysis examined the relationship between *growth* in the foreign-born population and *change* in social spending as a proportion of GDP between 1970 and 1998, an interesting result emerged: countries with large increases in the proportion of their population born outside the country tended to have smaller increases in social spending.

[8] This finding has been confirmed by a recent study of public opinion by Crepaz (2006), showing that countries with higher levels of MCPs have not seen an erosion in public support for redistribution in comparison with countries with lower levels of MCPs.

[9] Next steps here might involve re-examining the proposed causal mechanisms underlying the heterogeneity/redistribution and recognition/redistribution hypotheses, to see why the predicted effects did not occur. For example, while there is substantial cross-national evidence to support Putnam's (2007)

assertion that interpersonal trust declines as ethnic heterogeneity increases at the neighbourhoold level, this does not necessarily erode support for the welfare state, contrary to Putnam's causal model (Soroka et al, 2007). It would be interesting to study what variables mediate the link between interpersonal trust and support for the welfare state, and how public policies can affect this linkage.

References

Alesina, A. and Glaeser, E. (2004) *Fighting poverty in the US and Europe*, Oxford: Oxford University Press.

Banting, K. and Kymlicka, W. (eds) (2006) *Multiculturalism and the welfare state: Recognition and redistribution in contemporary democracies*, Oxford: Oxford University Press.

Banting, K., Johnston, R., Kymlicka, W. and Soroka, S. (2006) 'Do multiculturalism policies erode the welfare state?', in K. Banting and W. Kymlicka (eds) *Multiculturalism and the welfare state: Recognition and redistribution in contemporary democracies*, Oxford: Oxford University Press, pp 49-91.

Barry, B. (2001) *Culture and equality*, Cambridge: Polity Press.

Crepaz, M. (2006) '"If you are my brother, I may give you a dime!" Public opinion on multiculturalism, trust and the welfare state', in K. Banting and W. Kymlicka (eds) (2006) *Multiculturalism and the welfare state: Recognition and redistribution in contemporary democracies*, Oxford: Oxford University Press, pp 92-117.

Freeman, G. (1986) 'Migration and the political economy of the welfare state', *Annals of the American Academy of Political and Social Science*, vol 485, pp 51-63.

Gitlin, T. (1995) *The twilight of common dreams*, New York: Metropolitan Books.

Glazer, N. (1997) *We are all multiculturalists now*, Cambridge, MA: Harvard University Press.

Kitschelt, H. (1995) *The radical right in Western Europe*, Ann Arbor, MI: University of Michigan Press.

Kymlicka, W. (1995) *Multicultural citizenship*, Oxford: Oxford University Press.

Kymlicka, W. (2007) *Multicultural odysseys: Navigating the new international politics of diversity*, Oxford: Oxford University Press.

Miguel, E. and Gugarty, M. K. (2005) 'Ethnic diversity, social sanctions, and public goods in Kenya', *Journal of Public Economics*, vol 89, no 11-12, pp 2325-68.

Pearce, N. (2004) 'Diversity versus solidarity: a new progressive dilemma', *Renewal: A Journal of Labour Politics*, vol 12, no 3.

Putnam, R. (2004) 'Who bonds? Who bridges? Findings from the social capital benchmark survey', Presentation to the Annual Meetings of the American Political Science Association, Chicago, September.

Putnam, R. (2007) 'E pluribus unum: diversity and community in the twenty-first century', *Scandinavian Political Studies*, vol 30, no 2, pp 137-74.

Salter, F. K. (ed) (2004) *Welfare, ethnicity and altruism*, London: Frank Cass.

Soroka, S., Banting, K. and Johnston, R. (2006) 'Immigration and redistribution in a global era', in P. Bardhan, S. Bowles and M. Wallerstein (eds) *Globalization and egalitarian redistribution*, Princeton, NJ: Princeton University Press, pp 261-88.

Soroka, S., Johnston, R. and Banting, K. (2007) 'Ethnicity, trust and the welfare state', in F. Kay and R. Johnston (eds) *Social capital, diversity and the welfare state*, Vancouver, Canada: UBC Press.

Taylor-Gooby, P. (2005) 'Is the future American? Or, can Left politics preserve European welfare states from erosion through growing "racial" diversity?', *Journal of Social Policy*, vol 34, no 4, pp 661-73.

Wolfe, A. and Klausen, J. (2000) 'Other peoples', *Prospect*, December, pp 28-33.

FOUR

Structural injustice and the politics of difference

Iris Marion Young[1]

Introduction

It is now a truism – which I dispute – that a politics of difference is equivalent to 'identity politics', about claims of justice concerning cultural difference. There are at least two versions of a politics of difference: a politics of positional difference and a politics of cultural difference. They share a critical attitude towards a difference-blind approach to policy and politics. They differ, however, in how they understand the constitution of social groups, and in the issues of justice that they emphasise. While both versions of a politics of difference appear in contemporary political debates, over the last two decades the attention of both public discourse and that of political theorists has shifted from the politics of positional difference to a politics of cultural difference. This shift is unfortunate because it tends to obscure important issues of justice, limiting the framing of difference politics to a liberal paradigm. We should affirm both approaches but be clear on the conceptual and practical differences between them.

As a 1980s social movement tendency, the politics of difference involved claims of feminist, anti-racist and gay liberation activists that the structural inequalities of gender, race and sexuality did not fit well with the dominant paradigm of equality and inclusion. In this paradigm, the promotion of justice and equality requires non-discrimination: the application of the same principles of evaluation and distribution to all regardless of their particular social positions or backgrounds. In this ideal, which many understood as the liberal paradigm, social justice means ignoring gender, racial or sexual differences among people. Social movements asserted a politics of difference, theorists arguing that this difference-blind ideal was part of the problem. Identifying equality with equal treatment ignores deep material differences in social position, division of labour, socialised capacities, normalised standards and ways of living that continue to disadvantage members of historically excluded groups. Commitment to substantial equality thus requires attending to such differences.

In the context of ethnic politics and resurgent nationalism, a second version of a politics of difference gained currency in the 1990s, focusing on differences of nationality, ethnicity and religion. It emphasised the value of cultural distinctness to individuals, as against a liberal individualism for which culture is accidental to the self or something adopted voluntarily. Most modern societies contain multiple cultural groups, some of which unjustly dominate the state or other important social institutions, thus inhibiting the ability of minority cultures to live meaningfully in their own terms. Contrary to arguments for cultural neutrality, which until recently have been the orthodox liberal stance, the politics of cultural difference argues that public accommodation to and support of cultural *difference* is compatible with and even required by just institutions.

I have emphasised the politics of positional difference in structural position. Both *Justice and the politics of difference* (Young, 1990) and *Inclusion and democracy* (Young, 2000) critically assess the tendency of public and private institutions in contemporary liberal democratic societies to reproduce sexual, racial and class inequality by applying standards and rules in the same way to all who plausibly come under their purview. They consider how broad structures of the division of labour, hierarchical decision-making power, and processes of normalisation inhibit the ability of some people to develop and exercise their capacities while offering wide opportunity to others. Each book, however, also contains elements that relate more to the politics of cultural difference. *Justice and the politics of difference* (Young, 1990) refers to cultural claims of indigenous people, speaking approvingly of movements of structurally oppressed groups to resist stigma by constructing positive group affinities, as a means to the achievement of structural equality, rather than an end in itself.

Justice and the politics of difference was published earlier than most recent political theory focusing on a politics of cultural difference. That body of work might be said to begin with Charles Taylor's essay, 'Multiculturalism and the politics of recognition', and to receive its first book-length treatment in Kymlicka's (1995) *Multicultural citizenship. Inclusion and democracy* tries more explicitly to distinguish focus on structural inequality from focus on injustice through cultural difference and conflict. While most of that book theorises within the politics of positional difference, one chapter of *Inclusion and democracy* (Young, 2000) articulates a relational concept of self-determination, contrasting with more rigid notions of sovereignty and contributes to discussions on the politics of cultural difference. One motivation for this chapter is to sort out this distinction between two approaches to a politics of difference.[2]

In what follows, I therefore distinguish these two approaches. Both the politics of positional difference and the politics of cultural difference challenge commitments to political equality that tend to identify equality with sameness and which believe that the best way to pursue social and political equality is to ignore group differences in public policy and in how individuals are treated. They both argue that where group difference is socially significant for issues of conflict, domination or advantage, equal respect may not imply treating everyone in the same way. Public and civic institutions may be either morally required or permitted to notice social group difference, and to treat members of different groups differently for the sake of promoting equality or freedom. Despite these similarities, it is important to be clear on the differences between these two political stances. In recent discussions of a politics of difference, analysts sometimes either merge the two models or attribute to one features specific to the other. Readers consequently fail to notice important differences. For example, some critics aim objections at the wrong target. In his book, *Culture and equality*, for example, Barry (2001) fails to distinguish any strands in the thick ball of theoretical writing that he winds together. As a result, he levels criticisms at some writers that may be more apt for others, and he sometimes merges positions in a way that confuses the debate more than clarifies it. This chapter will attempt to sort out some of this confusion. A more important reason to elaborate the distinction between the two versions of a politics of difference, is to recover some issues of justice and ways of thinking about justice and difference that first motivated this line of thinking 25 years ago. As discussed below, a politics of positional difference primarily concerns issues of justice regarding structural inequality. Persons suffer injustice by virtue of structural inequality when their group social positioning means that the operation of diverse institutions and practices conspires to limit their opportunities to achieve well-being. Persons suffer specifically culture-based injustice when they are not free to express themselves as they wish, associate with others with whom they share forms of expression and practices, or socialise their children in the cultural ways they value, or when their group situation is such that they bear significant economic or political costs in pursuing a distinctive way of life. Structural inequalities then sometimes build on perceived cultural differences (see Craig, Chapter Eleven). To the extent that political thinking takes a politics of cultural difference as paradigmatic, however, thinking about justice and group difference focuses on issues of liberty and tends to obscure issues of inequality in opportunities structured by the division of labour, hierarchies of decision making and the norms and standards that institutions apply to reward achievement.

This chapter therefore also discusses how the tendency in much recent political theory to narrow consideration of a politics of difference to a liberal paradigm has at least three unfortunate consequences. First, where structural injustices do build on perceived cultural differences, a politics of cultural difference and its emphasis on liberty does not make visible enough issues of structural inequalities. Second, because the politics and theory of cultural difference tend to focus on what state policy properly should allow, forbid or remain silent on, it ignores civil society as a crucial site for working on injustice. Third, recent discussions of the politics of cultural difference, especially regarding the status of women within cultural minorities, too often themselves tend to elevate particular group-based standards as normative for a whole polity without acknowledging this normalising move.

Politics of positional difference

This approach defines social groups as constituted through structural social processes which position people differently along social axes. These axes generate status, power and opportunity for the development of capacities or the acquisition of goods. Important axes of structural social privilege and disadvantage concern the social division of labour, hierarchies of decision-making power, practices of sexuality and body aesthetic, and the arrangement of persons in physical and social space.

Persons in less-advantaged positions suffer injustice in the form of structural inequality, or what Tilly (1998) calls 'durable inequality'. Some institutional rules and practices, the operation of hegemonic norms, the shape of economic or political incentives, the physical effects of past actions and policies, and people acting on stereotypical assumptions, all conspire to produce systematic and reinforcing inequalities between groups. People differently positioned in structural processes often have unequal opportunities for self-development and access to resources, to make decisions about both the conditions of their own action and that of others, or to be treated with respect or deference.

These structural inequalities do not determine that every member of a less-privileged group suffers deprivation or domination. They do, however, make most members of structurally-disadvantaged groups more vulnerable to harm than others. They also put constraints on the ability of group members to achieve well-being. It is these vulnerabilities and limitations that define structural injustice more than the amount of goods or power individuals may have at a particular time (Young, 2001). The politics of positional difference argues that public and private institutional policies and practices that interpret equality as requiring being blind to group differences are not likely to undermine persistent structural group differences, and often reinforce them. Even in the absence of explicitly discriminatory rules, adherence to body aesthetic, struggle over power and other dynamics of differentiation will tend to reproduce given categorical inequalities unless institutions take explicit action to counteract such tendencies. Thus, to remove unjust inequality it is necessary explicitly to recognise group difference and either compensate for disadvantage, revalue some attributes, positions or actions or take special steps to meet needs and empower members of disadvantaged groups.

Socioeconomic class is a paradigm of such structural grouping, where class does not refer simply to income level, but also to position in the social division of labour, decision-making structures and group-segmented practices of fashion and taste. I elaborate below three additional forms of group difference that have motivated claims of a politics of difference: groups defined by disability, gender and institutional racism.

Disability as structural inequality

Most social justice theorists either do not notice disability at all or bring it up in order to assert that disability is an outlier category, which theories of justice may deal with after addressing disadvantages that supposedly raise issues of justice in a more obvious way. Rawls, for example, famously 'puts aside' those disabilities 'so severe as to prevent people from being cooperating members of society in the usual sense' until the theory deals with the easier and more generally shared issues of justice. It is better to begin theorising justice, he says, by assuming that 'everyone has physical needs and psychological capacities within the normal range' (Rawls, 1971, p 245).

Some philosophers recently have questioned this set of assumptions, and have begun to develop alternative analyses of both disability and justice (Kittay, 1999; Nussbaum, 2006). Considering the large number of people who have impaired physical and mental capacities at some point in their lives,[3] it is simply factually wrong to think of disability as a relatively uncommon condition not affecting how we should think about justice. We can learn much about social justice generally as concerning issues of structural inequality, normalisation and stigmatisation, if we decide to make disability *paradigmatic* of structural injustice, instead of considering it exceptional.

In his book attacking all versions of a politics of difference, Barry (2001) devotes considerable space to defending a standard principle of merit in the allocation of positions. Merit involves equal opportunity in the following sense: it rejects a system that awards positions explicitly according to class, race, gender, family background and so on. Under a merit principle, all who wish should have the opportunity to compete for positions of advantage, and those most qualified should win the competition. Positions of authority or expertise should be occupied by those persons who demonstrate excellence in particular skills and who best exhibit the demeanour expected of people in those positions. Everyone else is a loser in respect to those positions, and they suffer no injustice on that account (for responses to this position see, for example, Chambers, 2002; Kelly, 2002).[4] In this merit system, according to Barry (and others), it is natural that people with disabilities will usually turn out to be losers.

> Surely it is to be expected in the nature of the case that, across the group (disabled) as a whole, its members will be less qualified than average, even if the amount of money spent on their education is the average, or more than the average. (Barry, 2001, p 95)

In our scheme of social cooperation, certain skills and abilities can and should be expected of average workers, and it is 'in the nature of the case' that most people with disabilities do not meet these expectations. Thus, they do not merit the jobs in which we expect these skills, and do not merit the income, autonomy, status and other forms of privilege that come with those jobs. These people's deficiencies are not their fault, of course, and a decent society will support their needs, ensuring them a dignified life, despite their inability to contribute significantly to social production.

One of the objectives of the disability rights movements has been to challenge this 'liberal common sense'. Most people who have not thought about the issues very much tend to regard being 'disabled' as an attribute of persons: some people simply lack the functionings that enable normal people to live independently, compete in job markets and have a satisfying social life. Many in the disability rights movements, however, conceptualise the problem that people with disabilities face rather differently. The problem is not with the attributes that individual persons have or do not have. The problem, rather, is the *lack of fit* between the attributes of certain persons, and dominant societal structures, practices, norms and aesthetic standards. The built environment is biased to support the capacities of people who can walk, climb, see, hear, within what are thought of as the 'normal range' of functionings, and presents significant obstacles for people whose capacities are judged outside this range. Both interactive and technical ways of assessing the intelligence, skill and adaptability of people in schools and workplaces assume ways of evaluating aptitude and achievement that unfairly disadvantage many people with disabilities from developing or exercising skills. The physical layout and equipment in workplaces and the organisation of work process too often make it impossible for a person with an impaired functioning to use the skills they have. Hegemonic standards of charm, beauty, grace, wit or attentiveness position some people with disabilities as monstrous or abject.

These and other aspects of the division of labour, hegemonic norms and physical structures constitute structural injustice for people with disabilities. Many people with disabilities unfairly suffer limitation to their opportunities for living as autonomous adults. A difference-blind liberalism can offer only very limited remedy for this injustice. It is no response to the person who moves in a wheelchair or who tries to enter a courtroom accessible only by stairs that the state treats all citizens in the same way. The blind engineer derives little solace from an employer who assures him/her that they make the same computer equipment available to all employees. The opportunities of people with disabilities can be made equal only if others specifically notice their differences, cease regarding them as unwanted deviants from accepted norms and unacceptable costs to efficient operations, and take affirmative measures to enable them to function at their best and with dignity.

The 1990 Americans with Disabilities Act recognises this in principle, in as much as it requires that employers, landlords and public services make 'reasonable accommodation' to the specific needs of people with disabilities. It codifies a politics of positional difference. The law has generated significant controversy, of course, concerning who counts as having a disability and what kinds of accommodation are reasonable. As a group, people with disabilities continue to be unfairly excluded from or disadvantaged in education and occupational opportunities, and to have unfair difficulties in access to transportation, or in having simple pleasures like an evening at the theatre. Only continued pressure on many institutions to conform to principles of fair accommodation will improve this structural situation.

I began with the example of injustice towards people with disabilities because I wish to suggest that it is paradigmatic of the general approach I am calling a politics of positional difference. It represents a clear case where difference-blind treatment or policy is more likely to perpetuate than correct injustice. The systematic disadvantage at which seemingly neutral standards puts many people in this case, however, just as clearly does not derive from internal cultural attributes that constitute the group 'people with disabilities'. It may be plausible to speak of a Deaf Culture, to the extent that many deaf people use a unique language and sometimes live together in deaf communities. In a wider sense, however, there is no community or culture of people with disabilities. Instead, this category designates a structural group constituted from the outside by the deviation of its purported members from normalised institutional assumptions about the exhibition of skill, definition of tasks in a division of labour, ideals of beauty, built environment standards and comportments of sociability. The remedy for injustice to people with disabilities consists in challenging the norms and rules of the institutions that most condition the life options and the attainment of well-being of these persons structurally positioned as deviant.

Issues of justice raised by many group-based conflicts and social differences follow this paradigm. They concern the way structural social processes position individuals with similar physical attributes, socialised capacities, body habits and lifestyle, sexual orientations, family and neighbourhood resources, in the social division of labour, relations of decision-making power, or hegemonic norms of achievement, beauty or respectability. The politics of positional difference focuses on these issues of inclusion and exclusion, and how they make available or limit the substantive opportunities for persons to develop capacities and achieve well-being.

Racial inequality

I do not aim here to give an account of the structural inequalities of institutional racism but to comment on racial inequality and the politics of difference. Although I focus on racialised processes of structural inequality in the US, racial inequality clearly structures many societies in the world (see Chapter Eleven). Racism consists in structural processes that normalise body aesthetic, determine that physical, dirty or servile work is most appropriate for members of certain groups, produce and reproduce segregation of members of these racialised groups, and render deviant the comportments and habits of these segregated persons in relation to dominant norms of respectability.

What distinguishes 'race' from ethnicity or nation, conceptually? The former naturalises or 'epidermalises' the attributes of difference (Fanon, 1967, pp 110-12). Racism attaches significance to bodily characteristics – skin colour, hair type, facial features – and constructs hierarchies of standard or ideal body types against which others appear inferior, stigmatised or deviant. In Western structures of anti-black racism this hierarchy appears both as dichotomous and scaled. That is, racial categorisation is organised around a black/white dichotomy, and this dichotomy organises a grading of types according to how 'close' they are to black (most inferior) or white (the superior).[5] Processes of racialisation stigmatise or devalue bodies, body type, or items closely attached to bodies such as clothing; this stigmatisation and stereotyping appear in public images and the way some people react to some others. Racialisation also involves understandings of the proper work of some and its hierarchical status in relation to others. The stigma of blackness in the US, for example, has its origins in slavery (Loury, 2002, Chapter 3). The slave does hard labour under domination, from which owners accumulate profits; or the slave does servile labour to attend to the needs and elevate the status of the ruling group. While chattel slavery was (legally) abolished 150 years ago, racialised positions in the social division of labour remain. The least desirable work – the work with the lowest pay, least autonomy and lowest status – is the hard physical work, the dirty work and the servant work. In the US, these are racialised forms of work, that is, belonging to black and brown people primarily, and, increasingly, 'foreigners'. A similar process of racialisation has occurred in Europe, which position persons of Turkish, North African, South Asian, sub-Saharan African and Middle Eastern origin as 'Other', and tends to restrict them to lower-status positions in the social division of labour (Chapter Eleven).

Segregation is a third common structure of racial inequality. It is not uncommon for migrants to choose to live near one another in neighbourhood enclaves ('clustering'). The urban residential patterning it produces might be considered a manifestation of cultural differentiation. While residential segregation often overlaps with or builds on such clustering processes, segregation is a different and more malignant process. Even when not enforced by law, segregation is a structural process of exclusion from residential neighbourhood opportunity that leaves the worse residential options for members of denigrated groups. The actions of local and national government, private developers and landlords, housing consumers and others conspire – by intention or otherwise – to concentrate members of these denigrated groups. Dominant groups thereby derive privileges such as larger and more pleasant space, greater amenities and stable and often increasing property values.

With segregation, the stigma of racialised bodies and denigrated labour marks space itself and the people who grow up and live in neighbourhoods. People who live together in such neighbourhoods tend to develop group-specific idiom, styles of comportment, interests and artistic forms. These also are liable to be devalued and stigmatised by dominant norms. People who wish to appear respectable and professional, for example, had better shed the habits of walking, laughing and talking in slang they have learned on the home block. If these are properly considered 'cultural', they are better considered consequences of segregation and limitation of opportunity, rather than their causes. These structural relations of bodily affect, meanings and interests in the social division of labour, segregation and normalisation of dominant habitus operate to limit the opportunities of many to learn and use satisfying skills in socially recognised settings, to accumulate income or wealth, or to attain positions of power and prestige.

The main purpose of this brief account is to exhibit racism as a set of structural relations in which processes of normalisation have a large role. Being white is to occupy a set of social positions that privileges some people according to at least those parameters outlined, and sets standards of respectability or achievement for the entire society. Being black, or 'of colour', means being perceived as not fitting the standards, being suited for particular kinds of work, or that one does not belong in certain places. An anti-racist politics of difference argues that such liabilities to disadvantage cannot be overcome by race-blind principles of formal equality in employment, political party competition and so on. Where racialised structural inequality influences so many institutions and potentially stigmatises and impoverishes so many people, a society that aims to redress such injustice must *notice* the processes of racial differentiation before it can correct them.

Even when overt discriminatory practices are illegal and widely condemned, racialised structures are reproduced in many everyday interactions. It is important that persons positioned similarly by racial structures are able to organise politically together to bring attention to these relations of privilege or disadvantage. While such organising properly has some elements of the celebration of positive 'identity politics', the primary purpose of such group-based organising ought to be to confront and undermine the structural processes that perpetuate the limitation of opportunities (Young, 2000). Anti-racist movements ought to be directed at government policy to intervene in the structures. Government is not the only agent for institutional change, however.

Gender inequality

In the literature of political theory, the politics of positional difference and the politics of cultural difference conceive women's issues differently. Some proponents of a politics of cultural difference implicitly invoke gender justice under norms of equal treatment. As discussed by much of the literature, the political struggle consists in getting women recognised as the *same* as men in respect to having rights to autonomy. In the politics of positional difference, by contrast, feminist politics is a species of the politics of difference; that is, on this approach, in order to promote gender equality it is necessary to notice existing structural processes that differently position men and women. On this account, gender injustice also involves processes of structuring the social division of labour and the fit or lack of fit of bodies and modes of life with hegemonic norms.

In the last 25 years, there have been many changes in gendered norms of behaviour and comportment expected of men and women, with a great deal more freedom of choice in taste and self-presentation now available to members of both sexes. Basic structures of gender comportment, assumptions that 'normal' bodies are implicitly male, the structures of heterosexual expectations, and the sexual division of labour, nevertheless continue structurally to afford men more privilege and opportunity for access to resources, positions of power and authority, and the ability to pursue their own life plans.

People too often react to public evidence of female-specific conditions with aversion, ridicule or denial. Public institutions that claim to include women equally fail to accommodate to the needs of menstruating, pregnant and breastfeeding women, sometimes discouraging them from participation in these institutions. Sometimes the costs to women of being positioned as deviant in relation to normal bodies are small inconveniences, like remembering to carry tampons in anticipation that the women's room at work will not supply them but women may suffer serious discomfort, threats to their health, harassment, job loss, or forego benefits by withdrawing in order to avoid these consequences. Including women as equals in schools, workplaces and other institutions entails accommodating to their bodily specificity to the extent that they can both be women and excel in or enjoy the activities of those institutions. Aside from these stark examples of women's differences rendering them deviant in some settings, much contemporary feminist theory argues more broadly that society's social imagination projects onto women all the vulnerability and chaotic desire attendant on being embodied, sexual beings. The norms of many public professional institutions, however, exclude or repress acknowledgement of bodily need and sexuality. The presence of women or womanliness remains upsetting unless women can present themselves like men.

The social differences produced by a gendered division of labour constitute another access of gender difference that renders women vulnerable to domination, exploitation or exclusion. Although large changes in attitudes have occurred about the capacities of men and women, and most formal barriers to women's pursuit of occupations and activities have been removed, in at least one respect change has been slow. A structured social division of labour remains in which women do most of the unpaid care work in the family, and most people of both sexes assume that women will have primary responsibility for care of children and other family members, and for housecleaning. As Okin (1989) theorised it, this gendered division of labour accounts in large measure for injustice to women, whether or not they themselves are wives or mothers. The socialisation of girls continues to be oriented towards caring and helping. Occupational sex segregation continues to crowd women into relatively few job categories, keeping women's wages low. Heterosexual couples sometimes find it rational to depend on a man's pay for their primary income, if it is large enough. Thus, women and their children are vulnerable to poverty if the husband/ father ceases to support them.

The structural positioning of women in the division of labour offers another instance of gender normalisation. Most employers institutionalise an assumption that occupants of a good job – one that earns enough to support a family at a decent level of well-being and with a decent pension, annual leave and job security – can devote him/herself primarily to that job. Workers whose family responsibilities impinge on or conflict with employer expectations are deviants, and they find it difficult to combine 'real' work and family responsibility. Feminism construed as a politics of difference thus argues that real equality and freedom for women entail attending to embodied, socialised and institutional sex and gender differences in order to ensure that women – as well as men who find themselves similarly positioned – do not bear unfair costs of institutional assumptions about what women and men are or ought to be doing, who they feel comfortable working with or voting for, and so on. For women to have equal opportunities with men to attain positions of high status, power or income, it is not enough that they prove that their strength, leadership capacities or intelligence are as good as men's. This is relatively easy. It is more difficult to overcome the costs and disadvantages deriving from application of supposedly difference-blind norms of productivity, respectability or personal authority, which are structurally biased against women.

The problems of injustice to which the politics of positional difference responds arise, therefore, from structural processes of the division of labour, social segregation and lack of fit between hegemonic norms and interpreted bodies. I have emphasised injustice to people with disabilities, racial injustice and gender injustice in order to bring out social group difference not reducible to cultural difference, and illustrate some diverse forms that these structural inequalities take. Each form of structural inequality concerns relations of privilege and disadvantage where some people's opportunities for the development and exercise of their capacities are limited and they are vulnerable to having their conditions of their lives and action determined by others without reciprocation. A politics of positional difference holds that equalising these opportunities cannot rely on supposedly group-blind policies, because so many rules, norms and practices of many institutions have group-differentiating implications. Promoting justice requires attending to such structural differences and changing them, not only within law and public policy, but also in other social and economic institutions and practices.

The politics of cultural difference

A politics of positional difference continues to have proponents – myself included – among political theorists and those engaged in public discussion about the implications of group difference for values of freedom, equality and justice. What I call a politics of cultural difference has in recent years received more attention, both from political theorists, and in wider political debates.

Consider Kymlicka's (1995) book, *Multicultural citizenship*, an early, thorough theoretical statement of this distinctive approach to a politics of difference (see also Chapter Three). He explicitly distinguishes his approach to issues of group difference from one concerned with the situation of socially disadvantaged groups.

> The marginalization of women, gays and lesbians, and the disabled cuts across ethnic and national lines – it is found in majority cultures and homogeneous nation-states as well

as national minorities and ethnic groups – and it must be fought in all these places. (Kymlicka, 1995, p 19)

Kymlicka does not elaborate this distinction between his approach to multiculturalism and that concerned with marginalised groups. It seems clear, however, that one basis of the distinction is that he thinks that groups defined by what he calls 'societal culture' are different kinds of groups from the sort of group whose members face threats of marginalsation or social disadvantage like that faced by women, sexual minorities or people with disabilities. According to the terms I use here, the latter are *structural* social groups; what makes these groups is that their members are similarly positioned on axes of privileged and disadvantaged through structural social processes such as the organisation of the division of labour or normalisation.

The groups with which Kymlicka is concerned, face distinctive issues, according to him, just because what defines them as groups is 'societal culture'. In his theory this term refers only to differences of nation and ethnicity. A 'societal culture' is synonymous with 'a nation' or 'a people' – that is, an intergenerational community, more or less institutionally complete, occupying a given territory or homeland, sharing a distinct language and history. A state is multicultural

> [I]f its members either belong to different nations (a multi-nation state), or have migrated from different nations (a poly-ethnic state), and if this fact is an important aspect of personal identity and political life. (Kymlicka, 1995, p 18)

The societal culture to which a person relates is an important aspect of their personal identity; their personal autonomy depends in part on being able to engage in specific cultural practices with others who identify with one another as in the same cultural group; on being able to speak the language one finds most comfortable in the conduct of everyday affairs; on having the space and time to celebrate group-specific holidays and to display important group symbols. When the societal culture takes the form of nationality, this personal autonomy is tied to self-government autonomy for the group itself. Kymlicka, along with most who theorise the politics of cultural difference, thinks that most political societies today consist of at least two cultural groups, and often more than two. The question the politics of cultural difference poses is this: given that a political society consists of two or more societal cultures, what does justice require in the way of their mutual accommodation to one another's practices and forms of cultural expression, and to what extent can and should a liberal society give public recognition to these cultural diversities?

The politics of cultural difference assumes a situation of inequality common in contemporary polities in which members of multiple cultures dwell. It assumes that the state or polity is dominated by one of these cultural groups, which usually constitutes a majority of the polity's members. The situation of political conflict, according to the politics of cultural difference, is one in which this dominant group can limit the ability of one or more of the cultural minorities to live out their forms of expression; or more benignly, the sheer ubiquity of the dominant culture threatens to swamp the minority culture to the extent that its survival as a culture may be endangered, even though the lives of the individual members of the group may be relatively comfortable in other ways. Under these circumstances of inequality of freedom, members of embattled cultural groups frequently demand special rights and protections to enable their culture to flourish, and/or claim rights to a political society of their own either within a federated relationship or that of the dominant culture(s).

The politics of cultural difference explicitly rejects political principles and practices that assume that a single polity must coincide with a single common culture. This implies also rejecting the assumption held by many liberals that for the state and law to treat all citizens with equal respect entails that all be treated in the same way. Kymlicka distinguishes two kinds of cultural groups existing within today's multicultural politics: ethnic groups and national groups. Much of the response to his theory has focused on whether this distinction is viable, whether Kymlicka has made it correctly and whether he has correctly identified the requirements of justice appropriate for each. Neither this distinction nor the debates it generates concern the major argument of this chapter.

Kymlicka's theory receives wide attention because within it he has clarified many of the major issues of conflict and potential accommodation that arise in the contemporary politics of cultural difference. Most subsequent theories take up these issues and add to them. What does freedom of cultural expression require? Does it entail forms of public recognition of and accommodation to practices, symbols and ways of doing things, and not just allowing group members private freedom to engage in minority practices and forms of expression? Where the rules of public regulation, employers or others come into conflict with what members of cultural minorities consider culturally obligatory for the survival of their culture, does justice require exemption from those sorts of rules? Can cultural groups make a legitimate claim on the wider polity for resources necessary to memorialise their cultural past and the means to preserve its main elements for future generations? Do some cultural groups have legitimate claims to national autonomy, and if so, what does this imply for forms of self-government and relations with other groups? Does justice require that state and society take special measures to try to prevent members of cultural minorities from suffering a loss of opportunity or other disadvantage because they are committed to maintaining their cultural identity? Since cultural minorities often suffer political disadvantage in getting members elected to office and in voicing their interests and perspectives in representative bodies, does justice call for installing forms of group representation? Kymlicka considers the question of whether liberal polities ought to go so far as to tolerate practices that members of a culture regard as important but which a wider societal judgement finds violate standards of liberal accommodation and individual human rights.[6] He argues that such practices should not be tolerated.

Kymlicka more explicitly than others distinguishes the politics of cultural difference from what I call a politics of positional difference (see Chapter Three). With one important exception, moreover, the arguments he advances set an agenda of theorising that subsequent texts have continued to debate. To the issues Kymlicka treats, theorists of a politics of cultural difference have added another: the extent to which religious difference should be accommodated and affirmed in a multicultural liberal polity. No doubt, partly because issues of religious difference and perceived freedom of religious practice have become more prominent in political debates within most societies, some theorists of politics and group difference have put religion alongside ethnicity and nationality as paramount forms of deep diversity (see, for example, Parekh, 2000; Benhabib, 2002). The logic of religious difference and its implications for politics importantly diverges from ethnicity and nationality, at least because religious adherents often take doctrine and ceremony not simply to help define their identities, but as obligatory for them. This raises the stakes in potential conflicts between majority commitments and the commitments of religious minorities.

Much recent theorising about the politics of cultural difference takes issue with what writers charge is Kymlicka's overly homogeneous and bounded concept of societal culture. Carens (2000), for example, argues that Kymlicka's concept of societal culture implicitly follows the logic of the concept of nation state, even as the theory aims to challenge the singularity of one state for each nation. Ethnic and national groups, on his model, are each bounded by a singular understanding of themselves, in which place, language, history and practice line up, and are differentiated from other groups. The motive for Kymlicka's theory is precisely to challenge the singularity of the self-conception of the nation state; but his logic of group difference may follow a similar logic. Many others theorising a politics of cultural difference raise problems with what they fear is an 'essentialism' of cultural difference, where either participants or observers take a culture to be a coherent whole, relatively unchanging, and fully separate from other cultures. Against this, Parekh (2000) and Benhabib (2002) each offer a politics of cultural difference that puts dialogue among cultures at the centre. On the dialogic view, members of different cultural groups within a society often influence one another and engage in productive cultural exchange, and this interaction ought to be mobilised to resolve intercultural conflict.

Since both the theoretical approaches reviewed here are versions of a politics of difference, it should not be surprising that they share some features. I find two major similarities in the analyses and arguments of the politics of positional difference and the politics of cultural difference. Both worry about the domination some groups are able to exercise over public meaning in ways that limit freedom or curtail opportunity. Second, both challenge difference-blind public principle. They question the position that equal citizenship in a common polity entails a commitment to a common public interest, a single national culture, a single set of rules that applies to everyone in the same way. They both argue that commitment to justice sometimes requires noticing social or cultural differences and sometimes treating individuals and groups differently.

While they are logically distinct, each approach is important. The politics of cultural difference is important because it offers vision and principle to respond to dominant nationalist or other forms of absolutist impulses. We can live together in common political institutions and still maintain institutions by which we distinguish ourselves as peoples of cultures with distinct practices and traditions. Acting on such a vision can and should reduce ethnic, nationalist and religious violence. The politics of positional difference is important because it highlights the depth and systematic basis of inequality, and shows that inequality before the law is not a sufficient remedy. It calls attention to relations and processes of exploitation, marginalisation and normalisation that keep many people in subordinate positions.

I do not argue that political actors and theorists ought to accept one of these approaches and reject the other. Instead, my claim is that it is important to notice the difference between them, a difference sometimes missed in recent literatures. At the same time, the two forms of argument are compatible in practice. Indeed, for some kinds of issues of group-based politics and conflict, both forms of analysis are necessary. The oppression of minority cultures often, for example, merges into structural inequalities of racism in so far as it entails the limitation of opportunities for developing and exercising capacities.

I conclude this section by addressing a familiar question. To what extent is this distinction in theoretical approaches similar to the distinction that Fraser (Fraser and Honneth, 2003) has drawn between a politics of redistribution and politics of recognition? They are not in fact the same distinction at all. As I understand Fraser's categorisation, both forms of a politics of difference I have articulated here fall under her category of a politics of recognition. Fraser distinguishes what she calls a participatory parity approach – which roughly corresponds to what I call the politics of positional difference – and an identity politics approach – which roughly corresponds to what I am calling the politics of cultural difference. In so far as there can be any comparison, I think Fraser would categorise both approaches to the politics of difference I have described as different forms of a politics of recognition. Except for Taylor (1994), Fraser gives little attention to theorists of the politics of cultural difference, and she favours the approach she calls participatory parity as a response to structural inequalities of gender, race and sexuality. I find this distinction between different forms of recognition politics useful. However, it is too polarising to construct economic relations, or redistribution, and culture, or recognition, as mutually exclusive categories (Young, 1997). As I try to do above, it seems more useful to separate out different aspects of the production of structural inequality such as normalisation and the division of labour, each of which has both material effects on access to resources as well as the social meanings underlying status hierarchy.

Critical limits to the politics of cultural difference

The politics of cultural difference exhibits a different logic from the politics of positional difference. Each highlights important issues of justice relevant to contemporary politics and the two approaches are often compatible in a particular political context. To the extent that recent political theory and public discourse focus on the politics of cultural difference, however, they inappropriately narrow debates about justice and difference. Some issues of justice retreat from view, and the discussion brings those that remain squarely under a liberal paradigm, which sometimes distorts their significance.

I therefore conclude by discussing three such worries with the ascendancy of issues of ethnic, national and religious difference in debates about justice and social group difference. The paradigm of the politics of cultural difference tends to underplay important issues of group difference such as those discussed earlier in giving an account of the politics of positional difference. To take one example: the paradigm of cultural difference obscures racism as a specific form of structural injustice. Second, I discuss how the liberal framework under which the politics of cultural differences brings its issues focuses too much on the state in relation to individuals and groups, and does not see relations in civil society either as enacting injustice or as a source of remedy. Because many theorists of the politics of cultural difference define their issues in terms of tolerance, finally, I will argue that the politics of cultural difference easily slips into expressing and reinforcing a normalisation exposed and criticised by a politics of positional difference.

The tendency to obscure some issues of justice

As discussed earlier, the politics of positional difference conceptualises group difference primarily in structural terms. Social relations and processes put people in differing categorical social positions in relation to one another in ways that privilege those in one category in relation to others, in the range of opportunities for self-development available to them, the resources they have or can access, the power they have over the lives of others and the degree of status they have as indexed by others' willingness to treat them with special respect. Class and gender are important structural axes in most societies. I have argued that physical and mental ability are functionally similar in our society that normalises certain capacities. Race also names an important structural axis in most societies today.

The politics of cultural difference does not have a conceptual place for racial difference. To be sure, racialised social processes usually build on perceived differences in culture – language, religion, a sense of common lineage, specific cosmological beliefs, differing social practices and so on. As I have discussed above, however, racialisation and racism consist in a great deal more than that groups perceive themselves as distinct in relation to one another and refuse to recognise the equal legitimacy of the culture of others. It even consists in more than that groups that perceive themselves as ethnically or culturally different, have conflicts or are hostile to one another. Such ethnic or cultural difference becomes racial hierarchy when the groups interact in a social system where one is able to extract benefits by its hierarchical relation to the other. In the process of racialisation, norms construct members of a group as subordinate, stereotyped, despised, assigned to dirty work, excluded from high-status positions and segregated from the dominant group.

The politics of cultural difference obscures this process. Many political claims and conflicts in contemporary multicultural societies involve both issues of cultural freedom *and* issues of structural inequality such as racism. Where there are problems of a lack of recognition of or accommodation to national, cultural, religious or linguistic groups in liberal democratic societies (and others) today, these are often played out through dominant discourses that stereotype members of minority groups, find them technically inept or morally inferior, spatially segregate them and limit their opportunities to develop skills and compete for high-status positions (Young, 2000, pp 102-7).

Issues of justice for Latinos in the US, for example, concern not only cultural accommodation and acceptance, but also exposure and criticism of institutional racism, which many believe are deeply intertwined. Demands for and implementation of policies that mandate English only in public institutions such as courts and schools limit the freedom of some Latinos to express themselves freely and their ability to develop marketable skills and stigmatise them. The position of many Latinos is racialised, moreover, in that their brown skin and facial features place them together as a group in the eyes of many Anglos, in spite of the fact that they or their parents hail from different parts of Latin America and experience differences of language and tradition among themselves. Within the dominant structures, 'Hispanics' occupy particular positions in the social division of labour, and the benefits employers derive from this positioning are significant enough to limit the opportunities of members of this racialised group to move into other occupational positions.

Everywhere that indigenous people make claims to freedom of cultural expression and political self-determination, to take another example, they do so in the context of racialised structural inequality. Indians in North America, Aboriginals in Australia, indigenous people in Latin America, are all victims of historically racist policies of murder, removal, spatial concentration, theft of their land and resources, and limitation of their opportunities to make a living. Structures of racialised inequality run deep in these societies, and discrimination and stereotyping persist. Many conflicts over cultural toleration or accommodation in contemporary liberal democracies occur within a context of structural inequality between the dominant groups and cultural minorities. What is at stake in many of these conflicts is not simply freedom of expression and association, but substantively equal opportunity for individuals from marginalised groups to develop and exercise their capacities, and to have meaningful voice in the governance of the institutions whose policies condition their lives. When the politics of cultural difference dominates political discourse on group difference, however, these positional issues are harder to raise and discuss. The weight of felt grievance about structural injustice then may bear down on these cultural conflicts.

The example of political conflict between Latinos and Anglos in the US is not unique: it focuses on cultural difference, but still has roots in structural inequality. Some group political conflict in multicultural European societies focuses on cultural difference in a context where structural inequality is a primary but understated issue. Many Muslim people dwelling in European cities, for example, are victims of racial injustice. They are excluded from many opportunities for achieving status and income, they suffer stereotyping and objectification of their embodied presence, they lack recognised political voice, and they often live in segregated, less desirable, neighbourhoods (see Chapter Eleven). The claims of such Muslims that they should have the freedom to wear headscarves or make their prayer calls in the public squares in the cities where they live should not be divorced from this context of broad and entrenched structural privilege of majorities and social and economic disadvantage of minorities. Public debates seem to displace the structural problems onto issues of culture; the debates tend to ignore issues of poverty, unemployment, poor education and segregation among Muslims, at the same time that they magnify issues related to religion and culture. Structural racism is obscured by disputes over cultural symbols.

State and civil society

The paradigm situation assumed by the politics of cultural difference is that of a society in which there is a plurality of ethnic, national and/or religious groups; in the current moment one (or some) of them tends to wield dominant power through the state. These dominant groups tend to bias state action and policy in ways that favour their group members – for example, by declaring their language the official political language, or making only those religious holidays celebrated by members of their group recognised by the state. Cultural minorities resist this dominative power, making claims on the state and other societal members to recognise their right to freedom of expression and practice, to exempt them from certain regulations on religious or cultural grounds, to recognise their language as one among several constituting the political community, to support their children being educated in their language, to take special measures to assure representation of minority groups in political decision making, and many other claims for cultural recognition and freedom. Some minority groups claim to be distinct nations towards whom a right of self-determination should be recognised. An array of proposals and debates has arisen concerning what it can mean to accommodate such a right, not all of which involve creating a distinct sovereign state for the oppressed nationality; most, however, involve constitutional issues.

Critically, most of the issues that arise both in theoretical writing and public discussion about the politics of cultural difference concern state policy, regulation, or the organisation of state institutions. In this respect the politics of cultural difference usually comes within a liberal framework. One of the features of a liberal framework, as distinct from other political frameworks, such as critical theory, republicanism or communitarianism, is that it often presumes that political struggle is primarily about state policy. This liberal framework assumes a simple model of society as consisting of the public – coinciding with what is under the administrative regulation of the state – and the private, which is everything else. Under this liberal model, the main questions are, what shall the state permit, support or require, and what shall it discourage or forbid? Framing questions of the politics of difference largely in terms of what the state should or should not do in relation to individuals and groups, however, ignores civil society as an arena both of institutional decision making and political struggle, on the one hand, and processes of structural differentiation, on the other. It tends to ignore ways that non-governmental institutions often exercise exploitation, domination and exclusion, as well as ways that private organisations and institutions can design remedies for these wrongs. The relations in which individuals and groups stand to one another within civil society, even apart from their relations to state policy, are very important both as causes of injustice and resources for remedying this injustice (Young, 2000, Chapter 5).

The assumption that politics concerns primarily what the state allows, moreover, can generate serious misunderstanding about positions taken by proponents of a politics of difference, particularly with the politics of positional difference. Barry (2001, p 95) quotes disapprovingly my claim in *Justice and the politics of difference* (Young, 1990) that 'no social practices or activities should be excluded as improper subjects for public discussion, expression and collective choice', and then cites Fullinwider's (1996) interpretation of this statement to the effect that I advocate political intervention and modification into 'private choices'. The spectre haunting Barry and Fullinwider is the limitation of individual liberty backed by state sanction. Apparently they envisage no object of public discussion and collective choice other than state policies and laws. Certainly these are important objects of public discussion and choice in a democracy. A political theory concerned with the production and reproduction of structural inequalities even when laws guarantee formally equal rights, however, must shine its light on other corners as well. Movements of African Americans, people with disabilities, feminists, gay men and lesbians, indigenous people, as well as many ethnic movements, realise that societal discrimination, processes of segregation and marginalisation enacted through social networks and private institutions must be confronted in their non-state institutional sites. While law can provide a framework for equality, and some remedy for egregious violations of rights and respect, the state and law cannot and should not reach into every capillary of everyday life. A politics of positional difference thus recommends that churches, universities, production and marketing enterprises, clubs and associations all examine their policies, practices and priorities to discover ways in which they contribute to unjust structures and recommends changing them when they do. Such a position is not tantamount to calling the culture Gestapo and to police every joke or bathroom design. Numerous social changes brought about by these movements in the last 30 years have involved actions by many people that were voluntary, in the sense that the state neither required them nor sanctioned agents who did not perform them. Indeed, state policy as often follows behind action within civil society directed at undermining structural injustice as leads it.

Benhabib (2002) distinguishes such a 'dual track' approach to politics, which she associates with critical theory, and argues that liberal political theory typically ignores non-state dimensions of politics:

> In deliberative democracy, as distinguished from political liberalism, the *official* public sphere of representative institutions, which includes the legislature, executive and public bureaucracies, the judiciary and political parties, is not the only site of political contestation and or opinion and will formation. Deliberative democracy focuses on social movements, and on the civil, cultural, religious, artistic, and political associations of the *unofficial* public sphere, as well. (Benhabib, 2002, p 21, emphasis in original)

Barry and others who consider issues of difference under a liberal paradigm, ignore this non-official public sphere of contestation and action, and thus 'attempt(s) to solve multicultural conflicts through a juridical calculus of liberal rights' (Barry, 2001, p 92). A conception of justice able to criticise relations of domination and limitation of opportunity suffered by gender, racialised, ethnic or religious groups must consider relations within private activities and civil society and their interaction with state institutions.

Normalising culture

The logic of most theorising in the politics of cultural difference, as well as the logic of many political debates about multiculturalism, assumes the point of view of a power or authority that deliberates about what practices, forms of expression and forms of civic and political association should be allowed, encouraged or required, and which should be discouraged or forbidden. Both theoretical and political debates in the politics of cultural difference, often take the traditionally liberal form of debates about what should and what should not be tolerated. Framing issues of difference in terms of tolerance, however, often introduces a normalising logic in debates about multiculturalism. The political questions debated often have this form: shall we tolerate this expression or practice that we find of questionable value or morality, for the sake of mutual accommodation and civic peace? Should we allow methods of processing animals for food that require that the animals be awake at the time of slaughter? This form is typical in multicultural debates and assumes the following. The primary participants in the debate are members of the 'we', who argue among themselves for and against tolerance. This 'we' is the point of view of the dominant culture, which also assumes itself to have the power to influence the authorities who allow or forbid. While those holding the point of view debate among themselves whether tolerance is the appropriate stance in this case, they all presume themselves to occupy a position as normal, which means not only in the statistical majority, but also holding values that lie within the range of acceptable and even good. Those whose practices the normalised 'we' discuss have little or no voice in the debates. They are the object of the debates, but in it, if at all, only weakly as political subjects. The debate positions them as deviant in relation to the norm; as with all questions of tolerance, the question is only, are these practices so deviant as to be beyond a line of permissibility? Those who find themselves positioned in this normalising discourse often believe that the terms of the debate themselves are disrespectful, even before a resolution has been achieved. They also often believe that their being positioned as deviant makes them liable to other forms of denigration, exclusion or disadvantage.

An odd inversion often happens to gender issues in this politics of cultural difference, utilising the normalising logic implicit in many debates about tolerance. The politics of cultural difference obscures many issues concerning gender and justice that are matters of structural inequality. The politics of positional difference theorises gender as a set of structural social positions. These structures operate in complex ways to render many women vulnerable to gender-based domination and deprivation in most societies of the world, including Western liberal democracies. You might never know it, however, to listen to gendered debates among contemporary theorists of the politics of cultural difference. Many of the political debates currently taking place about multiculturalism focus on beliefs and practices of cultural minorities, especially Muslims, about women. These debates are especially salient in Europe, although George W. Bush used these issues to great rhetorical effect to legitimate the US-led 2001 invasion of Afghanistan (Young, 2003). A great deal of the recent political theoretical literature taking the approach of a politics of cultural difference devotes considerable attention to the treatment of women by cultural minorities.

In many theoretical writings on multiculturalism, gender issues serve as the test to the limits of tolerance. Can we tolerate rules of a national minority that refuse to recognise the women who marry outside its group members? Can we allow Muslim women to accede to the pressure or expectation that they wear the hijab? Surely we cannot permit arranged marriages of teenage girls or female genital cutting under any circumstances? My purpose in calling attention to the ubiquity of gender issues in contemporary political and theoretical debates on cultural difference is not to take a position but offer them as instances of the normalising discourse of tolerance typical of the logic of the politics of cultural difference. The 'we' in these questions occupies the position of the majority Western liberals. 'We' can raise these questions about the extent to which the gender practices of the minority culture can be tolerated because among 'us', women have (at least legally) the same freedom and autonomy as men. Our gender individualism is the norm against which the practices of many cultures come up deviant. Debates about gender in the politics of cultural difference thus serve the double function of positioning some cultural groups beyond the pale and encouraging a self-congratulatory arrogance on the part of the 'we' who debate these issues. Gender has moved from being a difference, to occupying the universal. In the process, the real issues of gendered structural inequality may be ignored.

Conclusion

This chapter set out to clarify differences in approaches to political and theoretical debates about justice: whether and to what extent justice calls for attending to rather than ignoring social group differences. The fact that the politics of cultural difference has more occupied political theorists in recent years than a politics of positional difference is lamentable, I have suggested, for several reasons. It tends to narrow the groups of concern to ethnic, national and religious groups, and to limit the issues of justice at stake to those concerned with freedom and autonomy more than equal opportunity of people to develop capacities and live a life of well-being. Its reliance on a liberal paradigm, moreover, tends to limit politics to shaping state policy and to reintroduce normalising discourses into what began as de-normalising movements. My objective in making these distinctions and arguments has not been to reject the politics of cultural difference, but to encourage political theorists to refocus their attention to group differences generated from structural power, the division of labour, and constructions of the normal and the deviant, as they continue also to reflect on conflicts over national, ethnic or religious difference.

Notes
[1] Very sadly, Professor Young died unexpectedly as this chapter was nearing completion. We are grateful to Cambridge University Press for permission to reproduce it. The original version is appearing in *Multiculturalism and political theory*, Anthony Laden and David Owen (eds). This version is edited, as had been agreed with Professor Young, and we hope that we have not distorted her key arguments in doing so.

[2] I have profited from discussions of versions of this chapter at a range of international meetings and I am grateful to the following individuals for comments on earlier drafts: David Alexander, Joseph Carens, Jon Elster, Fred Evans, David Ingram, Anthony Laden, John McCormick, Patchen Markell, David Owen and Jeremy Waldron.

[3] Approximately one in eight of the UK population at any one time, for example.

[4] I have argued that so-called merit standards often normalise attributes, comportments or attainments associated with particular social groups, and thus often do not serve the impartial purpose they claim.

[5] As was apparent in the gradation of 'mixed race' slaves. Gordon (1995) analyses the logic of the dichotomy of anti-black racism according to an existentialist logic of absolute subject and the Other.

[6] One example is what 'Western societies' call female genital mutilation (see Chapter Eleven).

References

Barry, B. (2001) *Culture and equality*, Cambridge, MA: Harvard University Press.

Benhabib, S. (2002) *The claims of culture: Equality and diversity in the global era*, Princeton, NJ: Princeton University Press.

Carens, J. (2000) 'Liberalism and culture', in *Culture, citizenship and community: A contextual explication of justice as evenhandedness*, Oxford: Oxford University Press, pp 52-87.

Chambers, C. (2002) 'All must have prizes: the liberal case for interference in cultural practices', in P. Kelly (ed) *Multiculturalism reconsidered*, Cambridge: Polity Press, pp 151-73.

Fanon, F. (1967) *Black skins, white masks*, New York: Grove Press.

Fraser, N. and Honneth, A. (eds) (2003) *Redistribution or recognition: A philosophical exchange*, London and New York: Verso.

Fullinwider, R. (ed) (1996) *Columbia encyclopaedia*, Cambridge: Cambridge University Press, pp 183-202.

Gordon, L. (1995) *Bad faith and anti-black racism*, Atlantic Highlands, NJ: Humanities Press.

Kelly, P. (2002) 'Defending some dodos: equality and/or liberty?', in P. Kelly (ed) *Multiculturalism reconsidered*, Cambridge: Polity Press, pp 62-80.

Kittay, E. F. (1999) *Love's labor: Essays on women, equality, and dependency*, New York: Routledge.

Kymlicka, W. (1995) *Multicultural citizenship: Inclusion and democracy*, Oxford: Oxford University Press.

Loury, G. (2002) *Anatomy of racial inequality*, Cambridge, MA: Harvard University Press.

Nussbaum, M. (2006) *Frontiers of justice*, Cambridge, MA: Harvard University Press, chapters 2-3.

Okin, S. M. (1989) *Justice, gender and the family*, New York: Basic Books.

Parekh, B. (2000) *Rethinking multiculturalism*, London: Macmillan.

Rawls, J. (1971) *A theory of justice*, Cambridge, MA: Harvard University Press.

Taylor, C. (1994) 'The politics of recognition', in A. Gutmann (ed) *Multiculturalism*, Cambridge, MA: Harvard University Press.

Tilly, C. (1998) *Durable inequality*, Berkeley, CA: University of California Press.

Young, I. M. (1997) 'Unruly categories: a critique of Fraser's dual systems theory,' *New Left Review*, no 222, pp 147-60.

Young, I. M. (1990) *Justice and the politics of difference*, Princeton, NJ: Princeton University Press.

Young, I. M. (2000) *Inclusion and democracy*, Oxford: Oxford University Press.

Young, I. M. (2001) 'Equality of whom? Social groups and judgments of injustice', *Journal of Political Philosophy*, vol 9, no 1, pp 1-18.

Young, I. M. (2003) 'The logic of masculinist protection: reflections on the current security state', *Signs: A Journal of Women in Culture and Society*, vol 29, no 1, pp 1-25.

FIVE

Recognition and voice: the challenge for social justice[1]

Ruth Lister

Introduction

This chapter addresses both the more theoretical and the more policy-oriented themes of this volume. It begins with an overview of how some of the theoretical literature on social justice has addressed the relationship between distributional and relational justice (couched in the language of recognition and voice). Is social justice about distribution or is it about relations of respect, recognition and voice – or a combination of the two?

The chapter then turns to its central concern, namely the recognition paradigm of social justice. The first issue it addresses is the association of this paradigm with social movements and identity politics. According to Barbara Hobson (2003, p 2), 'recognition has been grounded in normative political theories of justice, citizenship, and democracy in which inclusion, rights, and membership are the cornerstones'. 'Identity is at the core of the recognition paradigm', Hobson (2003, p 4) states, and recognition struggles 'make claims resulting from devalued statuses and misrecognized identities'. However, as will be argued, that does not mean that recognition struggles necessarily constitute identity politics (Lister, 2005).

Indeed, the chapter will contend that the recognition paradigm of social justice helps us to make sense of the contemporary politics of poverty, more typically associated with the distributive paradigm and certainly not a form of identity politics. Despite having worked within the distributive paradigm as both a campaigner and an academic for most of my adult life, through my readings of political, social and feminist theory and also through listening to and reading what people in poverty say about what poverty means to them, I have come to believe that a poverty politics of social justice must integrate distributive and recognition perspectives. This can be identified as 'a politics of redistribution and of recognition & respect', in acknowledgement of how people with experience of poverty themselves use the language of respect (Lister, 2004).

From an analytical perspective, 'recognition and redistribution become specific lenses for viewing the same struggles, rather than discrete categories' (Hobson, 2003, p 2). Anne Phillips (2003) reinforces this point. She observes that 'struggles for recognition are and have been very much struggles for political voice' (2003, p 265) and that understood in this way the struggles are less obviously about a particular *category* of injustice. 'Voice' is about the right to a say. It means being listened to and heard in democratic spaces.

The chapter concludes by outlining some possible policy implications of understanding poverty within the recognition paradigm of social justice.

Theoretical perspectives on the relationship between distribution and recognition

A frequently cited straightforward definition of social justice is that provided by David Miller (1999, p 1): 'how the good and bad things in life should be distributed among the members of a human society'. This conceptualises social justice firmly within the distributive paradigm. Nevertheless, Miller does make reference to recognition and cultural identities as 'issues of justice in the broad sense', but explains that 'they are not issues of distributional justice' as understood by political philosophers (1999, p 253). He also talks about 'social equality', that is, relations of equal recognition and respect, which he characterises as 'independent of justice' (1999, p 239). More recently, he seems to posit a closer connection in arguing that social justice depends on a culture of equal respect and that the question of voice belongs on the social justice as well as the democratic renewal agenda (2005). This does not mean, however, that Miller considers recognition and respect as matters of *social* justice.[2]

Among those who place greater emphasis on recognition, it is possible to identify four broad approaches to conceptualising its relationship to the distributive paradigm. These are explored through a brief overview of the writings of theorists whose work exemplifies these positions.

One approach is that found in an ambitious book on equality by John Baker and colleagues (2004). This attempts, in effect, to characterise questions of recognition, respect and voice in distributional terms as dimensions of equality. These dimensions do not, however, lend themselves to quantification in the way that inequalities of material resources do, as the authors acknowledge (Baker et al, 2004). At the opposite extreme, Iris Marion Young, in her most influential work, *Justice and the politics of difference*, challenges the reduction of social justice to the distributive paradigm. She does not reject that paradigm outright but she argues for its de-centring so that 'domination and oppression', that is the 'institutional constraints' on 'self-determination' and 'self-development', rather than 'distribution' are taken as 'the starting point for a conception of social justice' (1990, pp 37, 16; see also Chapter Four).

Her argument is twofold. First, that a focus on the allocation of material goods diverts attention from 'the social structure and institutional context that often help to determine distributive patterns' in particular 'decision-making power and procedures, division of labour, and culture' (1990, p 15). Second, that if the distributive paradigm is metaphorically extended to non-material social goods, such as recognition and respect, it misrepresents 'them as though they were static things, instead of a function of social relations and processes' (1990, p 16). In treating them as possessions and focusing on outcomes and patterns of possession, the distributional paradigm loses sight of social and power *relations* and the cultural meanings in which they are embedded.

A rather different challenge to the distributive paradigm can be found in the work of Axel Honneth. His theory of social justice is rooted in the recognition paradigm, which, he argues, is more fundamental than the distributive paradigm to the experience of injustice. 'What is needed', he opines, 'is a basic conceptual shift to the normative premises of a theory of recognition that locates the core of all experiences of injustice in the withdrawal of social recognition, in the phenomena of humiliation and disrespect' (2003, p 134).

Rather than counterpoise distributional and recognition conflicts, he argues that distributional conflicts are reducible to recognition conflicts because demands for redistribution cannot be 'understood independently of any experience of social disrespect' (2003, p 171). 'Even distributional injustices must be understood as the institutional expression of social disrespect' (2003, p 114). It is the experience of disrespect rather than the distribution of resources as such that fuels political claims for redistribution, he contends. The starting point for Honneth's theory of social justice is 'that the recognition of human dignity comprises a central principle of social justice' (2004, p 352). 'The justice or wellbeing of a society is measured according to the degree of its ability to secure conditions of mutual recognition in which personal identity formation, and hence individual self-realization, can proceed sufficiently well' (2004, p 354).

Honneth has developed his arguments partly through a dialogue with Nancy Fraser, which led to the publication of 'a political-philosophical exchange' (Fraser and Honneth, 2003). Here, contra Honneth, Fraser argues that problems of distribution cannot be subsumed within a recognition paradigm; nor can the distributive paradigm subsume problems of recognition. Instead, she develops what she calls a '"two-dimensional" conception of justice [which] treats distribution and recognition as distinct perspectives on, and dimensions of, justice ... within a broader overarching framework' (2003, p 35).

This framework is rooted in the notion of 'parity of participation'. This is a norm of justice that 'requires social arrangements that permit all (adult) members of society to interact with one another as peers' (2003, p 38). Participatory parity rests on two conditions: the 'objective condition' of a distribution of material resources such as to ensure 'independence and "voice"' and the 'intersubjective condition' of 'institutionalized patterns of cultural value [which] express equal respect ... and ensure equal opportunity for achieving social esteem' (2003, p 36). In her original *New Left Review* article, Fraser (1995, p 70) made clear that these are analytical distinctions used for heuristic purposes, as in the real world 'culture and political economy are always imbricated with one another'.

More recently, Fraser has added a third dimension to her analysis: the political. This refers to 'the nature of the state's jurisdiction and the decision rules by which it structures contestation. The political in this sense furnishes the stage on which struggles over distribution and recognition are played out' (Fraser, 2005, p 75). She points out that:

> [T]his means that there can be distinctively political obstacles to parity, not reducible to maldistribution or misrecognition, although ... interwoven with them. Such obstacles arise from the political constitution of society, as opposed to the class structure or status order. (2005, p 76)

Representation thus stands alongside distribution and recognition as a dimension of justice. This development in Fraser's position accords with Simon Thompson's argument for a synthesis between her and Honneth's recognition theories. In a helpful critical exposition of their theoretical positions, he suggests that 'Honneth's analysis of the political dimension of justice can make good a lack in Fraser's theory'

(Thompson, 2006, p 127). Voice represents a point of particularly thick interweave between representation and recognition.

Recognition, social movements and identity politics

Fraser's initial statement on recognition starts with the claim that:

> [T]he 'struggle for recognition' is fast becoming the paradigmatic form of political conflict in the late twentieth century. Demands for 'recognition' of difference fuel struggles of groups mobilized under the banners of nationality, ethnicity, 'race', gender and sexuality. (Fraser, 1995, p 68)

These, she contends, have supplanted social class struggles fuelled by exploitation and the unjust distribution of material resources.

This claim has generated considerable debate among fellow critical and feminist theorists (see, for instance, Phillips, 1997; Young, 1997). Leaving this debate aside, it seems clear that it is largely the non-materialist demands of social movements that have helped to underline the importance of recognition and voice to any theory and politics of social justice. However, acknowledgement of this fact is not to deny the links often made between distributive and recognition claims in both social movement and more traditional social class struggles.

Fraser posits a 'conceptual spectrum' in which all social differentiations involve economic and cultural forms of injustice but to differing degrees. Social class stands at one end in the primarily distributive frame of an unjust political economy. Sexuality stands at the other in the recognition frame of an unjust status order, where institutionalised heteronormality has accorded gays and lesbians the status of 'a despised sexuality' (Fraser, 1999, p 30). In between, she sets gender and 'race' as hybrid 'bivalent' differentiations subject to injustices rooted in both political economy and culture. Gender injustice reflects, on the one hand, the maldistribution of material resources and time between women and men and, on the other, cultural codes, which privilege traits associated with the 'masculine' and devalue those associated with the 'feminine'. The classic example is the devalued status of care work – both paid and unpaid.

Racial injustices, Fraser writes, 'include both maldistribution and misrecognition' (Fraser, 1999, p 32; see also Chapters Four and Eleven, this volume). The same is true of disability, which surprisingly Fraser virtually ignores in her work (Lister, 2007b) but which Young emphasises as 'paradigmatic' of structural injustice in this volume. Yet, arguably, disability politics provides a prime example of the integration of a politics of redistribution and recognition (see also Shakespeare, 2005). Disabled people have been subject to misrecognition, hostility and humiliation as 'different' and 'other'. Bert Massie, Chair of the former Disability Rights Commission, has spoken of 'a degree of social repulsion to disabled people that is unparalleled with any other group' (O'Hara, 2007). Disability pride politics challenge such misrecognition. Yet at the same time, disabled people suffer very real material disadvantage in terms of labour market position, access to public services and the failure of income maintenance provisions adequately to cover the additional costs associated with disability. Disabled people are still therefore much more likely than non-disabled to be in poverty. Their struggle is thus for greater equality and access as well as recognition of their difference: that is for both material and cultural forms of justice (see, for instance, Goodlad and Riddell, 2005; Witcher, 2005).

As observed earlier, identity is at the heart of recognition claims. Charles Taylor, a leading recognition theorist, explains the link with identity:

> ... a person's understanding of who they are, of their fundamental defining characteristics as a human being. The thesis is that our identity is partly shaped by recognition or its absence, often by the *mis*recognition of others, and so a person or group of people can suffer real damage, real distortion, if the people or society around them mirror back to them a confining or demeaning or contemptible picture of themselves. (Taylor, 1992, p 25)

This means, he contends, that recognition is 'a vital human need' (p 26). As such it 'is not a luxury that ranks lower than the satisfaction of material needs, but is essential for well-being' (Sayer, 2005, p 54).

Taylor is here describing what David Taylor (1998) calls 'ontological identity': a person's unique sense of self. All too often, however, recognition politics are conflated with identity politics, which speak to collective, 'categorical' and political identities shared with others. As the proliferation of politicised identities associated with identity politics gave rise to divisions and fragmentation in social justice politics, identity politics became increasingly discredited. This has led some feminist theorists to construct various versions of what might be described as 'a politics of solidarity in difference' (see Lister, 2005).

Fraser makes the case for disconnecting a politics of recognition from identity politics on the grounds that what is at issue is not group identity but the status subordination of individual group members, which impedes parity of participation in social life. She also makes clear that recognition claims are not necessarily claims for recognition of difference. The appropriate form of the recognition claim, she argues, depends on the nature of the misrecognition: 'in cases where misrecognition involves denying common humanity ..., the remedy is universalist recognition' (Fraser, 1999, p 38). Similarly, in his interpretation of Charles Taylor's theory of recognition, Thompson equates what Taylor terms the 'politics of universalism' with a 'politics of respect'. Such a politics 'holds that human beings, by their very nature, deserve to be treated with respect, and it argues that such respect should be enjoyed equally. Only in these circumstances will people be able to experience equal dignity' (Thompson, 2006, p 45).

The politics of poverty

Universalist recognition and respect are at the heart of the struggle waged by many poverty activists. This is one aspect of what Andrew Sayer (2005, p 53) identifies as the 'micro-politics of class [which] are very much about recognition and misrecognition'. Although recognition theorists do not tend to write about poverty as such, their work is helpful in thinking about social justice in this context. Fraser's notions of status subordination and participatory parity, in particular, help cast recognition politics in terms that make sense in relation to poverty. Similarly, the acknowledgement that recognition claims are not necessarily grounded in difference is a crucial move when applying the recognition paradigm to a group of people who most certainly do not want to be treated as different. On the contrary, what people living in poverty want is the universalist recognition of their common humanity and citizenship and of the equal worth that flows from that.

I would, however, place greater emphasis than Fraser does on the psychological effects of misrecognition, without subscribing to a 'psychologised' theory. Thus, it is possible to agree with her that 'the wrongness of misrecognition does not *depend* on the presence of such effects', as argued by recognition theorists, such as Honneth and Taylor (Fraser, 2003, p 32, emphasis added). However, at the same time we can also question her contention elsewhere that 'when misrecognition is identified with internal distortions in the structure of self-consciousness of the oppressed, it is but a short step to blaming the victim', thereby seeming 'to add insult to injury' (2001, p 27; Thompson, 2006).

Richard Wilkinson (2005, p 156) has also warned how 'those privileged to view these problems [of misrecognition] from above' can all too easily blame them on the victims, so that the fault lies with 'their self-esteem rather than with the humiliation they suffer'. He makes the point, however, in support of his own thesis, which emphasises the importance of psychosocial processes to the experience of poverty and inequality. 'The concept of the psychosocial is an attempt to recognize the primacy of emotional responses to human existence, particularly in relation to hierarchies of domination and subordination' (Charlesworth et al, 2004, p 51).

Participatory research in an international development context 'reveals that these psychological dimensions are central to poor people's definitions of poverty' (Narayan, 2000, p 267). The significance of the psychological dimension for understanding social justice from the perspective of people living in poverty is brought out in an in-depth study of poverty in Australia. The researcher spoke to participants in the study about their visions of social justice:

> What mattered to them was acknowledgment of capacity and intelligence. Their justice was distributive and procedural, and intimately connected with dignity and self-determination. Justice was about being respected, trusted and listened to because what you had to say was important. *If social justice is a response to poverty, they argued, it must be a response to poverty's psychological and emotional wounds, not just its financial consequences.* (Peel, 2003, p 167, emphasis added)

People with experience of poverty bring home the hurt caused by such wounds. For instance, Moraene Roberts, a poverty activist with ATD Fourth World,[3] speaking at a National Poverty Hearing organised by Church Action on Poverty, explained: 'The worst blow of all is the contempt of your fellow citizens. I and many families live in that contempt' (cited in Russell, 1996, p 4). An anonymous participant in a UK Coalition against Poverty Workshop described what the loss of self-esteem associated with misrecognition feels like:

> You're like an onion and gradually every skin is peeled off you and there's nothing left. All your self esteem and how you feel about yourself is gone – you're left feeling like nothing and then your family feels like that. (UKCAP, 1997, p 12)

A group of low-income parents told the All-Party Parliamentary Group on Poverty that 'the worst thing about living in poverty is the way it gives others permission to treat you – as if you don't matter' (Galloway, 2002, p 13). Another example is provided by Simon Charlesworth, who quotes an unemployed man: 'They look at you like you're muck don't they, like you're dirt on the floor ... I feel worthless in myself, I just feel worthless'. When asked what makes him feel worthless in particular, he replied: 'How people treat you in public' (Charlesworth, 2005, pp 302-3).

To acknowledge the psychological pain that these people are expressing as a result of misrecognition is not 'to add insult to injury'. Similarly, if we look at poverty from the perspective of children, we see how lack of participatory parity and the psychological impact of poverty are intertwined. Tess Ridge (2002, p 85) observes that:

> [I]nner worries, fears of social difference and stigma, and the impact of poverty on self-esteem, confidence and personal security may all exact a high price for children who are in the formative process of developing their self and social identities.

Vivyan C. Adair, an American who describes herself as a 'poverty class scholar', provides a vivid account of the impact of extreme poverty on the childhood she and her sister experienced:

> Our dirty and tattered clothing; posture that clearly reflected guilt, shame and lack of a sense of entitlement; scars and bodily disease; and sheer hunger, marked us as Others among our more fortunate working-class neighbours and colleagues.... Other students and even our working class teachers read us as 'trailer trash', as unworthy, laughable, and dangerous.... We were ... shamed and humiliated in our ragged and ill-fitting hand-me-downs, our very bodies signalling our Otherness. (Adair, 2005, p 823)

Of course, if our starting point were simply to say that people in poverty may have low self-esteem, as if this were somehow innate, then yes it would be to 'add insult to injury'. On the other hand, if, following Adair, we analyse such psychological effects as the result of the Othering of 'the poor' by the 'non-poor' then we can understand these effects in terms of misrecognition (Lister, 2004).[4]

Reframing the politics of poverty as a politics of recognition as well as redistribution has implications for how people in poverty are represented and treated at all levels of society (Lister, 2004). This includes the language and images that make up popular discourses of poverty. As a parent living on benefit has put it, 'we hear how the media, and some politicians, speak about us and it hurts' (APPGP, 1999, p 11). Participants in the Fourth European Meeting of People Experiencing Poverty (European Commission, 2005) were unanimous in their complaints about stereotyped images of poverty, particularly in the media. Terms such as the 'underclass' contribute to the process of Othering. More subtly perhaps, the unwritten subtext of New Labour's mantra of helping 'hard-working families' is that those who are not working hard in employment do not matter. One can almost hear the (usually) unspoken 'decent' before 'hard-working', recreating historically rooted divisions between the 'deserving' and 'undeserving' poor. By Othering those in poverty as different from the rest of us, such stigmatising language serves to distance 'us' from 'them'. The result is that the wider society is more likely to write 'the poor' off as beyond the bonds of common citizenship than to respond to appeals to support a concerted attack on poverty.

Some policy implications

The attack on poverty requires a multifaceted approach. This final section considers some possible broad implications for policy and practice of taking on board recognition, respect and voice as part of the social justice and anti-poverty agendas. In focusing on a recognition policy agenda, it is important to emphasise that this is not an alternative to a more traditional redistributive position. Sayer's warning against treating it as such needs to be borne in mind:

> [I]t is easy for the dominant to grant discursive recognition and civility to the dominated or socially excluded; giving up some of their money and other advantages to them is another matter. An egalitarian politics of recognition at the level of professed attitudes is easier for the well-off to swallow than an egalitarian politics of recognition-through-distribution, and it suits them to regard the former as progressive and the latter as passé. (Sayer, 2005, p 64)

Sayer's reference to 'recognition-through-distribution' signals that it is not a question of either-or. 'The grounds for an egalitarian politics of distribution', he argues, 'lie in an egalitarian politics of recognition: any argument for distributional equality must ultimately appeal to criteria of recognition – that all are of equal moral worth' (Sayer, 2005, p 65). Majid Yar makes a similar point: 'redistributive claims, *as moral claims upon others invoking the terms of justice and injustice*, irredeemably have the character of recognition claims', as they involve '*normative* concepts which are based upon specific self-understandings about what kinds of beings we are, what our worth is, and what kind of treatment we properly deserve' (Yar, 1999, pp 295, 294, emphasis in original). While, following Fraser, I would not go so far as to *reduce* all redistribution claims to recognition claims, the point made here is that the two are inextricably interwoven.

This is illustrated by the issue of low pay even though, on the face of it, demands for improvements in the wages of the low paid represent redistribution claims grounded in the material effects of poverty wages. An important lesson, learned by the journalist Polly Toynbee from her experience of living temporarily on low pay, echoes Yar. She observes that 'what a person is paid signifies their worth and it is of primary emotional and social importance' (2002, p 35).

> Low pay is low status…. Just as pay is a cause for boasting among the fat cats, it is equally a source of daily humiliation for the low paid, seeing how little one hour of their hard work is valued at. (Toynbee, 2002, p 14)

When low-paid workers frame their demands as a claim for dignity they reinforce the need for a public debate about the overall distribution of pay and the rewards attached to different kinds of work (Lister, 2007c).

Redistributive claims to improvements in social security benefits also appeal ultimately, even if not always explicitly, to recognition principles. The European Commission recommended in 1992 that member states 'recognise the basic right of a person to sufficient resources and social assistance to live in a manner compatible with human dignity' (Veit-Wilson, 1998, p 86). One participant in the Get Heard Scotland project stated that: 'I couldn't afford to live as I would like to live, yet everyone's entitled to dignity' (Burnett, 2006, p 45). Dignity was an issue raised by a number of participants in the project:

> It was strongly felt that dignity should not have to be earned…. People living on a low-income should not be expected to survive on lower quality services and products,

> yet frequently they felt deprived of their dignity because
> they are offered what might be defined as 'society's leftovers'.
> (Burnett, 2006, p 47)

Get Heard was a national UK participatory initiative, initiated by the
Social Policy Taskforce, which comprises a number of anti-poverty
organisations and networks, in conjunction with the Department for
Work and Pensions (DWP). It was prompted by governmental failure
to involve those affected in the drawing up of the first of regular
National Action Plans on Social Inclusion, as required by the European
Commission. The final report describes it as:

> one of the largest projects undertaken in the UK to involve
> people with first-hand experience of poverty to give their
> views on government policies designed to combat poverty
> – and in doing so to shape those policies which affect their
> lives. (Get Heard, 2006, p 4; Cochrane, 2006)

The initiative was, in part, a response to the growing demands among
people with experience of poverty for a say in decision making that
affects their lives or a 'voice with influence' (Gaventa, 2002, p 2). How to
remove the barriers to such participation was the key question addressed
by the Commission on Poverty, Participation and Power, half of whose
members had direct experience of poverty. The Commission's starting
point was the overwhelming message that it received concerning the
lack of respect accorded people living in poverty. For many of them
respect is tied in with being listened to. Lack of respect is identified as
the main barrier to participation in decision making and the ultimate
disrespect is seen as 'being involved in phoney participation, by people
who don't listen, when things don't change' (CoPPP, 2000, p 18).

A report published by the former Office of the Deputy Prime
Minister states that 'for social justice we must give everyone – and
especially the most deprived – more of a say' (ODPM, 2005, para 1.14).
As the Get Heard project shows, this is beginning to happen but there
is still a long way to go (Lister, 2007d). Thus, for instance, the DWP
may have started to listen, but there is no long-term mechanism for
enabling people with experience of poverty to feed their views into
and have influence on ongoing policy development.

Finally, returning to Iris Marion Young's emphasis on social relations
and processes, social justice is not just about outcomes but also about
how policy is delivered to marginalised groups. This was acknowledged

in a Social Exclusion Unit report on improving service delivery to disadvantaged groups. The report observes that:

> [P]eople from disadvantaged backgrounds who rely heavily on public services have the best experiences when they feel treated with respect and as individuals in a welcoming, non-intimidating environment. But our research has found that they do not always get this kind of positive treatment.... They feel they are not treated with respect; they are not spoken to politely; they are talked down to.... Lack of respect is a recurring issue. (SEU, 2005, p 58-9)

Among examples of good practice cited in the report is evidence that 'better training in the needs of disadvantaged groups can ... improve service delivery' (SEU, 2005, p 70). Members of the disadvantaged groups to whom the Social Exclusion Unit spoke

> suggested that more staff training should be delivered by people from disadvantaged groups. This would give staff [including senior managers] an opportunity to improve their understanding of disadvantaged people's experiences and needs through first hand contract. (SEU, 2005, p 70)

Participants at the Fourth European Meeting of People Experiencing Poverty similarly recommended 'training by "experiential experts", as is starting to be done in Belgium' (European Commission, 2005, p 3). 'Experiential experts' are people with experience of poverty who have been trained 'to become mediators in contacts with public services' (European Commission, 2005, p 40). A number of such experts have been employed by federal government agencies.

In the UK, poverty awareness training is beginning to be developed. In the same way that professionals and officials are now expected to have an understanding of equal opportunities and non-discrimination, so they need training in poverty-awareness.[5] A report of a joint project between ATD Fourth World, Family Rights Group and Royal Holloway, University of London provides some insights into how this might be pursued involving people with experience of poverty. The project brought together social service users with experience of poverty, social work practitioners and academics in order to develop a training module on poverty for social work students that would be delivered by people with experience of poverty (Perry, 2005).

Although, inevitably, the process was difficult, the evaluation concludes that it did demonstrate that 'the real-life perspectives of service user trainers are a huge resource for social work students to tap' (Perry, 2005, p 29). The trainers identified the impact of institutionalised, discriminatory, 'povertyism', which 'perpetuates a lack of knowledge and understanding about the lives of families experiencing poverty' (Perry, 2005, p 21). One participant summed it up: 'it is about how we are treated, we just want them to treat us the same way they want us to treat them – with respect' (Gupta, 2004, p 7).

Conclusion

Respect lies at the heart of the challenge to social justice posed by the principles of recognition and voice. This chapter has made the case for an ideal of social justice that incorporates recognition as well as redistribution so as to address the cultural and political as well as economic dimensions of injustice. It has used the example of poverty politics and policy, which traditionally have been understood in purely distributional terms. Application of the recognition paradigm of social justice illuminates the ways in which poverty politics are also a 'politics of recognition & respect' (Lister, 2004). This translates into policy demands for respectful treatment and genuine voice as well as for social security benefits and pay adequate to ensure dignity.

Notes

[1] An earlier, shorter version of this chapter has been published in Degener, U. and Rosenzweig, B. (eds) (2006) *Die Neuverhandlung sozialer Gerechtigkeit*, Wiesbaden: Vs Verlag für Sozialwissenschaften, and it draws in part on material in Lister (2007a, 2007b).

[2] He made this clear in his interventions at the ESRC seminar at the London School of Economics and Political Science, 21 March 2005, at which an earlier version of this chapter was presented. Brian Barry (2005) is another leading political philosopher who interprets social justice as essentially a distributional question.

[3] ATD Fourth World, a human rights organisation that works with families in severe and long-term poverty in a number of countries: www.atd-uk.org

[4] It should be noted here that some recognition theorists, notably Honneth, make a distinction between respect and esteem. Whereas 'respect is due to all humans in light of their universal capacity for rational agency', esteem is earned

by virtue of 'individual traits and abilities which help to advance "societal goals"' (Thompson, 2006, p 74; see also Sayer, 2005, pp 60-3).

[5] The Poverty Alliance in Scotland, for instance, carries out a programme of poverty awareness training.

References

Adair, V. C. (2005) 'US working-class/poverty-class divides', *Sociology*, vol 39, no 5, pp 817-34.

APPGP (All-Party Parliamentary Group on Poverty) (1999) *Policy, poverty and participation*, London: APPGP.

Baker, J., Lynch, K., Cantillon, S. and Walsh, J. (2004) *Equality from theory to action*, Basingstoke: Palgrave.

Barry, B. (2005) *Why social justice matters*, Cambridge: Polity Press.

Burnett, L. (2006) *'Dignity shouldn't have to be earned!' Get Heard Scotland final report*, Glasgow: The Poverty Alliance.

Charlesworth, S. (2005) 'Understanding social suffering: a phenomenological investigation of the experience of inequality', *Journal of Community & Applied Social Psychology*, vol 15, pp 296-312.

Charlesworth, S., Gilfilian, P. and Wilkinson, R. (2004) 'Living inferiority', *British Medical Bulletin*, vol 69, pp 49-60.

Cochrane, C. (2006) 'Involving people in poverty in the UK National Action Plan on Social Inclusion 2006-08', *Benefits: The Journal of Poverty and Social Justice*, vol 14, no 2, pp 147-9.

CoPPP (Commission on Poverty, Power and Participation) (2000) *Listen hear: The right to be heard*, Bristol: The Policy Press.

European Commission (2005) *Report of the fourth European meeting of people experiencing poverty*, Luxembourg: European Commission.

Fraser, N. (1995) 'From redistribution to recognition? Dilemmas of justice in a "post-Socialist" age', *New Left Review*, no 212, pp 68-93.

Fraser, N. (1999) 'Social justice in the age of identity politics: redistribution, recognition and participation', in L. Ray and A. Sayer (eds) *Culture and economy after the cultural turn*, London: Sage Publications.

Fraser, N. (2001) 'Recognition without ethics', *Theory, Culture & Society*, vol 18, no 2-3, pp 21-42.

Fraser, N. (2003) 'Social justice in the age of identity politics: redistribution, recognition and participation', in N. Fraser and A. Honneth (eds) (2003) *Redistribution or recognition? A political-philosophical exchange*, London and New York: Verso.

Fraser, N. (2005) 'Reframing justice in a globalizing world', *New Left Review*, no 36, pp 69-88.

Fraser, N. and Honneth, A. (eds) (2003) *Redistribution or recognition? A political-philosophical exchange*, London and New York: Verso.

Galloway, K. (2002) *A Scotland where everyone matters*, Manchester: Church Action on Poverty.

Gaventa, J. (2002) 'Exploring citizenship, participation and accountability', *IDS Bulletin*, vol 33, no 2, pp 1-11.

Get Heard (2006) *People experiencing poverty speak out on social exclusion*, London: UK Coalition against Poverty.

Goodlad, R. and Riddell, S. (2005) 'Social justice and disabled people: principles and challenges', *Social Policy and Society*, vol 4, no 1, pp 45-54.

Gupta, A. (2004) 'Involving families living in poverty in the training of social workers', *SWAP News*, no 7, p 7.

Hobson, B. (2003) 'Introduction', in B. Hobson (ed) *Recognition struggles and social movements*, Cambridge: Cambridge University Press.

Honneth, A. (2003) 'Redistribution as recognition', in N. Fraser and A. Honneth (eds) (2003) *Redistribution or recognition? A political-philosophical exchange*, London and New York: Verso.

Honneth, A. (2004) 'Recognition and justice', *Acta Sociologica*, vol 47, no 4, pp 351-64.

Lister, R. (2004) *Poverty*, Cambridge: Polity Press.

Lister, R. (2005) 'Being feminist', *Government and Opposition*, vol 40, no 3, pp 442-63.

Lister, R. (2007a) 'Social justice: meaning and politics', *Benefits: The Journal of Poverty and Social Justice*, vol 15, no 2, pp 113-25.

Lister, R. (2007b) '(Mis)recognition, social inequality and social justice: a critical social policy perspective', in T. Lovell (ed) *(Mis)Recognition, social inequality and social justice*, London and New York: Routledge.

Lister, R. (2007c) 'The real egalitarianism? Social justice "after Blair"', in G. Hassan (ed) *After Blair*, London: Lawrence and Wishart.

Lister, R. (2007d) 'From object to subject: including marginalised citizens in policy making', *Policy & Politics*, vol 35, no 3, pp 437-55.

Miller, D. (1999) *Principles of social justice*, Cambridge, MA: Harvard University Press.

Miller, D. (2005) 'What is social justice?', in N. Pearce and W. Paxton (eds) *Social justice: Building a fairer Britain*, London: Politicos.

Narayan, D. (2000) *Can anyone hear us?*, New York/Oxford: Oxford University Press/World Bank.

O'Hara, M. (2007) 'Living with a label', *Society Guardian*, 24 January.

ODPM (Office of the Deputy Prime Minister) (2005) *Sustainable cities: People, places and prosperity*, London: Cabinet Office.

Peel, M. (2003) *The lowest rung*, Cambridge: Cambridge University Press.

Perry, N. (2005) *Getting the right trainers*, London: ATD Fourth World.

Phillips, A. (1997) 'From inequality to difference: a severe case of displacement?', *New Left Review*, no 224, pp 143-53.

Phillips, A. (2003) 'Recognition and the struggle for political voice', in B. Hobson (ed) *Recognition struggles and social movements*, Cambridge: Cambridge University Press.

Ridge, T. (2002) *Childhood poverty and social exclusion*, Bristol: The Policy Press.

Russell, H. (ed) (1996) *Speaking from experience*, Manchester: Church Action on Poverty.

Sayer, A. (2005) *The moral significance of class*, Cambridge: Cambridge University Press.

SEU (Social Exclusion Unit) (2005) *Improving services, improving lives: Evidence and key themes*, London: ODPM.

Shakespeare, T. (2005) 'Disabling politics? Beyond identity', *Soundings*, no 30, pp 156-65.

Taylor, C. (1992) 'The politics of recognition', in A. Gutmann (ed) *Multiculturalism and the politics of recognition*, Princeton, NJ: Princeton University Press.

Taylor, D. (1998) 'Social identity and social policy', *Journal of Social Policy*, vol 27, no 3, pp 329-50.

Thompson, S. (2006) *The political theory of recognition: A critical introduction*, Cambridge: Polity Press.

Toynbee, P. (2002) *Hard work: A challenge to low pay*, London: Smith Institute.

UKCAP (UK Coalition against Poverty) (1997) *Poverty and participation*, London: UKCAP.

Veit-Wilson, J. (1998) *Setting adequacy standards*, Bristol: The Policy Press.

Wilkinson, R. (2005) *The impact of inequality*, London and New York: Routledge.

Witcher, S. (2005) 'Mainstreaming equality: the implications for disabled people', *Social Policy and Society*, vol 4, no 1, pp 55-64.

Yar, M. (1999) 'Beyond Nancy Fraser's perspectival dualism', *Economy and Society*, vol 30, no 3, pp 288-303.

Young, I. M. (1990) *Justice and the politics of difference*, Princeton, NJ: Princeton University Press.

Young, I. M. (1997) 'Unruly categories: a critique of Nancy Fraser's dual systems theory', *New Left Review*, no 222, pp 147-60.

SIX

Globalisation, social justice and the politics of aid

Christopher Bertram

Introduction

One of most important recent developments in theorising about social justice has concerned the extension of the conception of justice developed by Rawls in *A theory of justice* (1999a) to the global arena. In what follows I review some of this discussion and suggest that cosmopolitan critics are right, against Rawls himself, to suggest that we should treat the world as a whole (or at least the global economic system as a whole) as being in principle subject to evaluation according to a single distributive standard. But while that standard can be extended beyond the borders of nations to the wider arena of cooperation, the key mechanism that Rawls relied on to do the distributive work, the design and selection of an institutional structure, is not available to us in the same way as it is for the domestic sphere. It exists in one sense (there is a global basic structure that does much to explain distributive outcomes) but we cannot exercise very much control over it and could not reliably predict the effects of doing so if we could. We are therefore forced both to look more directly at social outcomes and at measures to change them after the event, and also to seek not the full achievement of social justice on a global scale but rather the avoidance of the most serious harms and injustices.

For and against cosmopolitanism: beyond the self-contained society

Rawls's original restriction of focus to a self-contained society, although made for methodological simplicity, had the important limitation of not corresponding to the world in which we live. No society is really self-contained: all societies engage in trade across borders and all permit, to varying degrees, the immigration of outsiders and the emigration of citizens. In addition, societies interact in other ways: through cultural contact, environmental effects, war, participation in global institutions of various kinds and so on. Indeed, we live in a world in which societies are less self-contained than at any time in history. The simplest of objects that a person consumes – a cup of tea for example – will have been produced by a process involving the cooperation of thousands of people in activities including mining, agriculture, transport and fuel production. In order to maintain those links, moreover, complex systems of payment and accounting are in place. All these people will be located across the planet, and the goods that they consume as they work to provide me with the constituent parts of my cup of tea will in turn draw on a similarly complex network of cooperation.

The people who are thus linked in cooperating together to fulfil their various needs will vary enormously in their levels of wealth, in their ability to enjoy various human goods, in their life expectancies and health outcomes and so on. And the location of any particular individual within that web of cooperation, with all the burdens and benefits that are associated with their position, is largely a matter of happenstance. Some babies are fortunate enough to be born in the wealthy suburbs of Boston Massachusetts, others come into the world in Burundi or Bangkok, and all to families at different levels of wealth and income. Small wonder, then, that many theorists have sought to extend the concern for social justice expressed by Rawls in his original theory to the wider subject of global society. Many have indeed thought that if the inequalities between persons who are co-citizens of a particular nation are troubling, and stand in need of justification, the inequalities between cooperators across borders (and among persons more generally) also require explanation and, then, either vindication or modification.

This might seem to be a simple enough matter. If cooperation takes place on a global scale then it looks obvious that the network of cooperation it constitutes is readily subject to evaluation from the point of view of justice. This was essentially the view taken by Charles Beitz in the first real attempt to extend Rawlsian ideas globally:

> The world economy has evolved its own financial and monetary institutions, which set exchange rates, regulate the money supply, influence capital flows, and enforce rules of international economic conduct. The system of trade is regulated by international agreements on tariff levels and other potential barriers to trade. To these global institutions should be added such informal practices of economic policy

> coordination among national governments as those of the
> Organization for Economic Cooperation and Development,
> which are aimed at achieving agreement on a variety of
> domestic policies of local and international relevance. Taken
> together, these institutions and practices can be considered
> as the constitutional structure of the world economy; their
> activities have important distributive implications. (Beitz,
> 1979, pp 148-9)

Beitz noticed the fact that there are institutions and practices that
are heavily implicated in distributive outcomes. His fundamental
contention was that if there is such a structure with such profound
effects, then that is something a theory of justice, and principles of
justice, have business dealing with. People are cooperating with one
another on a global scale, there are winners and losers, there are terms
of cooperation and there are moral questions to be raised about who
gets what and who does what. Beitz was surely right that the structure
of the world economy has such profound distributive effects. It is
possible to go further and add the point that it is not just the structure
of the economy that has such effects, but also the system of borders
and restraints on movement. Not only do children born in some parts
of the world have much worse life prospects than children born in
other parts, but if the first decide to relocate to the richer economies
they will often be forcibly prevented from doing so.

Rawls's own extension of his theory to the global arena was strikingly
different from that proposed by Beitz and by other Rawlsian theorists
(Rawls, 1999b). Instead of seeing the world as a single global system
of cooperation linking individuals, Rawls took his original model
of a well-ordered society and imagined it as inserted into a world
containing other states of various kinds. Taking 'peoples' rather than
individuals as his primary unit, Rawls asked what sort of principles
representatives of such peoples would agree to under a reworked version
of his original position thought-experiment. Rawls imagined such
representatives agreeing to rules rather similar to those embodied in
the United Nations charter and in international conventions regarding
human rights, as well as principles to adopt regarding 'outlaw states'
and 'burdened peoples'. When it came to global distributive justice,
he adopted a rather conservative view. Peoples were to be treated as
collectives taking responsibility for their economic and demographic
policies and, above a certain threshold, no redistributive duties were
to obtain between them. The exception was with regard to 'burdened
societies', whose absolute level of impoverishment was such that better-

off societies ought to aid them until such time as they could become self-sustaining.

Rawls's remarks have struck many critics as profoundly unsatisfactory (for example, Buchanan, 2000). First of all, his picture of how the world is and the way states operate within it looks curiously old-fashioned in an era of globalisation. He may have relaxed the idea that societies are self-contained, but he did not relax it very far. The 'peoples' of *The law of peoples* (Rawls, 1999b) are able to manage their domestic economies in relative isolation from the world beyond their shores, and such matters as the movement of migrants across borders are treated as aberrations. Second, Rawls endorses an explanation of the relative success and failure of 'peoples' in matters economic that is highly controversial. He treats such success and failure as explained largely by their internal policies and institutions and as having little to do with the way they interact with other societies. Third, Rawls's remarks are very sketchy by the standards of his earlier work, and there is no sustained attempt to defend his position against potential critics.

The anti-cosmopolitan view that envisages an international society of states that are not subject to strong redistributive duties has, however, not lacked for defenders. In contrast to Rawls, they have not necessarily bought into an unrealistic picture of the world but have rather sought to argue that, even if the world in some respects resembles the global system of cooperation described by Beitz, this is not sufficient to trigger a requirement of global redistribution. Those arguing on such lines have included Richard Miller (1998), Michael Blake (2002) and Thomas Nagel (2005). Notwithstanding important differences within their family of positions, the essential core of their arguments has been that in order for persons to be bound by redistributive principles they must be the common subjects of a legal authority, of coercive laws, and perhaps, in some sense, the authors of those laws. The idea being that a fair condition for agreeing to participate in a system of legal coercion is that one do so on reasonable distributive terms. All the citizens of a state agree to be bound by a common system of law and those who are the least advantaged in such an arrangement have, at least, the assurance that the cooperative system works to give them opportunities at least as good as would be available under any alternative scheme. But such arguments have not been short of critics, who can point to a number of difficulties.

The first and most obvious of these is that, while a legal system does indeed coerce citizens, those are not the only people it coerces. A world that is divided up into nation states that restrict access to their territory is one in which those who wish to migrate from one part of the world to another, perhaps in search of a better life, are subject to coercion. It seems odd to claim that the coercion of members of a state by that state triggers distributive principles but that the coercion of outsiders comes without a distributive payoff.

Second, a number of theorists, most notably Thomas Pogge (2002), have ably documented the distributive consequences of various features of the international legal system, particularly with respect to the recognition states grant to the rulers of other states regarding the right to borrow and the right to sell the natural resources of a country (see also below).

Third, as Beitz had already noticed, tariff agreements and supranational organisations of various kinds operate in ways that are distributively consequential and depend on the coercive power of states.

Perhaps the most effective riposte to such concerns is to insist, as Nagel does, on the importance and relevance of collective authorship of the law. The difficulty with such a move is that it has to rely either on a very weak conception of authorship that ends up including global institutions as 'authored' or with one that is too strong. It is surely a fiction to think of the citizens of France, India, the UK or the US as being in any real sense collectively the authors of the laws to which they are subject, let alone the citizens of non-democratic states such as China or supranational systems like the European Union. If we insist on using authorship in some weaker and more metaphorical sense, it is hard to see how we could then avoid the conclusion that the people or peoples of the world are in that weaker sense the authors of the distributively consequential features of the global order to which they are subject.

Global obstacles to the 'well-ordered society'

It looks, then, as if the cosmopolitan theorists have the better of the argument. They seem to have a more realistic conception of the way in which the world actually functions than their opponents do, and most of the opposing arguments look highly question-begging. There is, however, a profound obstacle to the idea that we should treat the world as a whole as having a single 'basic structure' distributing rights and duties, roles and responsibilities and, crucially, benefits and burdens. This arises from the fact that the basic structure in Rawls's work has a dual function. The side of things that Beitz, along with other cosmopolitan theorists, noticed, was that the basic structure has a role in explaining social outcomes. Who benefits from whom, the distribution of goods and opportunities, and so forth, are facts to be explained by the working of institutions. We can evaluate such sets of institutions from the point of view of justice by looking to the outcomes they produce. A set of institutions that routinely and systematically generates destitution for some and unimaginable riches for others looks, on this view, to be an unjust system.

But Rawls's institutional focus had a second motive besides that of being true to the findings of social science. While the evaluation of existing institutions was backward looking and explanatory, Rawls also hoped to use the notion of the basic structure as part of a social ideal and, thereby, to deflect criticisms of the whole idea of social justice that had been voiced by figures such as Friedrich Hayek (1976). Central to Rawls's conception of a just society was the idea that social justice would emerge from the routine functioning of the institutions constituting that society, such as its political constitution, legal system and economic structure. Hayek had argued that the achievement of social justice would require extensive ex post tinkering with the outcomes of market processes in ways that were both destructive of the epistemic function of markets and incompatible with the rule of law. Rawls showed how, in theory at least, this was not so, since the rules constitutive of the system could be chosen with a view to their propensity to achieve certain distributive outcomes. Citizens of a 'well-ordered society' could go about their business, making their individual choices about careers, how much to work, to invest and so on, secure in the knowledge that the basic structure would work behind their backs in the manner of the 'invisible hand' to deliver distributive justice (Rawls, 1993; see also Krouse and MacPherson, 1988; Pogge, 1989). Contra Hayek, a just distribution could be generated without the state coming along and overriding the decisions of citizens or seizing their property.

One thing worth noting here is that there is considerable vagueness about different writers' use of words like 'institution' and 'institutional'. When Beitz is writing about the distributive effects of institutions, he clearly includes various organisations and agencies. Rawls, on the other hand, when focused on the institutional structure of particular societies, is thinking more in procedural terms and about the application of rules.

Rawls developed these ideas during the heyday of Keynesianism and was much influenced by the work of the Keynesian economist James Meade (1964). In today's more globalised, post-Keynesian world, it is unclear, at best, how applicable is Rawls' vision of distributive outcomes emerging as the result of the routine functioning of institutional rules, since we are likely to have a much more sceptical view of the predictability of such processes than was common in the 1970s. What is clear, however, is that the idea that distributive justice on a global scale might be achievable principally by such 'invisible hand' mechanisms is utopian in a bad sense. If we decide that the global distribution of wealth and income is a fitting subject for evaluation in the light of a conception of justice then it may well be that our judgement of the justice of an outcome will come apart from any view about how procedures and systems of rights ought to be designed or, more weakly, that while we can think about how the rules constitutive of the global economy might be reformed to avoid bad outcomes we have little idea about how we might achieve ones that are close to what justice requires.

Structural reform and piecemeal amelioration

The concern then is that the Rawlsian hope of reconciling the achievement of a just distributive pattern with procedural justice via the design of basic social institutions is simply not a viable strategy for something as large and complex as the global economy. Faced with this obstacle, we might think about dropping the insistence on having just distributions emerge from processes that allocate rights, duties, roles and rewards procedurally. That is, we could simply use global agencies and organisations to intervene ex post, and take from the rich to give to the poor in the manner of a global Robin Hood. But this hardly seems satisfactory either. Individuals and states need to be able to pursue their legitimate aims within a framework that gives them reasonable predictability and security. The existence of a global levelling agency or extensive redistributive programmes by existing agencies might undermine such an environment, and might also have the effect of undermining prudent decision making by states and the democratic autonomy of their peoples. This in turn could lead to a growing sense of alienation and a lack of commitment to justice itself. We might also have a concern that powerful global redistributive agencies would be much too powerful, could not be subject to effective democratic control and would be a continual object of contestation among elites seeking to capture it. (For some further argument to this effect, see Bertram, 2005.)

These worries, however, pale beside the apparent political and practical implausibility of such agencies acting against the power of states. At least in the immediately foreseeable future, such extensive redistributive intervention on a global scale is a fantasy. Existing states are simply not going to consent to grant a global redistributive agency the kind of tax and transfer powers that would be necessary for it to do its job. This does not rule out, of course, that regional organisations such as the European Union might act redistributively within their own borders, although there are clearly limits to how far this can be done without coming up against problems of legitimacy. And, of course, regional groupings such as the European Union are as much actually an obstacle to global redistribution as they might be potentially facilitators of it.[1]

An alternative to the neo-Rawlsian idea of putting in place an automatically functioning procedural structure to achieve justice is to pursue the progressive reform of the existing global institutional framework with the aim of both avoiding the most unjust outcomes and of providing development aid. That is to say, we should look to the most damaging effects that the current basic structure generates and seek to alter it so as to avoid them, as well as favouring various ad hoc proposals that might generate real resources for development. There has been much recent literature along these lines. Prominent among proposals have been measures aimed at disincentivising the bad governance that so often accompanies and generates acute poverty, measures to remove tariffs, subsidies and other barriers to trade, or to reform various features of international property law, proposals aimed at compensating nations for the maldistribution of natural resources, and other measures such as the Tobin tax.[2]

Thomas Pogge and the borrowing and resource privileges

A focus on harm avoidance emerges in the way that Thomas Pogge argues against the damaging effects of the current structure and in favour of its reform on the basis of a negative duty not to harm the global poor (Pogge, 2002, 2005a). This has its background in Pogge's response to Rawls's (1999b) own attempt to extend his theory of justice to the global level, and to argue for a society of peoples as opposed to a cosmopolitan ideal. In that work Rawls had endorsed the arguments of David Landes (1998) according to which the social institutions of a people are the key to explaining why some countries succeed and others do not (see the remarks in Rawls, 1999b, p 117). On this view, the fact that, say, natural resources, are arbitrarily distributed over the world's surface area loses much of its importance for global distributive justice since most of the variation in wealth and poverty comes about because some peoples adopt legal systems, systems of property law and liberal democratic governance, and others do not. On this view, extensive redistribution would punish those who have adopted good institutions for their prudence and reward bad states.

Pogge mounted an influential challenge to this 'explanatory nationalism'. On his view, the observation that there is a correlation between good institutions and affluence may be a sound one, but the leap from this to the conclusion that it is factors internal to a state that explain its success or failure is unjustified. This is because the existence of bad governance may itself be a consequence of features of an unjust global system and the way in which different states relate to it. It has often been noted, including by Landes, that resource-rich states are often poor and despotic. According to Pogge, the explanation for this fact lies in the way that the international system incentivises dictatorship in such countries through the recognition it grants to the rulers of states. Since the effective rulers of a state are recognised as entitled to sell its natural resources on world markets, there are powerful reasons for the military in oil-rich countries (such as, for example, Nigeria) to take power in order to appropriate the income stream, perhaps diverting it to bank accounts in countries such as Switzerland. Even where such countries are nominally democratic, corruption is often endemic, simply because those who would otherwise be tempted to seize control need to be bought off. Moreover, the resource privilege is not the only such perverse incentive. The rulers of states also have the right to borrow money from international lenders. Here, the income stream can be diverted and misappropriated by rulers while responsibility for the debt remains in the hands of the state and its people even after they have ceased to rule (Pogge, 2002, on 'explanatory nationalism'; see also Tan, 2004, Chapter 5).

In Pogge's view such widely acknowledged facts support the claim that the global economic order is an unjust one. He points out that while the idea that the inhabitants of wealthy and developed countries have a positive duty to help the global poor is highly controversial, the thought that we have a negative duty not to harm others is not. If, on this view, wealthy democratic states act so as to sustain a global order incorporating elements such as the resource privilege and the lending privilege, they act in ways that harm the very poor and thereby violate that negative duty. It remains, however, somewhat controversial who is bound by this negative duty and how people should act on it. Pogge believes that citizens of wealthy democracies violate this negative duty because (or to the extent that) they fail to act to persuade their governments to reform the unjust system. Otherwise, they are to be held responsible for the governments that act in their name. We might think of this as an excessively stringent attitude, since ordinary citizens have very little possibility of affecting government policy and it might be thought to be supererogatory of them to make enormous efforts in this direction. There is also the question of what reform of the global system ought to be implemented. Many countries that are not democracies are regarded by others as reasonable trading partners – China, for example. One possibility is that democratic states might agree not to trade with those who seize power through the overthrow of a democratic government, and not to recognise the new rulers of such countries as entitled to sell that country's assets on global markets. Such measures might partly disincentivise coups, and, to the extent to which they did, this would help end the developmental curses based on the borrowing and resource privileges.[3]

Disincentivising dictatorship through the abolition of the borrowing and resource privileges would also have the effect of helping to secure democracy. Much has been made of the importance of democracy to disaster avoidance since Amartya Sen's (1981) work on famines. It remains true, however, that in countries where rulers depend for their position on the approval of their electorates, they have a rather powerful incentive to see to it that the most essential interests of those electors are not neglected and that people are protected from the most acute shortages and other disasters. This will not be so reliably the case in non-democratic states where even if rulers are relatively benign they may be insulated from the facts about how things are for citizens by the desire of subordinates not to be the bearers of bad news.

Reform of the global trading and property system

Among the most widely voiced ideas for the reform of the global basic structure is that trade restrictions and subsidies by the wealthy North have the effect of impoverishing people in the South. Oxfam claims that trade restrictions in the developed world cost the developing world $100 billion per year, which is twice what they receive in foreign aid. It also claims that the very poorest are particularly hard hit, with sub-Saharan Africa losing as much as $2 billion a year (Oxfam, 2002, p 11). In principle, many politicians in Europe and North America have paid lip service to the need to reform the global trade system that is encapsulated in the rules of the World Trade Organization, but in practice it has been hard to make progress with the Doha round of talks stalling in 2006. The precise measures that would help the global poor are, however, open to a good deal of argument. Much of the advocacy has been on behalf of poor farmers in the South, but, in fact, subsidies may have redistributive effects within poor countries. Not everyone in the South is a farmer; and even when they are, the effect of trade distortions may depend on precisely what they are producing.

So, for example, US subsidies of cotton farmers really do hurt cotton producers in Mali, one of the poorest countries in the world. Malian farmers could and would produce cotton more cheaply than US farmers, but they are prevented from doing so by the subsidy. But many other cases are less clear cut. For example, subsidies to grain and dairy producers in the North have the effect of making more cheap food available to consumers in the South. It is not the case that there are lots of Africans who are excluded from selling in the market for grain and dairy products by Northern subsidies, since Africa is not a particularly good place to be producing such foods in the first place.

A second area of argument has concerned intellectual property rights, particularly concerning pharmaceuticals. Powerful lobbies associated with the pharmaceutical industry have argued that without very strong protection there will be no incentive to do the research and development of life-saving medicines. But if such medicines are needed now by very poor people suffering diseases from malaria to AIDS, such protection also has the effect of denying them access. Many have argued that this feature of the global basic structure is also strongly redistributive, but in the wrong direction (Pogge, 2005b).

Global taxation measures

The third class of ideas about the reform of the global basic structure consists of various ideas for levying just taxes that might be redirected towards development goals or towards raising the incomes of poor individuals. Such ideas have been advocated by Charles Beitz and include the global resources tax suggested by Thomas Pogge. The first of these would seek to compensate countries that were the victims of the chance uneven distribution of natural resources, the second would seek to generate revenues by taxing natural resource use (Beitz, 1979, pp 136-43; Pogge, 2002, Chapter 8). To these we could add the Tobin tax. While widely canvassed in the political theory and philosophy literature, such measures have never attracted wide support, and their general effectiveness is a matter of dispute.

Direct transfer

Putting in place institutions that will ameliorate the most severe harms of the present global order is an important part of what justice requires. But even if such institutions functioned perfectly, the world would still appear a massively unjust place. The unfortunate accident of being born in one country rather than another would condemn some people to much worse prospects in life than others have: worse health, lower income, shorter life expectancy, lower educational achievement and so on. And all through no fault of their own. In order to address this deficit, enormous resources would have to be transferred from the North to the South. But even if they were thus transferred, there is no guarantee that global inequality would not simply reproduce itself within a very short period. This is because we really understand very little about what makes some countries rich and other countries poor, and that what we do understand cannot be turned into a recipe and easily applied. At one point economists and development specialists believed that a lack of education was what held countries back, at another it was a lack of investment, more recently democratic institutions have been pointed to as the framework from which growth is possible. All of these proposals have disappointed the hopes of their advocates.[4]

There remains the matter of our duty, as individuals and as citizens of states, to address directly the most severe harms: preventable disease, premature death, famine, polluted water supplies and so on. Some of the literature on this question, such as a famous paper by Peter Singer (1972), suggests that our duties here are very extensive, since they involve preventing great evils at costs to ourselves that are not of comparable moral importance. Other theorists, such as Liam Murphy (2000), have argued that our duty is to do no more than what our share would be if everyone similarly situated played their part. Even if we take the less demanding of these two standards, it is clear that most wealthy societies currently do very little to address a continuing human and moral catastrophe.

Conclusions

This chapter has argued that the cosmopolitans are right against Rawls that principles of distributive justice should be global in scope. There is no justification for thinking that redistributive boundaries only hold within the boundaries of states, because the network of cooperation stretches beyond their borders, as does the system of mutual legal recognition, and because the system of state borders itself constitutes a coercive order of global proportions. The idea that we should seek global justice does, however, falter a little at the procedural requirements of Rawlsian justice. In the domestic case, Rawls's hope was that just outcomes could emerge as the result of the normal process of individuals pursuing their goals within an institutional framework designed with distributive justice in mind. Such a procedural order is not a fetish but provides people with valuable goods that are threatened when we try to pursue redistribution ex post. If we are committed to legal and institutional structures that give individuals a measure of security and predictability and which provide for democratic states to pursue their reasonable objectives, then there will be limits to how far we should pursue global redistribution directly. As in the domestic case, we have to look to put just institutions in place. But whereas institutional design on a local or national level might reasonably hope to issue in just outcomes, the complexity and size of the global order and the intractability of the development problem means that our most immediate goal must be the prevention of really bad outcomes. It is to be hoped, however, that, over time we will be able to develop global institutions, including ones governing trade, that are bent less to the interests of the richest nation and which may give all the prospect of development and of the enjoyment of the political and material goods that ought to permit all of humanity to flourish at a reasonable level.

Acknowledgements

Much work on this chapter was done during my tenure of a British Academy/ Leverhulme Senior Research Fellowship, and I should like to acknowledge the support of the Academy and the Leverhulme Trust.

Notes

[1] Of course, this last objection is of a different order to the preceding ones. Those are objections based on the importance of other values, this is one of practicability.

[2] The 'Tobin tax' is a proposal originally floated by the US economist James Tobin (1982) for a levy on foreign exchange transactions. The levy, set perhaps as low as 0.1% of the value of each transaction, would have the effect of calming currency movements driven by speculation and could make available a fund for development, aimed at assisting the poorest and most vulnerable nations.

[3] For a series of challenges to Pogge's view, see Risse (2005a, 2005b, 2005c).

[4] For an illuminating discussion of the history, see Easterly (2001).

References

Beitz, C. R. (1979) *Political theory and international relations*, New Haven, CT: Princeton University Press.

Bertram, C. (2005) 'Global justice, moral development and democracy', in G. Brock and H. Brighouse (eds) *The political philosophy of cosmopolitanism*, Cambridge: Cambridge University Press, pp 75-92.

Blake, M. (2002) 'Distributive justice, state coercion, and autonomy', *Philosophy and Public Affairs*, vol 30, no 2, pp 257-96.

Buchanan, A. (2000) 'Rawls's *law of peoples*: rules for a vanished Westphalian world', *Ethics*, vol 110, no 4, pp 697-721.

Easterly, W. (2001) *The elusive quest for growth*, Cambridge, MA: MIT Press.

Hayek, F. (1976) *Law, legislation and liberty*, vol 2, London: Routledge and Kegan Paul.

Krouse, R. and MacPherson, M. (1988) 'Capitalism, "property-owning democracy", and the welfare state', in A. Gutmann (ed) *Democracy and the welfare state*, Princeton, NJ: Princeton University Press.

Landes, D. (1998) *The wealth and poverty of nations*, New York: W. W. Norton.

Meade, J. E. (1964) *Efficiency, equality and the ownership of property*, London: George Allen & Unwin.

Miller, R. W. (1998) 'Cosmopolitan respect and patriotic concern', *Philosophy and Public Affairs*, vol 27, no 3, pp 202-24.

Murphy, L. (2000) *Moral demands in non-ideal theory*, Oxford: Oxford University Press.

Nagel, T. (2005) 'The problem of global justice', *Philosophy and Public Affairs*, vol 33, pp 113-47.

Oxfam (2002) *Rigged rules and double standards: Trade globalization and the fight against poverty*, Oxford: Oxfam.

Pogge, T. (1989) *Realizing Rawls*, Ithaca, NY: Cornell.

Pogge, T. (2002) *World poverty and human rights*, Cambridge: Polity Press.

Pogge, T. (2005a) 'Recognized and violated by international law: the human rights of the global poor', *Leiden Journal of International Law*, vol 18, pp 717-45.

Pogge, T. (2005b) 'Human rights and global health: a research program', *Metaphilosophy*, vol 36, no 1-2, pp 182-209.

Rawls, J. (1993) *Political liberalism*, New York: Columbia.

Rawls, J. (1999a) *A theory of justice* (2nd edition), Cambridge, MA: Belknap Harvard.

Rawls, J. (1999b) *The law of peoples*, Cambridge, MA: Harvard University Press.

Risse, M. (2005a) 'Do we owe the poor assistance or rectification?', *Ethics and International* Affairs, vol 19, pp 9-18.

Risse, M. (2005b) 'How does the global order harm the poor?', *Philosophy and Public Affairs*, vol 33, pp 349-76.

Risse, M. (2005c) 'What we owe to the global poor', *The Journal of Ethics*, vol 9, pp 81-117.

Sen, A. (1981) *Poverty and famines: An essay on entitlement and deprivation*, Oxford: Oxford University Press.

Singer, P. (1972) 'Famine, affluence and morality', *Philosophy and Public Affairs*, vol 1, pp 229-43.

Tan, K.-C. (2004) *Justice without borders: Cosmopolitanism, nationalism and patriotism*, Cambridge: Cambridge University Press.

Tobin, J. (1982) 'A proposal for international monetary reform', in J. Tobin (ed) *Essays in economics: Theory and policy*, Cambridge, MA: MIT Press.

SEVEN

Social justice and the family

Harry Brighouse and Adam Swift

Introduction

The family is a problem for any theory of social justice. On the one hand, children born into different families face very unequal prospects. However those prospects are conceived – as chances of social mobility, of lifetime well-being or income, or simply in terms of quality of childhood experiences – the fact that children are raised in families generates inequalities between them that it is hard to defend as fair or just. On the other hand, any suggestion that we should do away with the family for the sake of social justice, instead raising children in centrally organised quasi-orphanages or the like, is immediately regarded as the kind of crack-pot idea that only a philosopher could possibly envisage. The objection is not simply that abolishing the family would be a recipe for disaster, flying in the face of plausible claims made by sociobiologists or evolutionary psychologists. Rather, the family is defended by appeal to the kind of rights and duties with which theories of social justice are themselves fundamentally concerned – a claim about the vital role that familial relationships play in human flourishing and the fundamental interest that people have in being able to experience them.

It seems, then, that the family is both an obstacle to the realisation of social justice (because of the unfair inequality it produces) and a key ingredient of a just society (because of the right to parent–child relationships). This kind of tension is familiar to political theorists who, like us, think of themselves as 'egalitarian liberals' (or 'liberal egalitarians'). For us, achieving social justice is essentially about getting the right balance between equality and liberty. Justice requires that people be treated as equals and that requirement has serious distributive implications. It matters that people have equal resources to devote to their life-plans, or that they have equal opportunity for well-being, and on any specification of the approach (egalitarian liberals differ on the details) it is clear that social justice demands that goods be distributed much more equally than they are in the UK today. But, as liberals, we recognise that it is valuable for people to choose their lives for themselves, and important that they be accorded the freedoms necessary for them to live well. These include the freedom to engage in relationships that depend crucially on treating oneself, and particular others, as special – to act partially in favour of oneself and one's loved ones. Egalitarian liberals care that people enjoy equal freedom or are given equal opportunity to flourish. The problem, of course, is that the freedoms liberals value, tend to disrupt the equality egalitarians value. The family, being the natural home of partiality rather than impartiality, is a particularly stark locus of this crucial tension.

Our aim here is to sketch a theory of 'family values'. This phrase is usually associated with a conservative, sometimes Christian, approach to the evaluation of family policy and family life. We use it here in a more precise way – to describe the values that justify the institution of the family and that explain why, precisely, it would be a bad idea to abolish it. That theory allows us to make some progress towards resolving the conflict between the 'equality' aspect and the 'freedom to be partial' aspect of our conception of social justice, but it also puts us in a position to say something about family policy more generally. There is a widespread sense that the family is in trouble, and recent years have seen all the major political parties in the UK seeking to present themselves as 'pro family'. Our view is that public policy, taken as a whole, does indeed hinder the realisation of family values; it provides insufficient support for children who need to be well parented and for adults who want to parent well. But it also distributes those values, or access to them, very unjustly. A full account of the place of the family in a theory of social justice will not only address the conflict between the familial partiality and distributive equality, it will also consider the way in which social arrangements currently make it much harder for some than for others to realise family values in their lives.

The normative dimensions of the family have mainly been scrutinised by feminist theorists (Okin, 1989), and a chapter with our title might reasonably be assumed to focus on gender inequality. We do not doubt that the family as it actually exists has been, and continues to be, a crucial site of gender injustice, but its gendered aspect is not our subject here. Our theory of the family makes no assumptions about how familial or domestic labour is, or should be, divided between men and women; indeed, we do not assume that the family consists of two parents at all, let alone that they be a man and a woman. Our focus is specifically on the family as a social institution in which one or more adults 'parent' one or more children. We are interested here in the issues for social justice and public policy raised by parent–child relationships, not parent–parent ones.

Family values and relationship goods

Normative theories of the family variously appeal to the interests of three different stakeholders: children, third parties and parents. Thinking about the apparently outlandish proposal to abolish the family – to replace it with well-run state orphanages – helps to illuminate the differences between these accounts. Most theorists oppose abolition, but their accounts offer *different reasons* for that stance. For some, what would be wrong with the state-run childrearing institution is simply that it would fail the children entrusted to it. We want children to be raised in a way that will best serve their interests, and entrusting children to the authority of particular parents in the family happens to be that way. For others, the family is justified because the rest of society benefits from children being raised to be cooperative, trustworthy and capable of trust, and it is only by experiencing the parent–child bond or attachment that people with those attributes will be produced. Still others, including us, think that the family importantly serves the interests that adults have in parenting. Even if the state-run childrearing institution did as well as the family does by children and third parties, still parenting relationships contribute significantly to the well-being of adults, and the family is justified partly for that reason.

Our account focuses particularly on the goods that the family provides for the participants in the parent–child relationships themselves, which is why we call it the 'relationship goods' account (see Brighouse and Swift, 2006a, for a fuller version). Children have both developmental and non-developmental (or immediate) interests, and the family is justified in part because no other institution will serve these interests sufficiently well. The developmental interests fall into four overlapping categories; physical, intellectual (or cognitive), moral and emotional. In addition, the institution of the family allows parents to have a relationship of a kind that cannot be substituted for by relationships with other adults. They enjoy an intimate relationship with a dependant who spontaneously loves them. The parent decides for the child, and even as the child comes to be a decision maker him/herself, the parent determines the context in which decisions are made. The parent has a special duty to promote the child's interests (including the interest most have in eventually becoming someone who has no need of the parent's care). Since John Locke, it has been a familiar idea that parents have duties of care towards their children (although the precise content of those duties is widely disputed). We claim further that parents themselves have an interest in being able to carry out those duties of care. The family is justified partly by the fact that it is the institution for raising children that provides this good to adults.

We should immediately clarify two things. First, we are not claiming that all adults have a significant interest in parenting. Parenting is important enough for enough people to warrant special standing when it comes to public policy – and certainly many go to great lengths to become parents and many who do not raise children feel that their lives have been diminished by that absence. But it makes only a relatively minor contribution to the well-being of some people, and no, or perhaps even a negative, contribution to the well-being of others. Second, it is important to remember that what we are justifying, by appeal to the relationship goods they make possible, are particular kinds of intimate-but-authoritative relationship between adults and children. We do not claim that parents must be biologically related to 'their' children, nor, as we mentioned above, that there must be two parents, nor, where there are two, that they must be a man and a woman. It is, for us, a virtue of our philosophical approach to 'family values' that it leaves open the question of which particular forms of the family, if any, are particularly well suited to producing the goods we have identified.[1]

Parental partiality vs equality of opportunity

This 'relationship goods' account of why the family is valuable can help us towards a resolution of the tension with which we started: the conflict between parental partiality and equality of opportunity. Our aim, simply put, is to leave room for parents and children to enjoy the goods that the family distinctively makes possible – goods that depend for their realisation on parents treating their children differently from other people's children – while mitigating the extent to which the family undermines equality of opportunity.[2] It is widely accepted that parents have a duty of care to their children. Assuming that they can, parents must ensure that their children's interests are adequately met – that they are adequately fed, sheltered, kept safe from harm; that they experience the parental love that is needed if they are to develop into people capable of enjoying stable loving relationships with others, and so on. If parents fail properly to discharge that duty, then they forfeit the right to parent.[3] But in addition to what they *must* do, morally speaking, for their children, there is the issue of what they *may* do for them. Given inequalities of resources (both economic and cultural) between parents of different children, and differences in the motivation to use those resources to benefit those children, parental acts to further their children's interests are likely to generate injustice. The question, then, is in what ways may parents treat their children as special, beyond what is required of them by their duty of care, without exceeding the bounds of permissible or legitimate partiality? Here the answer that follows from our theory of family values is rather more controversial.

Here is a non-exhaustive list of some somewhat overlapping mechanisms by which relatively advantaged parents tend to transmit their advantage to their children and that tend both to produce inequalities between children and to reproduce patterns of social inequality across generations:

- gift/bequest;
- elite schooling/private tuition;
- access to social networks;
- values transmission/ambition formation;
- parenting styles;
- reading bedtime stories.

We could discuss each of these in much greater detail, and social scientists might even try to estimate the relative importance of these different mechanisms in generating either the extent of the association between the position of parents and children in the distribution of advantage or the extent of the inequality between children.[4] For current purposes, the interesting point is that, roughly speaking, as one reads down the list one progresses from more impersonal or 'external' mechanisms, such as leaving money or other property to children, or investing in their education, to more informal and intimate mechanisms, the paradigm case here being parental reading of bedtime stories. Of course, a traditional way of marking the spectrum from impersonal to personal is to consider the impersonal end in the public sphere, and hence legitimately susceptible to regulation, and the more personal end in the private sphere, and hence protected from regulation. But simply stipulating that something falls in the private sphere settles nothing; we are interested in working out precisely what should be regulated, what should be protected, and why.

For us, the key distinction is between those kinds of activities that are crucial to the ability of families to produce the relevant relationship goods and those that are not. Noting the tendency of the family to obstruct fair equality of opportunity, John Rawls (1971, p 511) famously asked: 'Should the family be abolished, then?'. The account we have sketched answers that question negatively, because family values are more important than fair equality of opportunity. A society in which people had equal prospects for material advantage, say, but which lacked familial relationships, would be impoverished relative to a society in which there was a good deal of inequality of opportunity but plentiful family life. But only some of the advantage-transmitting and inequality-generating mechanisms in the list qualify as worthy of protection on 'family values' grounds.[5] While the state should protect those parent–child interactions that are needed for people to realise familial relationship goods, those goods do not justify protecting the full range of things that parents currently do to favour their children.

Why is parental reading of bedtime stories a paradigm case of a protected activity? The parent reading the bedtime story is doing several things simultaneously. He is intimately sharing physical space with his child; sharing the content of a story selected either by her or by him with her; providing the background for future discussions; preparing her for her bedtime and, if she is young enough, calming her; re-enforcing the mutual sense of identification one with another. He is giving her exclusive attention in a space designated for that exclusive attention at a particularly important time of her day. Our theory says that there must be ample space for parents to engage in activities with their children that involve this kind of thing. Bequeathing one's child property, by contrast, or sending her to an elite private school, does not stand in the same relation to the relationship goods that we have claimed justify the family as the institution in which children should be raised. Thinking about why children should be raised in families, rather than in (possibly more egalitarian) state-run quasi-orphanages, we are *not* tempted to answer: 'Because human beings have a vital interest in being able to bequeath property to their children, or to receive it from their parents'. *That's* not why the family beats the quasi-orphanage.

So far, we have offered a criterion for identifying those parent–child interactions that, although tending to generate unjust inequalities between children, are worthy of protection because they are important for the production of familial relationship goods. Our approach can be thought of as reconciling family values with an egalitarian theory of social justice because we claim that the scope of such interactions is considerably narrower than is commonly thought. We can properly respect the integrity of the family without permitting parents to bequeath property to their children or to invest in their children's education. The suggestion that the state should limit the transmission of advantage from parents to children in these and similar ways is sometimes rejected on the basis that doing so would violate the integrity of the family. If our account is right, no such violation need be involved.

But our theory also aims to reconcile family values and egalitarian justice in another way. Although all the parent–child interactions listed above do indeed, in contemporary societies, tend to generate unfair inequalities between children, it is the way those interactions themselves interact with the social environment that produces much of the inequality in question. Protecting the space necessary for the realisation of family values is quite consistent with efforts to reduce the unjust impact of legitimate familial interaction. We could, if we wanted, allow parents to read bedtime stories to their children, or to talk to them at the table, or to take them on holidays, or to share their various enthusiasms – all of which are protected on our account of family values and their primacy over equality of opportunity – without *also* allowing children who have enjoyed those experiences to convert the skills or characteristics that they thereby acquire into social positions characterised by the kinds of inequality that we currently tolerate. Intimate and informal interactions between parents and children may indeed be worthy of protection on 'family values' grounds, but the inequalities of wealth and health that those interactions tend currently to produce are not. Reducing inequalities between outcome positions would make it less unjust that children born to different parents had unequal opportunities to achieve those positions.

So we see strong reasons for protecting the intimate activities through which, in the social environment we currently inhabit, parents tend to transmit competitive advantage to their children, but we also reject, as unjustified, attempts by parents deliberately to transmit such advantage and we point to the possibility of a radical restructuring of that environment so as to reduce the un-equalising effects of such familial interactions on children's outcomes. But the following two qualifications are very important.

First, we have argued specifically that there is no 'family values' justification for respecting parental investment in elite education or bequest of money where, and to the extent that, respecting them would create better-than-fair prospects, relative to others.[6] The parents of a child whose prospects would otherwise be *inferior* to those they would have in a just society may create no injustice by paying for her to attend better schools or bequeathing her money that they have refrained from spending on consumption goods. So, in a world in which other mechanisms undermine justice between children, it might be quite acceptable for less advantaged parents to act in these ways. For most poor parents, or members of minority ethnic communities, or parents of disabled children, whose children suffer from various biases in education systems and labour markets, bequeathing money, or buying private tuition or elite private schooling, may not conflict with equality of opportunity at all. Rather than seeking competitive advantage for their children, they may be simply providing some of the opportunities that their children would have in a more just society (Swift, 2003).

Second, we are focusing specifically on arguments about social justice that appeal to the *value of the family*. As we have said, it is quite common for defences of inequality to run through an appeal to the importance of parents being permitted to favour their children in various ways, so we think it worth targeting those arguments and seeing quite what taking 'family values' seriously does generate by way of a defence of inequality. But of course *other* justifications of some of the injustices that we claim cannot be defended by appeal to the family may be available. Perhaps, for example, allowing those who can afford it to invest in their children's education, at a level beyond what the state would be willing to support, is good for productivity and will benefit even the less advantaged in the long run. Perhaps, if parents are allowed to bequeath their wealth, or some substantial part of it, to their children, they might work harder themselves, thus contributing (in an economy structured the right way) more to the benefit of the worse off. In that case, we might have an argument for permitting these inequality-generating transmission mechanisms that appeals to what philosophers call 'prioritarian' concerns, where special weight is given to helping the worse off. In our view, even if that were a valid justification for permitting those transfers (and we are doubtful about the empirical claims in both cases), we should be aware that we are being asked to accept unfairly favourable opportunities for some (and unfairly unfavourable opportunities for others) for the sake of the long-term well-being of the worse off. Egalitarian concerns are subjugated to prioritarian ones, and the two come apart because of parents' insistence on favouring the interests of their own children over those of others in ways that, for us, cannot be defended by appeal to family values.

Family values and family policy

We have argued that the conflict between the family and equality of opportunity is less sharp than is commonly thought. Thinking hard about why the family is valuable, and about what that value gives us reason to allow parents to do to, with, and for their children, has yielded two conclusions. First, the sphere of interaction between parents and children that must be protected if family values are to be realised is narrower than is widely acknowledged, containing fewer mechanisms by which relative advantage is currently transmitted to children than is widely thought. Second, while respect for family values will doubtless leave room for parent–child interactions that result in children enjoying (or enduring) unequal opportunities to attain unequal outcomes, it is possible to reduce the inequality between those outcomes, thereby mitigating the extent of the injustice generated as a result of respecting the family.

But one might approach the conflict in a third, quite different, way. Rather than framing the issue in terms of a tension between the family, on the one hand, and equality of opportunity for goods such as income, education and health, on the other, one might instead attend to questions about the distribution of family values themselves. Familial relationship goods are vital elements of human well-being, yet opportunities for those goods are unequally and unfairly distributed. So now we turn towards public policy, and consider what kinds of policy might better promote family values and their fairer distribution. Just as reform of the social environment can help to mitigate its adverse effects on equality of opportunity, so the design of the economy, and other features of social organisation, can make it easier, or harder, for family life to flourish.

We can think about the proper goals of policy by remembering the three sets of interests at stake. From a child-centred perspective, we want a policy regime that does not make it unduly difficult for parents to look after and raise their children properly. Policy should help parents do what is needed to realise their children's interests in developing into flourishing adults, with the capacity to regulate their emotional lives and engage in fulfilling and secure affective relationships, and the moral capacity to engage in cooperative activities with others. But, of course, as talk of cooperation makes clear, the rest of us also have an interest in how other people's children turn out. Indeed, much recent discussion on the crisis of the family has focused less on the ways in which we are failing children than on the social problems (lack of 'respect', 'lawlessness' and so on) generated by that failure. And a further third-party interest is at stake. We have reason to care not only about the quality of the children being produced but also about their quantity. Demographic 'time bombs', on the one hand, and complex worries about overpopulation and justice to future generations, on the other, mean that there is a legitimate public interest in framing policies with a view to the number of children that we would like ourselves collectively to be raising. But this, in turn, interacts with parent-centred concerns;

our claim that many adults have an interest in being parents implies that policy makers have also to consider the aim of maximising the extent to which those whose lives would go better for being parents do indeed choose to parent. Finally, parents have an interest not simply in raising children, nor even in raising them well (which is primarily a child-centred concern, albeit one in which the parent too has an interest) but also in having the time and energy to enjoy the familial relationship goods made possible by their being parents.

Clearly, identifying the proper balance between these different considerations is a complex task, even before we factor in the other desirable goals with which they might compete. Here we can offer no more than some general thoughts about the policy direction implied by our theory of the family. Our, non-expert, reading of the empirical evidence is that the social environment in the UK today provides disincentives for parents (a) to have children at all,[7] (b) to spend as much time with their very young children as would be optimal for their children's development and (c) to spend as much time with their children throughout their childhood as would be optimal for the parents' enjoyment of familial relationship goods. We do not claim any originality for these observations, nor, in the UK context at least, is our aim to suggest a radically different approach to family policy from that currently on the agenda.[8] Rather, our aim has been to provide a normative or philosophical framework for thinking about familiar policy issues.

The mechanisms that currently hinder the achievement of the goals we have identified include the following:

- There is a substantial 'fertility penalty', in terms of lifetime earnings, suffered by parents (usually women) who leave the full-time workforce to raise children.
- Too many parents are too poor, and income replacement policies too meagre, to enable them to leave the workforce and look after their children for long enough.
- Employers (rationally) prefer full-time over part-time work, and prefer insecure part-time over secure part-time work; working hours are too long.
- Policy has been focused rather on providing childcare than on facilitating parental leave.
- The gender pay gap makes it rational for women rather than men to take parental leave (see Davies et al, 2000; Grimshaw and Rubery, 2007).

Policy in the UK, as we have said, is certainly moving in the right direction. Things are changing quite fast with recent developments such as:

- an increase in parental leave to nine months paid and three months unpaid from April 2007 (with the avowed intention to increase this further to 12 months paid);
- the right to request flexible work arrangements;
- the right to request up to 12 weeks' unpaid parental leave during a child's first five years;
- manipulation of the tax code, especially increases in Child Tax Credits that particularly help children whose parents are out of work, to reduce child poverty;
- maintenance of, and currently talk about increasing, Child Benefit; and
- a new emphasis in the Sure Start policy initiative on parenting skills and child development.

These are all positive moves, as far as our account of family values is concerned, but our sense is that policy makers in the UK have still not taken all the steps necessary to regulate the labour market so that it adequately serves the interests of children and adults-as-parents. The interface between work–life and family–life has not yet been seriously addressed, and, despite the striking emergence onto the political agenda of 'well-being' or 'quality of life' issues, policy makers have yet wholeheartedly to re-conceive their understanding of what makes people's lives go well. Economic criteria have tended to dominate policy making. Thus, for example, childcare policy has until recently primarily been aimed at getting mothers back into the labour force – an aim that happily combines considerations of productivity and economic competitiveness with those of gender equality – rather than at giving parents of both genders the opportunity to spend time with their children. And such emphasis as has been given to children's interests has tended to focus rather on their cognitive development, and on equipping them to become productive citizens, than on their emotional and personal development, where parent–child relationships, or at least very high-quality (and very expensive) childcare arrangements, are widely agreed to be of crucial importance (Gerhardt, 2004; Harker, 2006).[9]

Our suggestion that more be done to promote the realisation of relationship goods and their fairer distribution raises a number of further problems. Any policy will distribute costs and benefits unequally between different people, and it is always appropriate to ask whether those costs and benefits are being allocated fairly. Here are three different perspectives from which to view the justice issues raised by any family policy.

Men and women

Although we have put gender to one side, we suspect that some readers will see it as our blind spot, identifying us with that branch of the 'family values' lobby that seeks to restrict women's labour market opportunities. Fully to respond to that charge would take another chapter, but here is the essence of our position: if permitting some kinds of gender inequality were the only way adequately to meet children's developmental interests, then we would face some very hard choices and, in our view, the onus would be on feminists to explain why gender equality was more important than the proper raising of children. But that is a very big if. We are not persuaded that permitting gender inequality is necessary for children to be raised well. Men can adequately parent even very young children, children can prosper through attachments to more than one adult, and, to the extent that it is more valuable, for children, that mothers rather than fathers spend time with them in the early months, that would be no reason for society to construct gender *inequalities* on that fact.

Still, we accept that these thoughts, envisaging shared parenting and/ or gender differences without gender inequalities, are a long way from current reality. Although we are optimistic about recent developments in fathering (Equal Opportunities Commission, 2006), we accept that getting from where we are now to a position that is good enough for children and gender-equal may be less realistic than getting to one that is good enough for children and gender-unequal. To move most directly and immediately, from here, to a position where children are well parented might indeed imply a backward step for gender justice. That would be an example of the kind of 'trade-off between values given actually existing feasibility sets' that makes the real, intransigent, world a more challenging place than the elastic worlds imagined and re-imagined by political philosophers.

Parents and non-parents

The policies we are proposing involve transfers from non-parents to parents, relative to the status quo. Why should the activity of parenting be subsidised in this way? If our proposals were justified solely on child-centred grounds, we could respond by pointing out that since the indirect target of the transfers are children, and all adults have been children, there need not be any deep worry about redistributive effects between types of people; rather we would be advocating redistribution of resources across the lifecourse in order to spend them where they are most valuable. If we appealed solely to third-party interests, to the benefits that children bring to people other than their parents, then we would need to consider the normative issue of whether it is legitimate to require people to contribute to the costs of producing goods from which they benefit, rather than freeriding on the productive contribution of others. But for us, policy should not be aimed solely at promoting children's interests, and parents cannot simply be conceived as incurring a cost that it may be reasonable to require others to share. On our account, parenting usually yields benefits, in terms of relationship goods, to those who do it. Given that parents reap that non-material good in any case, why should resources also be transferred from non-parents to parents?

This too is a big issue, and again we only have room to sketch a couple of points in response. First, empirical judgements about who is subsidising whom necessarily depend on some baseline of comparison, on some analysis of how resources would be distributed in the absence of the alleged subsidy. It may be true that, *relative to the status quo*, our proposed policies would involve a transfer from non-parents to parents, but we see little reason to regard the status quo as the appropriate baseline. Falling fertility rates might be evidence that, factoring in the full range of distributive effects that result from current policies, we have tilted the balance against parenthood.[10] If so, our policies might better be conceived as removing a bias against parents than as introducing a bias in their favour. Second, it is important to remember that much of the benefit that accrues to parents, on our account that gives parents an interest in acting as a fiduciary for the child, accrues to them because they are doing what is valuable for their children. If it is good for a parent to be home from work in time to read bedtime stories to their children, that is in large part (although not entirely) because it is good for children to have stories read to them by the parent. Parents' well-being is properly promoted, on our view, but to a great extent it is promoted through policies that might be justified primarily on child-centred grounds. This does not entirely deal with the problem; it might be thought that since parents benefit, in terms of relationship goods, from the exercise of the fiduciary duty, they *should* pay the cost of fulfilling it, or at least part of it. But nothing in our argument suggests that parents should suffer no costs, relative to non-parents, for their decision to raise children. The point is not to make sure that nothing is sacrificed when an adult chooses to invest in family life. It is to make that life sufficiently manageable that parents can provide what their children need, and find it a source of well-being for themselves, without risking unreasonably bad outcomes.

Rich and poor

We have argued that the goods realised by familial relationships are of very great value for all children and for many parents. Yet access to those goods is distributed unjustly between rich and poor. While many of our readers will have been thinking about our arguments in the context of their own difficulties in combining family and a career, and while we are sympathetic to anyone in that position and hope that the policies we advocate would indeed make that juggling act less fraught, those who really lose out when it comes to family values are those who do not have a career at all – those in poverty or those who have to work such long hours just to try to meet their children's basic interests in food and shelter that they have neither the time nor energy to provide or enjoy many of the relationship goods we have been discussing. There are many reasons to tackle poverty, especially child poverty, and tackling it has indeed been an explicit aim of New Labour policy (and one that it has pursued with considerable success). Our perspective adds simply the observation that poor parents find it particularly hard to both provide their children with what they need for healthy development – cognitive, emotional and moral – and experience the pleasures of family life themselves. So there is a distinctively 'family values' justification for focusing on the relief of poverty.[11]

There is, of course, much more to be said about the way in which various kinds of inequality between parents create injustices in the distribution of relationship goods. We end with just two of them. First, even where a family is not in poverty, economic necessities can obstruct the realisation of family values. One main reason why parents do not take up the parental leave to which they are entitled is that they simply feel that they cannot afford to do so. From a distributive perspective, it is not enough that the state formally guarantee a period of parental leave; that leave must be 'paid at a sufficient level to make it a meaningful option for all parents' (Harker, 2006, p 76). The level of payment also affects the distribution of take-up as between men and women; current levels of paternity pay make it hard for lower-income men even to take their two weeks of paternity leave, while the gender pay gap makes it rational for women rather than men to take time off work to look after the children. Second, quite apart from issues to do with economic resources and time, some parents lack the skills they need to parent their children well. Such skills used to be learned by observation and practice in large and/or extended families, which were in turn part of broader communities. Nowadays, most children do not have younger siblings (very few have *much* younger siblings) and tend to spend a good deal of time inside the home rather than in places where they can observe other young children, yet while many aspects of education have been taken on by schools and other institutions outside the home, it is still widely assumed that parenting will be learned privately, within the family.[12] While, of course, there are difficult normative issues around the issue of compulsion in the case of adult parents, and while some critics are suspicious of all attempts objectively to identify the skills in question, our own view is that there are some aspects of parenting that can be done well or badly, that it is good for people to have a sense of which is which, and that the state may helpfully, and quite legitimately, provide education for parenthood.

Conclusion

The family is often invoked in justifications of inequality. Parents, it is claimed, have a right, or even a duty, to promote their children's best interests, and the protection of their freedom to do that severely limits the scope of attempts to create more equal opportunities for children born into different families. We accept that the family is a key component of a just society, and that it essentially involves parents treating their children differently from, and better than, other people's children. But by considering precisely why the family is such a valuable institution, we can see that respect for it need not require acceptance of many of the inequalities it is standardly invoked to justify. On the one hand, the kinds of interaction between parents and children that must be protected if family values are to be realised are rather fewer than is widely acknowledged. On the other hand, we could respect the partiality constitutive of valuable parent–child relationships while altering the social environment so as massively to reduce its impact on the distribution of other goods. But we can also consider relationship goods as among the goods that our society should seek to distribute more fairly. Rather than conceiving of them as obstacles to egalitarian goals, those who care about 'family values' should think about the proper content of those values and focus on the needs of those least able to enjoy them.

Acknowledgements

We are grateful to Tania Burchardt and Ingrid Robeyns for helpful comments on a draft of this chapter.

Notes

[1] For a similar approach, see Burtt (2002, pp 231-52).

[2] For a fuller and more nuanced version of our argument, see Brighouse and Swift (2006b) and, for a similar approach, Macleod (2002).

[3] It does not follow that such parents should have their children taken away from them. It could still be better, all things considered, for a child to stay with a negligent or incompetent parent than for them to be taken into care.

[4] For sophisticated work along these lines, see Bowles et al (2005). Notice that here we are focusing on parent–child interactions that lead to inequalities of opportunity specifically with respect to economic or material outcomes. There are, of course, crucial 'family values' reasons to care about children's emotional or psychological well-being, and justice reasons to care about the distribution of those kinds of advantage, to which other interactions, such as 'parental availability to comfort a distressed child', might be more relevant.

[5] We provide arguments for the account and this answer in Brighouse and Swift (2006a, 2006b).

[6] Rawls' official statement of his principle of fair equality of opportunity leaves it open that inequalities of prospects that are entirely due to inequalities of natural talent may be fair (although, considered alone, it does not require inequalities of prospects on that basis).

[7] Analysis of longitudinal studies looking at the gap between the number of babies people in their twenties say they want and the number they actually have at age 40 suggests a 'baby gap' of 90,000 per year in England and Wales. Further analysis suggests that the high opportunity costs of having children explains a good deal of this gap (Smallwood and Jeffries, 2003; Dixon and Margo, 2006, pp 80-3).

[8] Things are rather different in the US, where the current policy regime makes it extremely difficult for many people to realise family values in their lives. To take just one example: unless one has a partner or spouse with appropriate cover, leaving the workforce to care for one's young child means relinquishing

health insurance at a time when one is particularly concerned to have it. This creates a strong incentive to return to the workforce earlier than would be optimal for the child, or for the parent's relationship with the child.

[9] However, we welcome an increasing number of policy documents from both the government and the Conservative Party that emphasise the importance of family life for well-being – see, for example, *Every child matters* (DfES, 2003), *Every parent matters* (DfES, 2007), *Breakthrough Britain* (Social Justice Policy Group, 2007) and, most explicitly, David Cameron's speech to the National Family and Parenting Institute in June 2007 (http://conservativehome.blogs. com/torydiary/files/cameron_family_speech.pdf). For an analysis of the new Conservative policy proposals, see Brighouse and Swift (2007).

[10] It is true that fertility rates standardly fall with economic growth, female education and improved opportunities for female labour market participation. But rich emancipated countries vary in their fertility rates, and the England and Wales figures cited above concerning the gap between the ambitions of people in their twenties and their actual birth rate by age 40 suggests cause for concern. The opportunity costs of having a child are high, and are influenced by tax-benefit policy. The amount of earnings an average mid-skilled woman forgoes if she has a baby at age 24 is £564,000, and reduces to £165,000 if she delays her first baby until age 28 (Dixon and Margo, 2006, p 76). But her ability to conceive also falls; and it is far from clear that there is a widespread understanding in the population of the rapidity of the decline of women's fertility after age 30, or of the costs and benefits associated with artificial reproductive technologies.

[11] We do not mean to imply that there is no reason grounded in family values to reduce inequality more generally, but we do see poverty (both absolute and relative) as a particularly urgent barrier to the realisation of relationship goods.

[12] We are grateful to David Piachaud for this observation.

References

Bowles, S., Gintis, H. and Osborne-Groves, M. (eds) (2005) *Unequal chances: Family background and economic success*, Princeton, NJ: Princeton University Press.

Brighouse, H. and Swift, A. (2006a) 'Parents' rights and the value of the family', *Ethics*, vol 117, no 1, October, pp 80-108.

Brighouse, H. and Swift, A. (2006b) 'Legitimate parental partiality', Centre for the Study of Social Justice Working Paper, Oxford: University of Oxford, http://social-justice.politics.ox.ac.uk/working_papers/index.asp

Brighouse, H. and Swift, A. (2007) 'The end of the Tory war on single parents?', *Public Policy Research*, vol 14, no 3, September–October, pp 186-92.

Burtt, S. (2002) 'What children really need: towards a critical theory of family structure', in D. Archard and C. Macleod (eds) *The moral and political status of children*, Oxford: Oxford University Press, pp 231-52.

Davies, H., Joshi, H., Rake, K. and Alami, R. (2000) *Women's incomes over the lifetime*, Report to the Women's Unit, Cabinet Office, London: The Stationery Office.

DfES (Department for Education and Skills) (2003) *Every child matters*, London: The Stationery Office.

DfES (2007) *Every parent matters*, London: The Stationery Office.

Dixon, M. and Margo, J. (2006) *Population politics*, London: Institute for Public Policy Research.

Equal Opportunities Commission (2006) *Twenty-first century dad*, Manchester: Equal Opportunities Commission.

Gerhardt, S. (2004) *Why love matters*, London: Routledge.

Grimshaw, D. and Rubery, J. (2007) *Undervaluing women's work*, EOC Working Paper 53, Manchester: Equal Opportunities Commission.

Harker, L. (2006) 'What is childcare for?', *Soundings*, vol 31, November, pp 66-77.

Macleod, C. (2002) 'Liberal equality and the affective family', in D. Archard and C. Macleod (eds) *The moral and political status of children*, Oxford: Oxford University Press, pp 212-30.

Okin, S. M. (1989) *Justice, gender and the family*, New York: Basic Books.

Rawls, J. (1971) *A theory of justice*, Boston, MA: Harvard University Press.

Smallwood, S. and Jeffries, J. (2003) 'Family building intentions in England and Wales: trends, outcomes and interpretations', *Population Trends*, no 114, pp 8-18.

Social Justice Policy Group (2007) *Breakthrough Britain*, London: Centre for Social Justice.

Swift, A. (2003) *How not to be a hypocrite: School choice for the morally perplexed parent*, London: Routledge.

EIGHT

Children, policy and social justice

David Gordon

Introduction

Children's needs and services are one of the current UK government's foremost policy priorities. In 1999, Tony Blair gave a commitment to end child poverty forever, within a generation. This was, arguably, the most radical and far-reaching policy commitment made by the New Labour governments. More recently, Children's Commissioners have been appointed in every country in the UK and the 2004 Children Act and the Every Child Matters framework (www.everychildmatters. gov.uk) are designed to coordinate services for children at all levels of government. The announcement of the Children's Plan by the new Secretary of State for Children late in 2007 takes this commitment even further.

Internationally, children's rights have received widespread policy support with every member state of the United Nations (UN) (193 countries) signing the UN Convention on the Rights of the Child (UNCRC). By contrast, both the social and the economic/ distributional justice literatures effectively ignore children – often relegating them to a mere property of their household or family, seeing their needs as, in effect, identical to those of their families (for example, in anti-poverty strategies). Children's agency is usually absent (but see Craig, 2002) and, where theory does engage with children, it is often as future workers or citizens rather than as actors with justice claims in their own right.

This chapter is primarily concerned with the policy and philosophy of distributional justice in relation to children in the UK. It first examines the political philosophy underlying current government policies for children, particularly anti-poverty and equality policies. The chapter then reviews the very limited political and economic philosophy literature on distributional justice for children before attempting to reach a conclusion. The focus of this chapter is child-centered, examining the justice of relationships between children, and between children and adults. This focus differs from that of Brighouse and Swift in Chapter Seven, which is primarily concerned with the potential tension between social justice and the family as an institution.

In this chapter, the term 'distributional justice' is taken to mean justice in the process and outcome of the distribution of economic and social goods (for example, money, wealth, educational services, health services and housing). It does not cover justice in the distribution of many other things that are very important to children (for example, love, happiness and friendship) but which are much less amenable to policy interventions.

New Labour and child policy in the UK

Since 1997, successive New Labour governments have arguably given child policies a greater prominence than any previous government over the past 100 years. It would take a whole chapter just to list and briefly describe all the policies aimed at children that have been implemented over the past decade. The New Labour governments have, at least rhetorically, placed the improvement in children's lives and well-being at the centre of their social justice policy agenda. There are, of course, many reasons for this emphasis on child policy. However, it is a logical outcome of the shift in the Labour Party's core beliefs – from a socialist party primarily concerned with 'equality of outcome' to a social democratic party primarily concerned with 'equality of opportunity'.

At the Beveridge Lecture in March 1999, Tony Blair, UK Prime Minister from 1997 to 2007, explained his concept of social justice in terms of the conditions needed for people (but primarily children) to have a chance of succeeding on the basis of their individual merits – talents and efforts:

> Social justice is as relevant today as it was for Beveridge. It is our aim. It is our central belief – the basis for a community where everyone has the chance to succeed. Social justice is about decency. It requires that any citizen of our society should be able to meet their needs for income, housing, health and education. Social justice is about merit. It demands that life chances should depend on talent and effort, not the chance of birth; and that talent and effort should be handsomely rewarded. The child born on a run-down housing estate should have the same chance to be healthy and well-educated as the child born in the

leafy suburbs. It is only when you put it like that you see the distance we have to go. Social justice is about mutual responsibility. It insists that we all accept duties as well as rights – to each other and to society. Social justice is about fairness. In a community founded on social justice, power, wealth and opportunity will be in the hands of the many not the few. These words come from the new Clause 4 of the Labour Party constitution and they are what New Labour is about. (Blair, 1999)

In this important speech, Blair contrasted New Labour's conception of how to achieve social justice with a 'straw man' position he attributed to the old Left, which he viewed as hostile to both policy change and wealth creation:

Social justice became, on the Left, identified with rigid policy prescriptions, good for the 40s, increasingly out of date for the 70s. Whereas the old Left regarded the application of social justice as unchanged, the Right regarded it as irrelevant. They believed it didn't matter; and that it had no connection with economic efficiency. Indeed, it is that curious alliance of the Right and old Left that I have witnessed and struggled against all my political life, both far Left and Right divorced economic efficiency from social justice. Both saw wealth creation as in opposition to social justice. (Blair, 1999)

Blair concluded his speech with a historic and time-limited commitment to eradicate child poverty forever within a generation (that is, by 2020).

We need to break the cycle of disadvantage so that children born into poverty are not condemned to social exclusion and deprivation. That is why it is so important that we invest in our children. But our reforms will help more than the poorest children. All parents need help. All children need support.... Our plans will start by lifting 700,000 children out of poverty by the end of the Parliament. Poverty should not be a birthright. Being poor should not be a life sentence. We need to sow the seeds of ambition in the young. Our historic aim will be for ours to be the first generation to end child poverty, and it will take a generation. It is a 20 year mission but I believe it can be done. (Blair, 1999; see Walker, 1999, for a detailed discussion of this speech.)

A large number of the child policy initiatives introduced since 1999 have been designed to help meet this social justice agenda, for example: increases in child and maternity benefits; large increases in funding initially for early years care and primary education and, more recently, for secondary education; the Working Families' Tax Credit; programme interventions such as Sure Start; and Child Trust Funds. The government's current child poverty policy strategy has four main planks, which were laid out in 2004 in the HM Treasury (2004) *Child poverty review:*

- work for those who can, helping parents participate in the labour market;
- financial support for families, with more support for those who need it most, when they need it most;
- delivering excellent public services that improve poor children's life chances and help break cycles of deprivation; and
- support for parents in their parenting role so that they can confidently guide their children through key life transitions.

This policy package is primarily designed to achieve distributional justice for children through paid work for parents and some redistribution via cash benefits and improved services. The main aim of this redistribution appears to be to increase equality of opportunity of children's life chances rather than redistribution to increase equality of outcome of the distribution of economic goods resulting from an unjust economic and social system. To understand the political thought behind this distributional justice policy package for children, it is necessary briefly to look at the history of the Labour Party's political thought about distributional justice.

The Labour Party and distributional justice

Social justice has always been a key aspiration of the UK Labour movement – although the meaning of the term 'social justice' has changed significantly. In 1883, the Social Democratic Federation (SDF) became the first organisation in Britain to adopt a socialist/Marxist ideology and began to publish the journal *Justice*. The last 'official' history of the Labour Party records that:

> Hyndman, in a silk hat and frock coat, did not disdain to
> sell *Justice* every week in the Strand, nor did William Morris
> consider it beneath his dignity to hawk the journal and
> Socialist pamphlets at the propaganda meetings. (Tracey,
> 1948, p 43)

This influential journal on the early Labour Party's political thought
had many contributors including George Bernard Shaw. Its ideas on
how to achieve 'justice' included improving housing conditions for the
working classes, free compulsory education for all, free school meals, an
eight-hour working day, nationalisation of the land, banks and railways,
abolition of the national debt and the organisation of agricultural and
industrial workers under state control, run on cooperative principles.

The Labour Party, founded at a conference in 1900, was followed
by a Labour Representation Committee (LRC), which included two
members from the SDF, two members from the Independent Labour
Party, one member of the Fabian Society and seven trade unionists. The
new party had no particular ideology or guide to its actions apart from
the words of the motion proposed by Keir Hardie to 'agree upon their
policy, which must embrace a readiness to cooperate with any party
which for the time being may be engaged in promoting legislation in
the direct interests of labour' (Foote, 1985, p 41).

Labour Party leaders would thus often make speeches that assured
their audience that socialism would bring a better world, particularly
for children, but which were also very vague on how this would be
achieved. Hardie's speech below is typical:

> [T]he ugliness and squalor which now meets you at every
> turn in some of the most beautiful valleys in the world
> would disappear, the rivers would run pure and clear as they
> did of yore ... and in the winter the log would glow on the
> fire the while that the youths and the maidens made glad
> the heart with mirth and song, and there would be beauty
> and joy everywhere. (Johnson, 1922, p 11)

The First World War (1914-18) and the Russian Revolution had a
dramatic impact on the Labour Party's political thought. During the
final year of the war, Arthur Henderson joined with Sidney Webb
and Ramsay MacDonald in the Labour Party National Executive
Committee to create a national party with a socialist programme on
internal and international affairs. They were the key men who drafted
the new constitution of the party, which was adopted in 1918 (Winter,

1972). Clause IV of this constitution was subsequently printed on the back of the membership cards:

> To secure for the workers by hand or by brain the full fruits of their industry, and the most equitable distribution thereof that may be possible, upon the basis of the common ownership of the means of production and the best obtainable system of popular administration and control of each industry or service.

This was a relatively clear socialist conception of distributional justice in terms of equitable distribution of the '*full fruits*' of labour. This constitutional aim remained in place until 1995 when Tony Blair, after being elected Labour leader, called for a Special Conference to change the Labour Party's constitution. Blair had criticised the old Clause IV for confusing 'ends with means'. After this constitutional change, the leaders of New Labour (Blair and Gordon Brown in particular) repeatedly described the government as now being committed to equality of opportunity rather than equality of outcome. For example, in 2001, Blair 'invoked the experience of his own communist-turned-Conservative father to explain why he had rejected both Thatcherism and traditional socialism in order to embrace a meritocratic vision of equal opportunity for all' (White, 2001).[1] Similarly, Gordon Brown, in his first speech to the Labour Party Conference as leader stated his beliefs:

> Not the old equality of outcome that discounts hard work and effort. Not the old version of equality of opportunity – the rise of an exclusive meritocracy where only some can succeed and others are forever condemned to fail. But a genuinely meritocratic Britain, a Britain of all the talents. Where all are encouraged to aim high. And all by their effort can rise. (Brown, 2007)

Labour Party leaders are well aware that poor children do not have the same opportunities as rich children. There is a vast amount of scientific evidence that shows that poor children are much more likely to suffer from ill-health and have worse educational outcomes than their more economically fortunate peers (Bradshaw, 2001). Hence, in order to attempt to achieve equality of opportunity while at the same time embracing flexible labour markets, privatisation, less market regulation and other neoliberal prescriptions, it is logical to attempt to eradicate child poverty and improve children's well-being. Extensive child poverty and a genuine meritocratic vision of equal opportunity are clearly incompatible. Thus, in order to facilitate a just distribution of economic goods among adults on the basis of merit, New Labour must try to distribute economic goods among children on the basis of need for those children who merit/deserve it.

Titmuss (1974) argued that, if society wants to move towards greater equality, then decisions are needed on which of the following four maxims should determine the provision of welfare services:

- to each according to individual *need*;
- to each according to individual *worth*;
- to each according to individual *merit*; and
- to each according to individual *work*.

Titmuss also argued that it was not possible to follow all four maxims simultaneously. Labour governments – prior to Tony Blair's leadership – mainly espoused the distributional justice principles of allocation on the basis of work ('full fruits of labour') and need. By contrast, New Labour has clearly prioritised the distributional principle of merit (primarily among adults) and need (primarily among children). However, New Labour does not seem to believe that the redistribution of economic resources to children on the basis of need should be unconditional. Only children who merit it should receive additional resources. For example, although during the past decade educational resources have been significantly increased for all children, the idea that these resources should go to the children who merit them most (rather than need them most) has not wholly disappeared. In 1995, David Blunkett, as Shadow Education Secretary, stated at the Labour Party Conference: "Watch my lips. No selection either by examination or interview under a Labour government". He later claimed that this statement in his speech was meant as a 'parody' and a 'joke' (Blunkett, 2000), and state-funded highly selective grammar schools remain to this day. There has been little laughter in the wider Labour movement at what is seen as the continuation of unjust selection that grammar schools represent.

Hendrick (1994, 1997, 2003) has argued that one of the enduring principles of UK social policy for children in the 20th century was the dual and paradoxical perception of children as both victims and a threat to society.[2] New Labour has continued this trend into the 21st century. Their 'needs'-based distributional justice agenda for children goes hand in hand with a significant increase in criminal justice legislation designed to reduce the 'threat' posed by children (for example Anti-Social Behaviour Orders, Dispersal Orders and Child Curfews). New Labour's distributional justice policies to redistribute economic resources to poor children are accompanied by a policing agenda that increasingly criminalises poor children whose behaviour does not conform to the government's requirements (Goldson, 2002).

Child rights, policy and justice

An additional driving force behind social justice policies for children in the UK has been the UNCRC. The core principles of the UNCRC are:

- the right to life, survival and development;
- non-discrimination;
- devotion to the best interests of the child;
- respect for the views of the child; and
- the right to an adequate standard of living and social security.

The UK signed the Convention in 1990, ratified it in 1991 and it came into force in the UK in 1992, although the UK government opted out of conditions applying to the detention of children in prisons with adults (Article 37) and to asylum-seeking children (Article 22). However, during the past decade, policy compliance with the UNCRC has accelerated and the government states that its 'commitment to implementing the Convention remains unwavering' (HM Government, 2007). Nevertheless, it would still require some profound ideological changes for the government fully to implement the Convention. For example, children are the only section of the UK population who can still legally be physically hit, and prison officers and teachers are the only professional groups allowed to shout at their clients.

The UNCRC has received near-unanimous consensus on its objectives and values and every country in the world (193 UN member states) has signed the Convention with only two countries failing to ratify it to date – Somalia and the US.[3] In the UK, non-governmental organisations and civil society organisations have campaigned widely for implementation and policy initiatives, such as the appointment of Children's Commissioners in England, Northern Ireland, Scotland and Wales as a direct response to UNCRC requirements. Dissent about the UNCRC has come from the more 'conservative' parts of the medical establishment. For example, in 2004, an editorial in *The Lancet* argued that UNICEF's focus on child rights had been detrimental to international campaigns to improve child survival (Horton, 2004). In particular, the editorial claimed that the outgoing UNICEF Director had focused on 'girl's education, early childhood development, immunisation, HIV/ AIDS, and protecting children from violence, abuse, exploitation, and discrimination', and that in doing this she had 'failed to address the essential health needs of children' (Horton, 2004, p 9451).

Although the UNCRC does not contain a specific right to freedom from poverty for children, there is little doubt that full implementation of the Convention would require much greater distributional justice of economic goods among children in the UK. Rights-based language can help to direct social justice policy (Falk, 2000). It shifts the focus of debate from the personal failures of the poor to the failure of macro-economic structures and policies implemented by nation states to eradicate poverty. Hence, child poverty in this context is no longer described as a 'social problem' but a 'violation of rights' (Pemberton et al, 2007).

Economic theory and children

So what insights can be found in the work of economic theorists about social justice and children that could be used to inform current UK policy? Unfortunately, it does not take very long to survey the philosophical work on this subject as it is mainly conspicuous by its absence. Where academic debate does exist it ranges from the mildly embarrassing to the downright ridiculous.

The ancient Greek philosophers (Plato, Aristotle and so on) viewed justice as a male personal attribute – the highest virtue of man. Women and children needed to be ruled by men because of their 'imperfect' reason. Plato, in the *Republic*, argues that in order to achieve unity among men, women and children should be shared and that children should literally be taken from their mothers. Aristotle objects to these ideas only on the grounds of practicality (Mayhew, 1997). The lack of any concept of distributional justice or rights for children in the world of Ancient Greece has always been startling to modern perceptions. For example, Adam Smith noted disapprovingly in 1790:

> [T]he murder of new-born infants was a practice allowed
> of in almost all the states of Greece, even among the polite
> and civilized Athenians; and whenever the circumstances of
> the parent rendered it inconvenient to bring up the child,
> to abandon it to hunger, or to wild beasts, was regarded

> without blame or censure.... Aristotle talks of it as of what
> the magistrate ought upon many occasions to encourage.
> The humane Plato is of the same opinion, and, with all that
> love of mankind which seems to animate all his writings,
> nowhere marks this practice with disapprobation.

Economic theory of distributional justice is also unhelpful from the perspective of children. Neoclassical economic theory has a simple and elegant explanation for both poverty and wealth. Wealth is a result of work, waiting and economic efficiency and poverty is a result of the absence of productivity and the inability or unwillingness to work and wait (Clark, 2002). Child poverty (and wealth) are entirely absent from this theory – children are not economically productive, they should not work and they cannot wait. Children do make an appearance in neoclassical economic theory in discussions of human capital. Investment in children's health, nutrition and education is needed so that they can grow up to become productive adult workers in the future. Children's current needs, agency and economic rights are invariably entirely absent from such discussion.

The absence of any useful economic theory of child poverty is not a result of the complex nature of this subject. In fact, the economics of child poverty are very simple and are entirely concerned with redistribution – where sufficient resources are redistributed from adults to children there is no child poverty; where insufficient resources are redistributed from adults to children child poverty is inevitable.

Almost all neoclassical economic literature treats children as a property of their families or households, which has an influence on the family's preferences (for example, Becker, 1991). There is a very limited economic theory literature on distributional justice that addresses children as individuals rather than merely as an influence on the consumption preferences of adults. It ranges from the very offensive views of Rakowski (1993, p 153) who sees children as an extravagant lifestyle choice: 'If the cultivation of expensive tastes, or silly gambles, or any other intentional action cannot give rise to redistributional claims, how can procreation?', to the slightly less offensive views of Folbre (1994a) who sees children as a necessary public good whose future income will benefit all adults in their old age, that is, their future work will pay for pensions and other services. Thus, parents have a redistributional justice claim as, 'Those who benefit from children's future income do so partly at the expense of present-day parents' (Folbre, 1994b, p 87).

Rakowski's misanthropic viewpoint runs counter to that of many philosophers with both 'left-wing' and 'right-wing' views who argue that procreative liberty is a fundamental right that is integral to any concept of social justice (for example, see Robertson, 1994; Roberts, 1995). Reproduction is both a biological and a social imperative; societies that do not have enough children inevitably become extinct. The historical and archaeological records show that most societies eventually collapse – there are no more Aztecs, Romans, Saracens or Vikings – sometimes as a direct or indirect result of raising insufficient children to adulthood. Indeed, with the notable exceptions of China, India, Korea, the Jews and Zoroastrians few societies or social groups can trace a continuous history back to the Bronze Age when detailed historical records began.

What is almost entirely lacking from the economic theory literature is the concept of children as individuals with agency who have independent distributional justice claims on adults (Levison, 2000). Neither the neoclassical nor, more surprisingly, the feminist economics literature addresses the political concept that children have a right to sufficient economic resources to meet their needs and that this is a fundamental requirement for a just society. The notable exception is the work of the Norwegian feminist economist Hilde Bojer (2000, 2003), which attempts to span both economic and political philosophy theory on social justice. Her work is discussed below.

Political philosophy and children

Unfortunately, the political philosophy literature pays no more attention to social justice for children than the economics literature. Children are completely ignored in Nozick's (1974) libertarian theories of justice, and Rawls (1997), in his liberal theory of justice, specifically excludes children from his ideas of a social contract[4] as he considers the family to be outside the public sphere. For Rawls (1971), the social contract drawn up behind the veil of ignorance is only concerned with the rights and duties of adult citizens (Bojer, 2000). *A theory of justice* assumes that the people who meet to negotiate the social contract are heads of families: 'It is not necessary to think of the parties as heads of families, although I shall generally follow this interpretation' (Rawls, 1971, p 128). In his later work, Rawls, in response to feminist critics (for example, Moller Okin, 1989), specifically addresses the rights of women and children. He argues that:

> Just as the principles of justice require that wives have all the rights of citizens, the principles of justice impose constraints on the family on behalf of children who as society's future citizens have basic rights as such.... The equal rights of women and the basic rights of their children as future citizens are inalienable and protect them wherever they are. Gender distinctions limiting those rights and liberties are excluded. (Rawls, 1997, pp 790-1)

Thus, Rawls does not view children as current citizens in their own right with valid justice claims on society. He views children as future citizens who are entitled to basic rights only by virtue of their future citizenship.

Nozick's (1974) libertarian theory of justice is also only applicable to adults and, arguably, only to adults who had never been children (Bojer, 2000). Libertarian justice theory holds sacrosanct the right to property fairly acquired and the retention of the fruits of individuals' labour. Taxation by society is therefore viewed as tantamount to theft, with the exception of the need for some organised policing to protect life and property rights – the 'night watchman state'. Nozick imagines a natural situation made up of a group of solitary hunters who would be willing to give up a minimum amount of their freedoms to a state that could protect them from robbery and murder. Children (and non-hunting women) would have no rights to economic goods in this theory of justice – children literally become the property of their parents – the 'fruits of their labour'. Bojer (2003, p 60) expresses puzzlement

> that the solitary hunter must have forgotten his own childhood. Otherwise, he would surely have chosen to organise society in a way that at least guaranteed his survival to adulthood; probably also that conditions during his childhood were such as to enable him to become a fit hunter.

Of course, Nozick's theory of justice among 'man the hunter' is a product of its time. During the 1970s, the idea of 'man the hunter' in a 'natural state of nature' was prominent in sociobiological writings (for example, Wilson, 1975; Ardrey, 1976). Janson-Smith (1980, p 75) argues that sociobiologists during the 1970s portrayed

> the quintessential female is an individual specialised for making eggs (whereas the perfect male – human, dominant

> – is according to Robin Fox, 'controlled, cunning, attractive
> to the ladies, good with children, relaxed, tough, eloquent,
> skilful, knowledgeable and proficient in self-defence and
> hunting.' It must be the aftershave!).

Bojer sees little hope of adapting libertarian justice theory to include children, although she is optimistic that the liberal justice theory of Rawls could be appropriately modified. In particular:

> Children may well be considered the weakest group in
> society, the group most unconditionally dependent on
> the goodwill of others. The group 'children' is therefore a
> strong candidate for the position of the least advantaged in
> the maxi-min principle. (Bojer, 2000, p 35)[5]

However, Bojer has to date 'only been able to indicate the general outlines of the social contract as extended to children' (Bojer, 2000, p 38).

In her most recent work, Bojer (2003) is more optimistic about extending the capabilities theory of Sen and Nussbaum to include children:

> The capability approach seems the most promising way of
> defining children's good. Children's capabilities as children
> must of course be conceived as different in many ways from
> the capabilities as adults. (Bojer, 2003, p 62)

Capabilities, children and poverty

Amartya Sen (1979, 1985a) developed capability theory. He argued that Rawls' focus on the justice of the distribution of primary goods should be replaced by a focus on the distribution of basic capabilities, saying: 'The focus on basic capabilities can be seen as a natural extension of Rawls's concern with primary goods, shifting attention from goods to what goods do to human beings' (Sen, 1979, pp 218-19).

Sen's (1993) idea is that distributional justice equality should be concerned with a person's 'actual ability to achieve various valuable functionings as a part of living' (p 30) that is, distributional justice should be mainly concerned with what people can do rather than with what economic and social goods they have.

As discussed above, one of the prime concerns of the UK government's social justice agenda has been the eradication of child poverty. So a key question is – how helpful is a capability approach for this task? Unfortunately, the capability approach to poverty is an absolute approach that is arguably non-sociological, oversimplistic and inadequate. A detailed debate on the merits of the capability approach conception of poverty occurred between Amartya Sen and Peter Townsend in the 1980s. Sen (1983, p 159) argued that 'There is ... an irreducible absolutist core in the idea of poverty. If there is starvation and hunger then, no matter what the relative picture looks like – there clearly is poverty'.

Examples of this absolutist core are the need 'to meet nutritional requirements, to escape avoidable disease, to be sheltered, to be clothed, to be able to travel, to be educated ... to live without shame' (Sen, 1983, pp 162-3).

Townsend (1985) has responded that this absolutist core is itself relative to society. Nutritional requirements are dependent on the work roles of people at different points of history and in different cultures. Avoidable disease is dependent on the level of medical technology. The idea of shelter is relative not just to climate but also to what society uses shelter for. Shelter includes notions of privacy, space to cook, work and play and highly cultured notions of warmth, humidity and segregation of particular members of the family, as well as different functions of sleep, cooking, washing and excretion. Sen (1985b, p 673) responded by arguing that:

> [T]he characteristic feature of absoluteness is neither constancy over time nor invariance between societies nor concentration on food and nutrition. It is an approach to judging a person's deprivation in absolute terms (in the case of a poverty study, in terms of certain specified minimum absolute levels), rather than in purely relative terms vis à vis the levels enjoyed by others in society. But on the space of the capabilities themselves – the direct constituent of the standard of living – escape from poverty has an absolute requirement, to wit, avoidance of this type of shame. Not so much having equal shame as others, but just not being ashamed, absolutely.

If we view the problem of conceptualising poverty in this light, then there is no conflict between the irreducible absolutist element in the notion of poverty (related to capabilities and the standard of living) and the 'thoroughgoing relativity' to which Peter Townsend refers, if the latter is interpreted as applying to commodities and resources.

Sen's semantic argument is that poverty is absolute in terms of capabilities, but relative in terms of commodities, resources and incomes. A fundamental problem with this argument is that it is non-sociological, it assumes that a person's capabilities and functionings (that is, what they can do) can be determined and interpreted independently of the society in which they live. It is hard to understand what Sen means when he argues that, in order to not be poor, there is an absolute requirement to have the capability not to be ashamed, that to be equally ashamed as the rest of the people in your society would be insufficient to avoid poverty. Townsend has consistently argued for over 50 years (for example 1954, 1962, 1970) that all conceivable workable definitions of poverty – even those that purport to be absolute definitions – only have meaning relative to the society in which a person lives. If Townsend is correct, then Sen's claim that poverty is absolute in the 'space of the capabilities' is understandable in the same way that the concept of unicorns, fairies and a loving god are understandable. However, there is no more real world meaning to the claim that poverty is absolute in capability space than the claim that poverty is absolute in fairy space.

It is hard to evaluate the validity of Sen's argument as he has consistently refused to propose a list of capabilities and functionings that could be used to evaluate the utility of his theory for policy purposes. Several authors have raised concerns about the practicality of operationalising Sen's capability framework (Beitz, 1986; Sugden, 1993; Alkire, 2002). It is therefore unsurprising that Streeten– one of the pioneers of basic needs measures of poverty – has proposed that it might be better to 'look at poverty and deprivation in terms of observable achievements' rather than capabilities (Streeten, 2000, p 159).

Nussbaum (1999, 2003) has proposed a list of 10 capabilities and functionings:

- life;
- bodily health;
- bodily integrity;
- senses, imagination and thought;
- emotions;
- practical reason;
- affiliation;
- other species;
- play; and
- control over one's environment, political and material.

Nussbaum further identifies three types of capabilities and functionings: basic capabilities, such as the senses – hearing and seeing; internal capabilities, which are the result of the development of the basic capabilities, for example speech that requires suitable external inputs such as socialisation, education and so on; and combined capabilities, which are internal capabilities combined with suitable external conditions that enable functionings. It is unclear in what sense child or adult poverty is an absolute phenomenon in terms of Nussbaum's list. Clark (2003) attempted to evaluate the usefulness of the capabilities approach to development using a survey of 157 poor people's views (aged 12 and over) in South Africa. Clark found that the majority of respondents agreed that many of Sen and Nussbaum's capabilities and functionings were necessary for a good life. However:

> The survey findings also confirm that Nussbaum and Sen's list pays insufficient attention to the importance of free time, sleep and rest, relaxation and opportunities for recreation. ... [It also] appears to overlook many of the harsh realities facing ordinary poor people. This tends to direct attention away from the capabilities that matter most. For example, consider the function of education. If the items included in Nussbaum and Sen's development ethic are interpreted literally, then the only obvious role for education is to promote the cognitive functions and the power of practical reason. No explicit provisions are made for acquiring practical skills, improving job prospects or raising earnings; but as we have seen, achieving these objectives are the primary reasons for valuing education and have the potential to make a big difference to the quality of life. (Clark, 2003, pp 189, 191)

Furthermore, Clark (2003, p 193) argues that:

> So far Sen has explored the moral and political implications of conceptualizing poverty in terms of capability failure. He has not yet developed a comprehensive list of basic capabilities on which to base his concept of poverty.

Given these profound and significant problems with a capability approach to issues of poverty and distributional justice for children, it is very hard to see how this theory could currently be used as a basis for practical policy advice or evaluation. Nevertheless, significant attempts have been made by several researchers to operationalise Sen's capability framework in a manner relevant to policy in the UK (for example, Seymour, 2000; Burchardt, Chapter Ten, this volume). Burchardt developed an operational list of capabilities using a rights-based approach[6] in conjunction with participatory workshops and in-depth interviews with adults from a range of social groups. Seymour's work was similarly informed by the results of five workshops and meetings held in various parts of the UK.[7] Burchardt modified her provisional list of capabilities for children (but not for other sociodemographic groups). For example, she excluded capabilities 'like participation in elections or freedom in matters of marriage and reproduction' (page 218). The justification for this was because in childhood the period of 'capability-formation – including the capabilities of being knowledgeable and engaging in critical reflection – is not yet complete' (page 218).

Burchardt's methods and arguments with regard to children are highly problematic. As she acknowledges, she was not able to consult children or organisations that represent children when drawing up her provisional capability list or include analysis of the UNCRC. A fundamental principle of the UNCRC is that children have rights that are independent but co-equal to adults, therefore by not considering human rights conventions that specifically address children's needs, Burchardt's methods are inconsistent with a rights approach for children. Finally, the argument that children's rights/ capabilities for political participation and freedom in marriage and reproduction should be curtailed because children may have limited knowledge and critical reflection abilities, does not stand up to critical scrutiny. Children are not the only social group said to have limited knowledge and critical reflection abilities and the definition of these groups has changed over time as our understanding of, for example, people's ability to communicate knowledge has changed. In the 20th century some governments implemented forcible sterilisation policies (for example, Germany, Sweden and the US) for adults deemed to have a low IQ. Similarly, voting rights have been restricted by some governments based on literacy tests or the perceived lack of critical reflection abilities of women or members of certain ethnic groups. These discriminatory policies have been condemned by the UN as human rights violations.

There may be good reasons why a socially just society would restrict certain children's rights and capabilities but stronger justifications for these restrictions on rights or capabilities are required. This is particularly the case in a country like the UK, which allows children between the ages of 16 and 18 legally to marry, have children and join the armed forces (as child soldiers). It could be argued that it might be more the case in countries where governments tolerate working by children at much younger ages.

Conclusions

A space alien visiting the Earth and reading the economic theory and political philosophy literature on distributional justice for children would be unlikely to discern that children are citizens with human rights that are independent and co-equal to the adults with whom they live. The space alien might also conclude that these academic authors had never been children and were unlikely to have children of their own, or at least if they did have children they were completely unconcerned with the distributional justice of the economic goods their children received.

This chapter has examined whether the limited political and economic philosophy literature on distributional justice for children provided a basis for evaluating current government social justice policies in the UK that affect children's well-being. The answer is clear: the academic literature on social justice for children is wholly inadequate.

The lamentable lack of a social justice literature that considers children is echoed by a similar lack of empirical and scientific literature on poverty from the viewpoint of the child. Most studies of poverty ignore children (but see Craig et al, 2000; Gordon et al, 2003) and where child poverty is estimated, it is usually indirectly with children treated as a property of their households or families. There are virtually no studies with direct measurements of what economic goods children receive. In a recent survey of the literature on the concept and measurement of child poverty, Minujin et al (2006, p 481) found that

> there is a lack of consideration of children's issues in the debate on poverty. The lack of visibility has negative implications for anti-poverty strategies, which seldom consider that children and their rights are central to their design and implementation.

Child poverty is unjust and a violation of children's rights. This issue is apparently of considerable concern to policy makers in the UK. Unfortunately, while some academics have paid significant attention to the issue of childhood poverty and a few have addressed children's agency, the academy as a whole does not seem to be as concerned about social justice for children in their own right.

Notes

[1] The term of 'meritocracy' was invented by Michael Young (who drafted the 1945 Labour Manifesto 'Let Us Face The Future') in his dystopian book *The rise of the meritocracy* (1958). This was a satirical history of British society from 1870 to 2033, which becomes divided on the basis of IQ with resulting gross and unjust inequalities and undesirable elitism.

[2] The idea that even young children are both innocents who need protection and a threat to society has a long history in European Christian thought. Cunningham (2005, p 49) quotes from a German sermon from 1520: 'Just as a cat craves mice, a fox chickens, and a wolf cub sheep, so infant humans are inclined in their hearts to adultery, fornication, impure desires, lewdness, idol worship, belief in magic, hostility, quarrelling, passion, anger, strife, dissension, factiousness, hatred, murder, drunkenness, gluttony, and more'.

[3] In some countries, however, the UNCRC is honoured only in the breach with, for example, some countries turning a blind eye to the existence of child slavery. The International Labour Organisation estimates that there may be hundreds of millions of children worldwide working and in slave-like conditions. (See special issue of journal *Children & Society*, 'Child Slavery Worldwide', 2008, vol 3).

[4] See Introduction, this volume, for a discussion of Rawls' theory of justice.

[5] Bojer is referring to Rawls' 'difference principle', in which social and economic inequalities are considered as long as they are of greatest benefit to the least advantaged (Bojer, 2000).

[6] Specifically, the rights in the International Covenant on Civil and Political Rights (ICCPR), and the International Covenant on Economic, Social and Cultural Rights (ICESCR).

[7] The author of this chapter chaired some of these meetings.

References

Alkire, S. (2002) *Valuing freedoms: Sen's capability approach and poverty reduction*, Oxford: Oxford University Press.
Ardrey, R. (1976) *The hunting hypothesis*, London: Collins.
Becker, G. (1991) *A treatise on the family*, Cambridge, MA: Harvard University Press.

Beitz, C. R. (1986) 'Amartya Sen's resources, values and development', *Economics and Philosophy*, vol 2, no 2, pp 282-91.

Blair, T. (1999) 'Beveridge revisited: a welfare state for the 21st century', Beveridge Lecture, Toynbee Hall, London, 18 March.

Blunkett, D. (2000) *Hansard*, 'Selection in education', 15 March, vol 315, col 302, London, www.parliament.the-stationery-office.co.uk/pa/cm199900/cmhansrd/vo000315/debtext/00315-04.htm

Bojer, H. (2000) 'Children and theories of social justice', *Feminist Economics*, vol 6, no 2, pp 23-39.

Bojer, H. (2003) *Distributional justice: Theory and measurement*, London: Routledge.

Bradshaw, J. (ed) (2001) *Poverty: The outcomes for children*, London: Family Policy Studies Centre.

Burchardt, T. (2008) 'Monitoring inequality: putting the capability approach to work', in G. Craig, T. Burchardt and D. Gordon (eds) *Social justice and public policy: Seeking fairness in diverse societies*, Bristol: The Policy Press.

Brown, G. (2007) Speech to the Labour Party annual conference, www.labour.org.uk/conference/brown_speech

Brighouse, H. and Swift, A. (2008) 'Social justice and the family', in G. Craig, T. Burchardt and D. Gordon (eds) *Social justice and public policy: Seeking fairness in diverse societies*, Bristol: The Policy Press.

Clark, C. (2002) 'Wealth and poverty: On the social creation of scarcity', *Journal of Economic Issues*, vol 36, no 2, pp 415-21.

Clark, D. A. (2003) 'Concepts and perceptions of human well-being: some evidence from South Africa', *Oxford Development Studies*, vol 31, no 2, pp 173-96.

Craig, G. (2002) 'Children's participation through community development: assessing the lessons from international experience', in C. Hallet and A. Prout (eds) *Hearing the voices of children*, London: Routledge.

Craig, G., Wilkinson, M. and Alcock, P. (2000) *Involving children in anti-poverty work*, London: Children's Society.

Cunningham, H. (2005) *Children and childhood in western society since 1500*, Harlow: Pearson Education.

Falk, R. (2000) *Human rights horizons: The pursuit of justice in a globalizing world*, New York: Routledge.

Folbre, N. (1994a) *Who pays for the kids? Gender and the structures of constraint*, New York: Routledge.

Folbre, N. (1994b) 'Children as public goods', *The American Economic Review*, vol 84, no 2, pp 86-90.

Foote, G. (1985) *The Labour Party's political thought: A history*, London: Croom Helm.

Goldson, B. (2002) 'New Labour, social justice and children: political calculation and the deserving-undeserving schism', *British Journal of Social Work*, vol 32, no 6, p 683-95.

Gordon, D., Nandy, S., Pantazis, C., Pemberton, S. and Townsend, P. (2003) *Child poverty in the developing world*, Bristol: The Policy Press.

Hendrick, H. (1994) *Child welfare: England 1872-1989*, London: Routledge.

Hendrick, H. (1997) *Children, childhood and English society, 1880-1990*, Cambridge: Cambridge University Press.

Hendrick, H. (2003) *Child welfare: Historical dimensions, contemporary debate*, Bristol: The Policy Press.

HM Government (2007) *The consolidated 3rd and 4th periodic report to the UN Committee on the Rights of the Child*, London: The Stationery Office, www.everychildmatters.gov.uk/_files/09796A5425218FB5DB5FEEE49AC9E858.pdf

HM Treasury (2004) *Child poverty review*, London: The Stationery Office.

Horton, R. J. (2004) 'UNICEF leadership 2005-2015: a call for strategic change', *The Lancet*, vol 364, p 9451.

Janson-Smith, D. (1980) 'Sociobiology: so what?', in Brighton Women and Science Group (eds) *Alice through the microscope: The power of science over women's lives*, London: Virago, pp 62-88.

Johnson, F. (1922) *Keir Hardie's socialism*, London: Independent Labour Party.

Levison, D. (2000) 'Children as economic agents', *Feminist Economics*, vol 6, no 1, pp 125-34.

Mayhew, R. (1997) *Aristotle's criticism of Plato's Republic*, Lanham, MD: Rowman and Littlefield.

Minujin, A., Delamonica, E., Davidziuk, A. and Gonzalez, E. D. (2006) 'The definition of child poverty: a discussion of concepts and measurements', *Environment and Urbanization*, vol 18, no 2, pp 481-500.

Moller Okin, S. (1989) *Justice, gender and the family*, New York: Basic Books.

Nozick, R. (1974) *Anarchy, state and utopia*, Oxford: Blackwell.

Nussbaum, M. C. (1999) *Sex and social justice*, Oxford: Oxford University Press.

Nussbaum, M. C. (2003) 'Capabilities as fundamental entitlements: Sen and social justice', *Feminist Economics*, vol 9, no 2-3, pp 33-59.

Pemberton, S., Gordon, D., Nandy, S., Pantazis, C. and Townsend, P. (2007) 'Child rights and child poverty: can the international framework of children's rights be used to improve child survival rates?', *PLoS Medicine*, vol 4, no 10, p 307, http://medicine.plosjournals. org/perlserv/?request=get-document&doi=10.1371/journal. pmed.0040307&ct=1

Rakowski, E. (1993) *Equal justice*, Oxford: Oxford University Press.

Rawls, J. (1971) *A theory of justice*, Oxford: Oxford University Press.

Rawls, J. (1997) 'The idea of public reason revisited', *University of Chicago Law Review*, vol 64, no 3, pp 765-807.

Roberts, D. E. (1995) 'Social justice, procreative liberty, and the limits of liberal theory: Robertson's children of choice', *Law & Social Inquiry*, vol 20, no 4, pp 1005-21.

Robertson, J. A. (1994) *Children of choice: Freedom and the new reproductive technologies*, Princeton, NJ: Princeton University Press.

Sen, A. K. (1979) *Equality of what?: The Tanner Lecture on Human Values*, Stanford, CA: Stanford University, www.tannerlectures.utah.edu/ lectures/documents/sen80.pdf

Sen, A. K. (1983) 'Poor, relatively speaking', *Oxford Economic Papers*, vol 35, no 2, pp 135-69.

Sen, A. K. (1985a) *Commodities and capabilities*, Oxford: North-Holland.

Sen, A. K. (1985b) 'A sociological approach to the measurement of poverty: a reply to Professor Peter Townsend', *Oxford Economic Papers*, vol 37, no 4, pp 669-76.

Sen, A. K. (1993) 'Capability and well-being', in M. Nussbaum and A. Sen (eds) *The quality of life*, Oxford: Clarendon Press, pp 30-53.

Seymour, J. (2000) *Poverty in plenty: A human development report for the UK*, London: Earthscan.

Smith, A. (1790) *The theory of moral sentiments*, London: A. Millar, www. econlib.org/Library/Smith/smMS.html

Streeten, P (2000) 'Freedom and welfare: a review essay on Amartya Sen, Development as Freedom', *Population and Development Review*, vol 26, no 1, pp 153-62.

Sugden, R. (1993) 'Welfare, resources, and capabilities: a review of Inequality Reexamined by Amartya Sen', *Journal of Economic Literature*, vol 31, pp 1947-62.

Titmuss, R. E. (1974) *Social policy*, London, Allen and Unwin.

Townsend, P. (1954) 'Measuring poverty', *British Journal of Sociology*, vol 5, no 2, pp 130-7.

Townsend, P. (1962) 'The meaning of poverty', *British Journal of Sociology*, vol 13, no 3, pp 210-27.

Townsend, P. (ed) (1970) *The concept of poverty: Working Papers on methods of investigation and life-styles of the poor in different countries*, London: Heinemann.

Townsend, P. (1985) 'A sociological approach to the measurement of poverty: a rejoinder to Professor Amartya Sen', *Oxford Economic Papers*, vol 37, pp 659-68.

Tracey, H. (ed) (1948) *The British Labour Party: Its history, growth, policy and leaders*, 3 vols, London: The Caxton Publishing Company Ltd.

Walker, R. (ed) (1999) *Ending child poverty*, Bristol: The Policy Press.

White, M. (2001) 'Party politics: Blair sets out his faith', *The Guardian*, 14 May, http://politics.guardian.co.uk/election2001/story/0,9029,490405,00.html#article_continue

Wilson, E. O. (1975) *Sociobiology, The New Synthesis*, Cambridge, MA: Belknap Press.

Winter, J. M. (1972) 'Arthur Henderson, the Russian Revolution, and the reconstruction of the Labour Party', *The Historical Journal*, vol 15, no 4, pp 753-73.

Young, M. (1958) *The rise of the meritocracy: 1870-2033. An essay on education and equality*, London: Thames and Hudson.

NINE

Social justice in the UK: one route or four?

Katie Schmuecker

> You can't have Scotland doing something different from the rest of Britain. (Tony Blair, on tuition fees policy, quoted in Ashdown, 2001, p 446)

Devolution to Scotland, Wales and Northern Ireland was one of the earliest and most radical Acts of the 1997 Labour government, opening up new and more democratically legitimate centres of decision-making power in Edinburgh, Cardiff and Belfast. Such constitutional changes are often regarded as dry, arcane matters of interest to a select few. But constitutional changes can have profound implications for policy and practice. Since the devolved administrations came into being in 1999, the achievement of overarching aspirations – such as progressing social justice – have required a different approach, one that takes account of policy differences in different parts of the UK.

For many, devolution to the nations of Scotland and Wales embodied a recognition of the different cultural and national identities in the multinational state that constitutes Great Britain. The debates that took place in the run-up to the referendums in 1997 focused heavily on creating a new kind of inclusive politics, voice, representation and, particularly in the case of Scotland, national identity. In terms of social justice, the issues that the debate turned on sat well within the more recent pluralistic approach to social justice, with its concern for representation and recognition of different groups (Fraser, 2003; Chapter Five, this volume).[1] The referendum debates paid less attention to the consequences of the greater policy divergence that devolution could bring. The debate in Northern Ireland was somewhat different, with conflict resolution acting as the key driver of devolution. The circumstances in Northern Ireland are exceptional, with the project stalling and restarting a number of times, meaning that devolution has been interspersed with periods of suspension and the re-imposition of direct rule. As a result, Northern Irish policies will not be discussed in detail here.

Finding local solutions to local problems and addressing specific territorial needs is a key rationale for devolution. Devolution of powers can create opportunities for policy experimentation, innovation and learning, with new and successful ideas shared. In this sense, devolution is said to create 'policy laboratories'. However, this also means different administrations pursuing different policies, a logical consequence of devolution that some – seemingly including Tony Blair – gave little thought to. Even in the first eight years of devolution, when Labour was either in power or the dominant partner in a coalition across all parts of Great Britain, there were some high-profile policy divergences. Some – such as the policies on tuition fees and proportional representation for local government elections in Scotland – were the result of coalition politics. But the May 2007 devolved elections resulted in a new political landscape, with a Nationalist administration in Scotland (albeit a minority one), Labour and the Nationalists sharing power in Wales, and the Unionists and Nationalists sharing power in Northern Ireland. With different parties in power in different parts of the UK the likelihood of divergent policy paths is surely increased.

It is the prospect of different parts of the UK developing different policy directions and spending decisions that has caused some to have concerns about the impact of devolution on the grounds of distributive social justice, and the ability to deliver common minimum standards (Walker, 2002). This could undermine what Marshall (1950) referred to as the 'social rights of citizenship', essentially a common minimum of social benefits and public services delivered by the welfare state, which are available to all citizens on the same terms, no matter where they live. While this chapter will challenge the view that devolution undermines social justice, these concerns do point to the conundrum that devolution poses for those concerned with social justice: how to reconcile equity with diversity (Morgan, 2001).

This chapter will explore the relationship between devolution and social justice. The next section will give an overview of the degree of devolution to Scotland, Wales and Northern Ireland, particularly in those policy areas that are important to distributive social justice and Marshall's 'social rights of citizenship'. The following section will give an overview of the theoretical debates about the relationship between devolution and distributive social justice, before the third section considers the actual scope for divergence in the UK. The final section will consider the relationship between devolution and social justice in practice by looking at two specific examples: first, policies to combat poverty and social exclusion across the UK; and second, the impact of transparency and public opinion on policy making in a devolved UK using the example of NHS waiting times.

The UK devolution settlement and distributive social justice

In order to understand the relationship between devolution and distributive justice, it is important to understand the extent of devolution, and how fully powers are devolved in different areas. Each of the devolved settlements differs (see the appendix to this chapter for a summary of powers), as does the level of autonomy available to each administration. All of the administrations exercise significant powers in the areas of health, education, housing, local government, social care and planning. But while Scotland enjoys some limited tax-raising powers,[2] and both Scotland and Northern Ireland have primary legislative powers, the Welsh government has less autonomy. It has secondary legislative and executive powers, and the 2006 Government of Wales Act conferred some legislative competence, although permission must be sought from Westminster on a case-by-case basis.

Two of the most important policy instruments for tackling poverty, and also for progressing equity and distributive justice, are the redistributive powers of taxation and benefits. These are the very foundation of the welfare state, and are fundamental to shared social citizenship rights if we follow the thinking of Marshall, or what David Miller (2005) has more recently called the 'social minimum' necessary for social justice. These are areas that remain reserved to the UK level, with the Treasury and Department for Work and Pensions (DWP) exercising significant powers for the whole of the UK.[3] Policies essential to distributive justice such as social security levels, the state pension, minimum wage, and tax credits all remain reserved. In this respect there arguably remains one main route to distributive social justice for the whole of the UK post-devolution.

However, distributive social justice is broader than simple measures of income distribution. Despite the differences in the devolved settlements, each of the devolved administrations exercises substantial powers over social policy, including how education and health services are designed and delivered, housing policy and substantial parts of 'early years' policy. Access to good-quality public services, particularly those just mentioned, also have an important role to play in delivering more equal life chances (Pearce and Paxton, 2005), and it is here that the devolved administrations have a substantial role to play.

In this respect, devolution has made progressing social justice more challenging in two ways. The first is a challenge of coordination, as there are some important areas of overlap between devolved and reserved powers. For example, while housing policy is largely devolved, responsibility for Housing Benefit remains reserved. This means that successful policies for social housing are likely to require coordination across different levels of government. Such coordination may be made more challenging still with different parties in power in different parts of the UK. The second is that democratic devolution has enhanced the likelihood of divergent approaches to policy in areas where the devolved administrations exercise powers, especially when there are different parties in power in different parts of the UK. This could lead to unequal progress towards social justice and differing social citizenship rights in different parts of the UK.

Does devolution undermine social justice?

Traditionally, some on the Left have regarded devolution as a threat to social justice, fearing that national identities could undermine class solidarity – Bevan (1944) summed up this view when he declared that there is no 'Welsh problem' (see also Kinnock, 1975). To allow devolution of power is to risk creating diverse standards – or 'postcode lotteries' – undermining equity, social citizenship and national solidarity (Walker, 2002). The social democratic welfare state, to this line of thinking, is a strong, centralised state ensuring even provision across the country. It has symbolic power, conveying national solidarity that underpins and reinforces attachment to the state as a nation, providing the basis on which redistribution can occur (McEwen, 2002).

Through devolution the UK has evolved into a quasi-federal state, and a brief survey of federalist theory would seem to uphold the concerns about the impact of devolving powers on the welfare state. Comprehensive comparative studies (Swank, 2002) have concluded that federalism has negative effects on levels of public spending on welfare. However, these arguments must be treated with caution for a number of reasons. First, where the welfare settlement pre-dates democratic federalism the impact on the welfare state is less likely to be negative, as in Austria or Germany. Also, as Keith Banting (2005) argues, the nature and scope of the settlement are important, as where there is a mature welfare state, and key social security and welfare powers are reserved to the highest level, equity almost always trumps diversity.

Second, concerns about the impact of devolution on the welfare state too often unquestioningly accept the ability of a strong centralised state to deliver uniformity, or at least national minimum standards. This has not been the case in practice, and decades of centralised state provision in the UK has not resulted in common high standards and equal access. Indeed, the centralised approach in the UK has tended to produce rigid and inflexible services that are not well equipped to respond to change (Paxton and Gamble, 2005). It is usually the worst-off who suffer most as a result of such failings.

Third, as Paxton and Gamble (2005) and Simeon (2005) argue, far from undermining the welfare state, devolution can act as a 'progressive brake', with sub-state communities often forming the principal opposition to welfare state retrenchment. In this respect, public opinion may also act as a progressive break, with social surveys indicating a high level of support for common standards in key areas. As Table 9.1 shows, over half of respondents in England, Scotland and Wales agree that standards for key services should be the same in every part of Britain. More nuanced research by the Office for Public Management (OPM, 2006) based on deliberative workshops found people at least expect common minimum standards beyond which they are more comfortable with variation. This desire for a degree of uniformity in key areas may mean that a 'better' welfare settlement in one part of the UK leads to demands for the same level of provision in other parts of the UK. This could result in a virtuous circle of policy improvement across the territories, particularly in areas of high salience to voters, or those that have a high profile.

This prospect for policy learning means that those concerned with social justice should look to devolution as an opportunity. In theory, devolution allows space for democratically mandated policy experimentation, innovation and learning. New and successful ideas can be adopted by other territorial administrations – as we have already seen with the introduction of free bus travel for older people and the smoking ban. Policy learning between administrations can push up

Table 9.1: Attitudes towards policy variation in Great Britain (2003) (%)

Standards for services, such as health, schools, roads and police should:		
	be the same in every part of Britain	be allowed to vary
England	66	33
Scotland	59	40
Wales	55	44

Source: Jeffery (2005, Table 2.3)

overall standards so any inequalities produced by policy divergence may prove to be a temporary aberration in a general drive towards higher standards all round.

A key factor that differentiates the pre-devolution era from post-devolution in the UK is *transparency*, and it is transparency that is vital to devolution's contribution to social justice. It is a fallacy to think of the UK as a unitary state before devolution. In reality there has been policy divergence ever since the Scottish Office was created in 1885, followed by the Welsh Office in 1964, and the Northern Ireland Office in 1972 after the dissolution of the Northern Ireland Government. These administrative territorial departments had responsibility for a wide range of domestic policy, although there is some disagreement within the academic community about the degree of policy autonomy enjoyed by the territorial offices (see, for example, Keating, 2002; Mitchell, 2006). There is, however, agreement that the UK, even before democratic devolution, could not be described as a classic unitary state as there were policy differences under administrative devolution.

An important difference now is the context within which divergence occurs. Under administrative devolution policy differences – such as they were – were opaque and managed behind closed doors in Whitehall, Belfast, Cardiff and Edinburgh. Democratic devolution has brought both greater opportunities for policy divergence, and more transparency to these differences, enabling comparisons to be made more easily by journalists, researchers and policy communities – not to mention devolved administrations themselves seeking to underline the 'better deal' they are pursuing for their populations. This is particularly the case in salient policy issues. This greater transparency reinforces the opportunities for policy learning, and for a virtuous circle of rising standards.

The scope for divergence in the UK

Given the permissive nature of the UK devolution settlement in legal terms – particularly in the field of social policy – the scope for policy divergence seems high. Certainly there have been a number of high-profile policy differences – free personal care for the over 65s and the early smoking ban in Scotland, a different approach to university tuition fees and greater reluctance towards PFI contracts in Scotland and Wales, and the abolition of school league tables in Wales among others. Such policy variations could result in different outcomes dependent on where you live. However, a legally permissive settlement does not mean there will necessarily be radical divergences. Policy changes take place in a constrained environment, and generally tend to be incremental, with the weight of existing commitments limiting the scope for innovation (Keating, 2002).There are in fact a range of competing pressures acting on the UK and devolved administrations, some likely to lead to policy divergence, and others convergence.

Forces for divergence

Democratic devolution has accorded the devolved administrations legitimacy, giving a mandate to pursue different policies. Under administrative devolution the same political party governed all parts of the Britain (and indeed all parts of the UK following the suspension of Stormont in 1974).This is no longer the case, and in the new political landscape with different parties – or combinations of parties – in power in Cardiff, Belfast, Edinburgh and Westminster, the likelihood of greater policy divergence is increased. Furthermore, it is not just the party in power but the party political system in each of the devolved territories that acts as a potential force for divergence. In Scotland and Wales the main battle is between Labour, the Liberal Democrats and the Nationalist parties, which pulls the centre of gravity of political debates towards the Left. In England, the main opposition to Labour is from the centre–Right Conservative Party.This certainly results in divergent rhetoric in the devolved administrations, although the impact on actual policy divergence is less clear (Lohde, 2005; Wincott, 2005).

The creation of institutions in Edinburgh and Cardiff has also created new forums for debate and lobbying, which has increased points of access into policy making.While much of the policy community already operated at a variety of geographical levels, civic society has generally been quick to adapt and form new policy communities or build the capacity of existing policy communities in order to interact with these new centres of power (Keating, 2002).

There are also constitutional and institutional factors that may serve to further enhance the permissive nature of the devolution settlement.The UK devolution settlement has no agreed principles of service, common standards of provision or floor targets built into it. It also does not make use of concurrent legislation or framework legislation,[4] which enables central governments to set state-wide standards in other decentralised states, making the UK relatively unusual internationally.This means that for the centre to progress social justice it must negotiate and work with the devolved administrations. In theory, Westminster retains sovereignty, and could therefore impose such minimum standards, however to do so would be deeply politically divisive and not in the spirit of devolution.

It would be a gift to the Nationalist parties, and most likely invoke a fierce backlash from Scotland and Wales.

That is not to say the UK is without institutions to manage policy coordination. The Council of the Isles (or British Irish Council as it is also known),[5] set up under the Good Friday Agreement, provides a forum for the exchange of ideas and best practice, with a remit to promote harmonious and mutually beneficial relationships across the islands of Britain and Ireland, and a view to reaching consensus on common policies or common actions in areas of mutual interest. Within the UK, a Memorandum of Understanding between the centre and the devolved administrations sets out the principles that underlie intergovernmental relations; a series of concordats between Whitehall departments and their counterparts set out how relations will be managed; and Joint Ministerial Committees (JMCs) exist to coordinate policies and manage disputes. However, to date they have rarely been used and have not been properly tested. Informal contact between officials and within political party structures has been relied on to manage differences – a practice that is no longer viable with different parties in power. Elsewhere we have argued for the creation of a Department for Nations and Regions to better manage territorial relations within the UK and ensure that the full benefit of policy learning is harnessed (Lodge and Schmuecker, 2007).

The existence of such forces for divergence still does not necessarily mean there will be significant policy divergences within the UK. As Banting (2005) finds, even where there is a lack of formal minimum standards, equity tends to win out over diversity. Furthermore, there are equally significant countervailing forces, pushing the UK towards convergence, which we turn to next.

Forces for convergence

Some welcomed the advent of devolution to Scotland and Wales as an opportunity for social democratic countries to flourish, freed from having to pander to the concerns of (middle) England. However, such a notion is predicated on the view that the Scots and Welsh have a more progressive or 'left-wing' set of values, a view that is seemingly bolstered by the different party political landscape of the devolved territories, where left of centre parties dominate. However, analysis of British Social Attitudes data dispels this popular myth, by revealing that there is very little difference between the Scottish, Welsh and English in terms of values (Adams and Robinson, 2002; Jeffery, 2005). These common values, when allied with the desire for common standards and the greater transparency that devolution brings, can create a powerful force for convergence.

Another force for convergence is the shared context of European integration, with all parts of the UK subject to EU framework policies. Globalisation too has a constraining effect, with dominant narratives and ideas – not least neoliberal economics – influencing thinking in numerous countries. For example, as Adams and Robinson (2005) argue, the similar approach taken to economic development policy across England, Wales and Scotland seemingly has more to do with each independently adopting ideas of sectoral clustering and nurturing a 'knowledge economy' leading to a process of parallel policy evolution rather than explicit policy learning.

Finally, important constraints on divergence can be found in the UK's common market, welfare state and common security area. For example, as Raffe (2005) argues, while education policy is nearly fully devolved, in practical terms the scope for divergence is somewhat constrained in some areas. He points to the common Great Britain labour and higher education markets as a force for convergence, particularly in post-16 qualifications as universities and employers prefer a standard approach – or at least one that is directly comparable – to ease the comparison of candidates for university places or jobs.

Devolution in practice

The context for policy making in the UK post devolution is a complex one, with competing forces for divergence and convergence at work. This presents a number of challenges and opportunities for progressing social justice. In this section, this complexity will be explored through the prism of two policy areas: tackling poverty and social exclusion; and waiting times in the National Health Service (NHS). The intention of the section is not to judge which part of the UK can claim to be most socially just, rather it is to illustrate some of the challenges and opportunities for furthering social justice in the UK post devolution.

Poverty and social exclusion

Poverty remains the most obvious affront to social justice, and, unlike its predecessor, the 1997 Labour government was quick to accept the existence of poverty in the UK. In policy terms, efforts have particularly focused on tackling child poverty, driven by the bold pledge to eradicate child poverty by 2020, which has been an important statement of values as well as a key target for the UK government. A narrative of social exclusion has also been adopted, arguing that disadvantage must be understood as more complex and dynamic than simply income poverty, emphasising individuals' capacity to participate in a range of ways – socially, economically and politically – and the impact that this has on communities where there are concentrations of social exclusion (Burchardt et al, 2002).

Many of the most important policies to tackle social exclusion and deliver the target to eradicate child poverty remain reserved at the UK level, most notably employment, tax and benefit policies. So far a range of tools has been utilised to achieve the fall in child poverty that has occurred: increasing Child Benefit; welfare-to-work policies, especially those for lone parents; the introduction of the national minimum wage; Child Tax Credits and Working Tax Credits. However, tackling social exclusion requires joining up across a broad a range of policy areas, from health, education and training to housing, community regeneration and childcare. This gives the devolved administrations an important role due to their significant powers in these areas, and creates potential for different outcomes in different parts of the country. Achieving the child poverty target and tackling social exclusion in all parts of the UK will require policy coordination and learning across Westminster, Edinburgh, Cardiff and Belfast (Lohde, 2005). This could be made more challenging if different parts of the UK begin to take substantially different approaches to poverty and exclusion, especially when different parties are in power.

For example, the DWP's (2007) Green Paper *In work, better off: Next steps to full employment* proposes greater integration between Jobcentre Plus and skills training in response to the Leitch Review of Skills (2006). This aims to better assist those who are out of work to re-enter the labour market and find sustainable employment. However, the Green Paper acknowledges that while there is a desire to expand this approach to Scotland and Wales, doing so will depend on discussions with the devolved administrations, as skills policy is a devolved matter.

Coordinating policy is not the only challenge of devolution, there is also the question of greater policy divergence, leading to a different understanding of social citizenship in different parts of the UK. However, how far this is happening is a moot point. To date there is certainly evidence of divergent rhetoric in the approaches to poverty and social exclusion. Under Labour (or the Labour/Liberal Democrat coalition in the case of Scotland) both devolved administrations wrapped their social exclusion policies in a narrative of social justice, and in the case of Scotland 'closing the opportunity gap' (Scottish Executive, 1999, 2002; WAG, 2003). So far this has not changed under the new governments in Scotland and Wales. This manifests itself in a number of ways from the Scottish Executive's emphasis on social *inclusion* rather than *exclusion* (Scottish Executive, 1999); to the Welsh Assembly Government's greater emphasis on equality of outcome, compared to the Scottish and English emphasis on equality of opportunity (Scott et al, 2005). However, it should not be assumed that differences in *rhetoric* will necessarily result in differences in *policy* or indeed policy *outcomes.*

There are also differences in the way that Scotland and Wales have structured their administrations compared to the UK government. Wales has a Minister for Social Justice and Local Government, a role with direct responsibility for regeneration, communities and housing, as well as a cross-cutting role to promote social inclusion within the Welsh Assembly Government. Scotland has previously had a Minister for Social Justice, but under Jack McConnell (First Minister 2001-07) social inclusion was absorbed into a Communities portfolio. Under the Scottish National Party's (SNP's) restructured Executive, now called the Scottish Government, social inclusion falls into the Health and Well-being portfolio, along with a number of other responsibilities, including the NHS, public health, community care, older people and housing.

While creating a Minister for Social Justice may signify the importance of social justice to the administrations, again it should not be assumed that this will necessarily be translated into policy difference. Indeed, there have been many similarities in actual policy content, and the types of programmes that are being pursued to tackle poverty and social exclusion in different parts of the UK. In a short chapter such as this it is not possible to review all the policies that contribute to tackling poverty and social exclusion, however there are some general conclusions that can be drawn. All parts of the UK have accepted paid work as the best route out of poverty and exclusion (Scottish Executive, 2002; WAG, 2003; Lohde, 2005; Scott et al, 2005), and have tailored specific programmes to try to move particular groups from welfare to work – especially lone parents as they (and their children) are more likely to experience poverty. A comparison of the administrations' flagship regeneration policies also reveals few differences, with all emphasising area-based working and community participation (Laffin, 2007). However, this may change as the new administrations in Scotland and Wales are currently reviewing their existing policies. Furthermore, the SNP government in Scotland is committed to reducing income disparities, setting a target to 'increase overall income and the proportion of income earned by the three lowest income deciles as a group by 2017' (Scottish Government, 2007, p 17). However, it is far from clear how this target will be achieved with the limited policy tools currently on offer, a point noted by the Scottish Government.

There is, however, one area where important policy differences seem to be emerging, which is in the approach to public services. In England the approach to public service reform has been to emphasise choice, and introduce a greater diversity of providers. Means testing and targeting have also been a central feature (Wincott, 2005). In Scotland and Wales (and especially in Wales) choice and diversity of providers has largely been rejected in the reform of public services. Both nations have shown a preference for a universal approach to public services provided predominantly by the state. The introduction of free personal care for the over 65s in Scotland is perhaps the best example of this, although the Welsh policy abolishing prescription charges, and the earlier introduction of free bus travel for all pensioners in both countries and their different approach to university tuition fees also indicate their universalist tendencies. In this respect they have extended to their citizens social rights that do not exist in other parts of the UK.

This may indicate evidence of the more socially democratic approach that some expected from Scotland and Wales prior to devolution. As Korpi (1983) argues, universal services can be an effective way to lock middle-class people into a social democratic pro-welfare coalition, which can in turn ensure a higher standard of service provision – services that are exclusively for poor people tend to be poor services as the dictum goes. On the face of it this may point to the development of a more generous welfare settlement in Scotland and Wales compared to England, and a different route to social justice for those nations.

However, critics have argued that these policies simply use scarce public money to subsidise the relatively wealthy. Furthermore, there is a real question mark over whether these policies are sustainable and affordable in the long run, in part due to the way that devolution is currently funded through the Barnett Formula (for an explanation of this much misunderstood formula see Heald and McLeod, 2002; McLean et al, 2008). Under the formula Scotland and Wales have both enjoyed considerably higher spending per head compared to England, but if strictly applied (although for political reasons it often is not) the formula should bring about convergence in spending levels over time, 'squeezing' the size of the budgets available in Scotland and Wales. Furthermore, and crucial in this context, the block grant that the devolved administrations receive is calculated on the basis of the increase or decrease in spending by the UK government for England. This means that a budget-cutting UK government, or one that introduces greater charging or private provision of public services, would have a serious knock-on effect, via the Barnett Formula, for the size of the budget available to the devolved administrations, particularly as they currently have limited options for raising their own revenue.

This is put into particularly sharp focus by questions that are already emerging about the affordability of these policies at a time when there have been sustained increases in spending. In Wales, Labour's 2003 Assembly election manifesto pledged to eliminate all charges for home care services for disabled people. However, following an independent costing in 2006 the universal policy was deemed too expensive and the threshold at which charges are paid was raised instead (Chaney, 2006). Furthermore, in Scotland there are reports that 25% of local authorities do not have sufficient budget to deliver free personal care for older people (Poole and Mooney, 2005), and the SNP minority government currently plans to freeze Council Tax rates from April 2008. Its longer-term aim is to replace Council Tax with a local income tax.

It is questionable whether these universal policies can offer a sustainable approach to combating poverty and social exclusion, unless the fiscal settlement underpinning devolution is reformed. Under the current arrangements the opportunities for the devolved administrations to pursue higher spending policies to deliver a social justice agenda are constrained.

Health waiting times

The NHS is one of the most iconic and important parts of the UK welfare settlement, with its offer of care free at the point of delivery. Along with the BBC it is often cited as a symbol of British national identity and citizenship (Stone and Muir, 2007).

While the NHS looms large in many people's sense of Britishness, in reality the 'national' in the NHS has referred more to the home nations than the UK for some years (Greer, 2005). Both the Scottish and Welsh administrations, on establishment in 1999, inherited significant and different challenges, not only in terms of differences in provision resulting from years of incremental policy divergences dating back to administrative devolution, but also as a result of the greater health challenges faced by the two nations. However, under administrative devolution these pre-existing differences went relatively unnoticed. The introduction of new centres of decision making has opened new channels for lobbying by patient groups and professional bodies, and arguably increased the scope for divergence. But the transparency that devolution has brought has made comparison across territories easier, and health policy remains a highly visible and salient issue for voters, where a high degree of uniformity is expected. This increased transparency has made health policy a challenging area since devolution, and one that illustrates well the tension between forces for convergence and divergence. To explore this tension this section discusses the Welsh experience of policy on waiting times in NHS, in the run-up to the 2005 General Election.

Health waiting times have been a totemic target for the NHS since 1997, although health targets set by Whitehall since 1999 have largely only applied to England. While there has been significant criticism about the way the NHS in England is being reformed, and of the perverse incentives targets can have on some areas of service delivery, it is undeniable that targets focus minds on outputs and outcomes, and that the consistent focus on waiting times in England has contributed to the significant reduction that has been seen. In Wales the approach to health policy has diverged substantially. The Assembly has tended to reject competition, consumerism and targets (Davies, 2003), focusing instead on localism, and emphasising equality of outcome over choice (Morgan, 2002). There has also been a much greater focus on public health (Greer, 2005). While waiting times were on the Welsh policy agenda early in the life of the Assembly, *Wales a better country* (WAG, 2003), which set out the targets for the second Assembly government, made no mention of a specific target to reduce waiting times in Wales as part of this new approach to Welsh health policy.

By the time of the General Election in 2005, health waiting times were considerably higher in Wales compared to England, as they generally were prior to devolution, but they seemed stuck at a stubbornly high rate at a time when English waiting times were falling. In 2004, it was estimated that 10% of the Welsh population was on some sort of waiting list (Greer, 2005). This was followed by a highly critical report from the Wales National Audit Office (Auditor General for Wales, 2005), and substantial media coverage both in Wales and in the London-based media. The health service, and waiting times in particular, became a key political issue during the General Election, with reports that the Secretary of State for Wales, Peter Hain, made an unprecedented call for Welsh health policy to emulate English policy on waiting times (Seaton and Osmond, 2005). However, this is a claim that Assembly ministers have repeatedly denied (Drakeford, 2006).

This pressure for convergent performance in relation to waiting times in part reflects the fact that in many aspects of health policy demands are similar across the UK, with interest groups operating across borders and making comparisons between different levels of service. This highlights the competing stresses and tensions at play in the way that policy diverges and converges in a post-devolution UK. The fact that the English approach has reduced waiting times, and was perceived in Scotland and Wales to have reduced waiting times, created a powerful force for convergence (Schmuecker and Adams, 2005). This placed pressure on the devolved administrations to alter their policies (Greer, 2005). Indeed, following this episode in Wales, a new target to cut waiting times was set, along with a pledge to spend £32 million on achieving it. This suggests that the transparency that comes with devolution, combined with public opinion that tends to favour common standards in policy areas of high salience, may act as a powerful de facto force for convergence despite the lack of formal coordination mechanisms in the UK.

Conclusion

The title of this chapter asks whether there is one route or four to social justice in the UK since devolution. With some of the most important policies for pursuing social justice reserved to the UK level, most notably in relation to income redistribution, there arguably remains one primary route to distributive social justice in the UK. But that is only a partial answer. There is scope for the devolved administrations to carve out their own distinctive routes to social justice through their significant discretion in areas of social policy and public services. But as the policy examples discussed here suggest, scope for divergence does not necessarily mean there will be radically different policies in different parts of the UK, and there are considerable countervailing forces pushing the UK towards convergence. This chapter highlights the complex policy-making environment following devolution. The UK devolution settlement is not so clear cut and watertight that many policy areas can be straightforwardly said to be 'devolved' or 'reserved', as is ably demonstrated by housing policy, where Housing Benefit is reserved while social housing policy is devolved. Coordination across different tiers of government as well as across policy areas will become increasingly important in order to pursue overarching policy aspirations like social justice.

In some respects in the UK there has always potentially been more than one route to social justice, due to administrative devolution. A key difference between then and now is the increased transparency that elections have brought. Transparency has a key role to play in helping to realise the opportunity for devolution to raise standards across the board through greater policy learning. When combined with the public's general preference for common standards in highly salient policy areas, it is likely to act as a powerful de facto force for convergence. However, our understanding of how much divergence is acceptable to the public and in what areas is currently limited, and must be improved.

An interesting test to this conclusion may be pending, as there are signs that English indifference towards devolution to Scotland and Wales may be coming to an end (Lodge and Schmuecker, 2007). While they may not put it in the language of social citizenship, or a social minimum, some sections of the English press are beginning to stoke grievances about policy differences between the nations of Great Britain. Differences in approaches to university tuition fees, Welsh abolition of prescription charges, Scottish free personal care for the over 65s and the availability of different drugs on the NHS in different parts of the country are all finding coverage. This may just be the first stirrings from the English dog that is yet to bark.

To date the UK government has struggled to get to grips with its new quasi-federal coordination role, and is ill equipped to deal with territorial relations. But it is a role that is increasingly important in the current context. The early 21st century finds the UK with different parties in power in different parts of the country, and an ongoing debate about further devolution for Scotland,[6] Wales and English local government. One of the first things Gordon Brown did on becoming Prime Minister was publish a Green Paper on further constitutional reform, *The governance of Britain* (Ministry of Justice, 2007). While it had little to say about the current devolution settlement, it is a welcome indication from Brown's government that we have not had the last word on constitutional reform. As the constitutional reform process moves forward, how to reconcile equity with diversity in order to further social justice must be an important consideration. To strike a judicious balance between these two goals requires all parts of the UK – not just the UK government – be engaged with deliberating where the balance should lie. To do so would be to ensure that the real opportunities devolution offers for furthering social justice are maximised.

Appendix: overview of devolved and reserved matters

(from Keating, 2002)

Scotland

The 1998 Scotland Act expressly reserves a number of matters, and all other matters are implicitly devolved.

Reserved matters:
- The Crown, the Union of the kingdoms of Scotland and England, the Parliament of the UK
- International relations, including foreign trade except for observing and implementing European Union and European Convention on Human Rights matters
- Defence and national security, treason, provisions for dealing with terrorism
- Fiscal and monetary policy, currency, coinage and legal tender
- Immigration and nationality, extradition
- The criminal law in relation to drugs and firearms
- Elections except local elections
- Official Secrets
- Law on companies and business associations, insurance, corporate insolvency and intellectual property; regulation of financial institutions and financial services
- Competition, monopolies and mergers
- Employment legislation including industrial relations, equal opportunities, health and safety
- Most consumer protection; data protection
- Post Office, postal and telegraphy services
- Most energy matters
- Railways* and air transport; road safety
- Social security
- Regulation of certain professions, including medical, dental, nursing, veterinary surgeons, architects, auditors and estate agents
- Transport safety and regulation
- Research councils
- Designation of assisted areas
- Nuclear safety, control and safety of medicines, reciprocal health agreements
- Broadcasting and film classification, licensing of theatres and cinemas, gambling
- Weights and measures; time zones
- Abortion, human fertilisation and embryology, genetics
- Equality legislation
- Regulation of activities in outer space

Note: * There was a significant transfer of rail powers to the Scottish Executive following the 2005 Railways Act (HM Government, 2005).

Devolved matters therefore include:

- Health
- Education and training
- Local government, social work, housing and planning
- Economic development and transport; the administration of the European Structural Funds
- The law and home affairs including most civil and criminal law and the criminal justice and prosecution system; police and prisons
- The environment
- Agriculture, fisheries and forestry
- Sport; the arts
- Research and statistics in relation to devolved matters

Northern Ireland

The 1998 Northern Ireland Act specifies the matters that the Northern Ireland Assembly does not have power over, but it also differentiates between excepted matters (matters that Westminster retains control of) and reserved matters (matters that Westminster retains control of but that might be devolved at a later date). As with the Scotland Act all other matters are implicitly devolved.

Excepted matters:

- The Crown, the Union of the kingdoms of Scotland and England, the Parliament of the UK
- International relations, but not the surrender of fugitive offenders between Northern Ireland and the Republic of Ireland
- Participation in the all-Irish institutions
- Observing and implementing European Union and European Convention on Human Rights matters
- Defence and national security, treason, provisions for dealing with terrorism or subversion
- Dignities and titles of honour
- Immigration and nationality
- Taxes under UK laws or existing stamp duties in Northern Ireland
- Social security
- The appointment and removal of judges and director of Public Prosecutions for Northern Ireland
- Elections, including local elections
- Coinage, legal tender and bank notes

- The National Savings Bank
- National security

Reserved matters:
- Navigation but not harbours or inland waters
- Civil aviation but not aerodromes
- The foreshore and the sea bed and subsoil and their natural resources
- Domicile
- Postal services
- Qualifications and immunities of the Assembly and its members
- Criminal law; the surrender of fugitive offenders between Northern Ireland and the Republic of Ireland
- Public order, police, firearms and explosives, civil defence
- The 1926 Emergency Powers Act (Northern Ireland) or any similar enactment
- Court procedure and evidence
- Foreign trade
- Regulation of building societies; banking; friendly societies; the investment and securities business
- Competition, monopolies and mergers
- Some consumer protection matters
- Trademarks, copyright, patent and topography rights, weights and measures
- Telecommunications and wireless telegraphy
- Human fertilisation and embryology, surrogacy, human genetics
- Consumer safety, some environmental matters, data protection
- Nuclear installations
- Designation of assisted areas
- Research councils
- Regulation of activities in outer space

Devolved matters therefore include:
- Health
- Education and training
- Social work, housing and planning
- Economic development and transport; the administration of the European Structural Funds
- The environment
- Agriculture, fisheries and forestry
- Sport; the arts

Wales

The 1998 Wales Act differs from the Northern Ireland and Scotland Acts in that rather than specifying reserved matters, it specifies devolved matters, with all other matters implicitly reserved.

Devolved matters:
- Economic development
- Agriculture, fisheries, forestry and food
- Industry and training
- Education
- Local government
- Health and personal social services
- The environment
- Planning
- Transport and roads
- Arts, culture, the Welsh language
- Built heritage
- Sport and recreation

Acknowledgements

Thanks to all those who have contributed ideas and comments on this chapter, in particular to Guy Lodge, John Adams, Stephen Sinclair, Gerry Mooney, Dave Gordon, Olga Mrinska and Kate Stanley for their helpful comments on earlier drafts.

Notes

[1] In some respects, this was written into the devolution settlements for Wales and Northern Ireland. The 1998 Government of Wales Act states that the Assembly will exercise its functions with 'due regard' to securing equality of opportunity for all people. The 1998 Northern Ireland Act is more specific, with Section 75 requiring public authorities to have due regard for promoting equality of opportunity: between persons of different religious belief, political opinion, racial group, age, marital status or sexual orientation; between men and women generally; between persons with a disability and persons without; and between persons with dependants and persons without.

[2] Including the 'tartan tax', as yet unused, which enables the Parliament to vary the basic rate of income tax by up to three pence in the pound.

³ The exception here is Northern Ireland, where the administration of social security is devolved; however, there is an agreement that policy will mirror that of the rest of the UK.

⁴ A common practice in federal countries – concurrent legislation gives both the state and federal level policy competence in a given area, but legislation passed by the federal level can overrule that of the state in specific circumstances. Framework legislation enables federal governments to set out common minimum standards, leaving the detail to the state level.

⁵ The Council of the Isles brings together the Irish government, British government, Scottish Executive, Northern Ireland Executive, Welsh Assembly Government, and representatives from Guernsey, Jersey and the Isle of Man.

⁶ The SNP government is also leading a debate on Scottish independence through its *National Conversation*, and the Unionist parties are setting up a Scottish Constitutional Commission to consider more power for the Scottish Parliament.

References

Adams, J. and Robinson, P. (2002) 'Divergence and the centre', in J. Adams and P. Robinson (eds) *Devolution in practice: Public policy differences within the UK*, London: IPPR.

Adams, J. and Robinson, P. (2005) 'Regional economic development in a devolved United Kingdom', in J. Adams and K. Schmuecker (eds) *Devolution in practice 2006: Public policy differences within the UK*, London: IPPR.

Ashdown, P. (2001) *The Ashdown diaries: 1997-1999, vol 2*, London: Allen Lane.

Auditor General for Wales (2005) *NHS waiting times in Wales*, Cardiff: National Audit Office Wales.

Banting, K. (2005) 'Social citizenship and federalism: is the federal welfare state a contradiction in terms?', in S. L. Greer (ed) *Territory, democracy and justice: Territorial politics in advanced industrial democracies*, Basingstoke: Palgrave Macmillan, pp 44-66.

Bevan, A. (1944) *Hansard*, 10 October, col 2312.

Burchardt, T., Le Grand, J. and Piachaud, D. (2002) 'Degrees of exclusion: developing a dynamic, multi-dimensional measure', in J. Hills, J. Le Grand and D. Piachaud (eds) *Understanding social exclusion*, Oxford: Oxford University Press.

Chaney, P. (2006) 'Public policy', in R. Wyn and R. Scully (eds) *Wales monitoring devolution report: May 2006*, London: Constitution Unit.

Davies, S. (2003) 'Inside the laboratory: the new politics of public services in Wales', *Catalyst*, www.catalystforum.org.uk/pubs/paper17.html

Drakeford, M. (2006) 'Health policy in Wales: making a difference in conditions of difficulty', *Critical Social Policy*, vol 26, no 3, pp 543-61.

DWP (Department for Work and Pensions) (2007) *In work, better off: Next steps to full employment*, Green Paper, Cm 7130, London: DWP.

Fraser, N. (2003) 'Social justice in the age of identity politics: redistribution, recognition and participation', in N. Fraser and A. Honneth (eds) *Redistribution or recognition? A political-philosophical exchange*, London: Verso.

Greer, S. L. (2005) 'The politics of health policy divergence', in J. Adams and K. Schmuecker (eds) *Devolution in practice 2006: Public policy differences within the UK*, London: IPPR.

Heald, D. and McLeod, D. (2002) 'Beyond Barnett? Financing devolution', in J. Adams and P. Robinson (eds) *Devolution in practice: Public policy differences within the UK*, London: IPPR, pp 147-75.

HM Government (2005) *Railways Act*, London: The Stationery Office.

Jeffery, C. (2005) 'Devolution and divergence: public attitudes and institutional logics', in J. Adams and K. Schmuecker (eds) *Devolution in practice 2006: Public policy differences within the UK*, London: IPPR.

Keating, M. (2002) 'Devolution and public policy in the UK: divergence or convergence?', in J. Adams and P. Robinson (eds) *Devolution in practice: Public policy differences within the UK*, London: IPPR.

Kinnock, N. (1975) *Hansard*, 3 February, col 1031.

Korpi, W. (1983) *The democratic class struggle*, London: Routledge and Kegan Paul.

Laffin, M. (2007) 'Comparative British central–local relations', *Public Policy and Administration*, vol 22, no 1, pp 74-91.

Leitch Review of Skills (2006) *Prosperity for all in the global economy – world class skills*, London: HM Treasury.

Lodge, G. and Schmuecker, K. (2007) 'The end of the union?', *Public Policy Research*, vol 14, no 2, pp 90-6.

Lohde, L. (2005) 'Child poverty and devolution', in J. Adams and K. Schmuecker (eds) *Devolution in practice 2006: Public policy differences within the UK*, London: IPPR.

McEwen, N. (2002) 'State welfare nationalism: the territorial impact of welfare state development in Scotland', *Regional and Federal Studies*, vol 12, no 1, pp 66-90.

McLean, I., Lodge, G. and Schmuecker, K. (2008) *Barnett and the politics of public expenditure*, London: IPPR.

Marshall, T. H. (1950) 'Citizenship and social class', in T. H. Marshall and T. Bottomore (eds) *Citizenship and social class*, London: Pluto Press.

Miller, D. (2005) 'What is social justice', in N. Pearce and W. Paxton (eds) *Social justice: Building a fairer Britain*, London: IPPR.

Ministry of Justice (2007) *The governance of Britain*, Cm 7170, London: The Stationery Office.

Mitchell, J. (2006) 'Evolution and devolution: citizenship, institutions and public policy', *Publius*, vol 36, no 1, pp 153-68.

Morgan, K. (2001) 'The new territorial politics: rivalry and justice in post-devolution Britain', *Regional Studies*, vol 35, no 4, pp 343-8.

Morgan, R. (2002) Third Anniversary Lecture to the Centre for Public Policy, University of Wales, Swansea National, 11 December.

OPM (Office for Public Management) (2006) *Lyons inquiry – public deliberation events: Final report for the Lyons inquiry team*, London: OPM.

Paxton, W. and Gamble, A. (2005) 'Democracy, social justice and the state', in N. Pearce and W. Paxton (eds) *Social justice: Building a fairer Britain*, London: IPPR, pp 219-39.

Pearce, N. and Paxton, W. (2005) 'Introduction', in N. Pearce and W. Paxton (eds) *Social justice: Building a fairer Britain*, London: IPPR, pp ix-xxiii.

Poole, L. and Mooney, G. (2005) 'Governance and social policy in the devolved Scotland', in G. Mooney and G. Scott (eds) *Exploring social policy in the 'new' Scotland*, Bristol: The Policy Press, pp 21-52.

Raffe, D. (2005) 'Devolution and divergence in education policy', in J. Adams and K. Schmuecker (eds) *Devolution in practice 2006: Public policy differences within the UK*, London: IPPR.

Schmuecker, K. and Adams, J. (2005) 'Divergence in priorities, perceived policy failure and pressure for convergence', in J. Adams and K. Schmuecker (eds) *Devolution in practice 2006: Public policy differences within the UK*, London: IPPR.

Scott, G., Mooney, G. and Brown, U. (2005) 'Managing poverty in the devolved Scotland', in G. Mooney and G. Scott (eds) *Exploring social policy in the 'new' Scotland*, Bristol: The Policy Press, pp 85-110.

Scottish Executive (1999) *Social justice … a Scotland where everyone matters*, Edinburgh: Scottish Executive.

Scottish Executive (2002) *Closing the opportunity gap: Scottish budget for 2002-2006*, Edinburgh: Scottish Executive.

Scottish Government (2007) *The government economic strategy*, Edinburgh: Scottish Government.

Seaton, N. and Osmond, J. (2005) 'Assembly government', in J. Osmond (ed) *Nations and regions: The dynamics of devolution*, Quarterly Monitoring Programme, Wales, April 2005, www.ucl.ac.uk/constitution-unit/monrep/wales/wales_april_2005.pdf

Simeon, R. (2005) 'Federalism and social justice: thinking through the tangle', in S. L. Greer (ed) *Territory, democracy and justice: Territorial politics in advanced industrial democracies*, Basingstoke: Palgrave Macmillan, pp 18–43.

Stone, L. and Muir, R. (2007) *Who are we? Identities in Britain, 2007*, London: IPPR.

Swank, D. (2002) *Global capital, political institutions, and policy change in developed welfare states*, Cambridge: Cambridge University Press.

WAG (Welsh Assembly Government) (2003) *Wales a better country: The strategic agenda of the Welsh Assembly Government*, Cardiff: WAG.

Walker, D. (2002) *In praise of centralism*, available at www.catalystforum.org.uk/pdf/walker.pdf

Wincott, D. (2005) 'Devolution, social democracy and policy diversity in Britain: the case of early childhood education and care', in J. Adams and K. Schmuecker (eds) *Devolution in practice 2006: Public policy differences within the UK*, london: IPPR.

TEN

Monitoring inequality: putting the capability approach to work

Tania Burchardt

Introduction

The capability approach offers an account of equality based on the distribution of substantive freedom. It has been developed by Amartya Sen and, in a somewhat different version, by Martha Nussbaum, over a period of several decades. The approach has been used extensively in international development, most notably in the United Nations Human Development Index, but until recently has rarely been applied to policy or analysis in the global North. Indeed, one of the recurring complaints about the approach is that, while it may be attractive in theory, it is unworkable in practice other than in a crude form. This chapter presents a case study of its application to monitoring inequality in Britain, offering an analysis of the difficulties encountered in translating the theory into a measurement framework and proposing some ways forward.

The context for this study was the creation of the Equality and Human Rights Commission, which in October 2007 took up statutory powers for monitoring and promoting equality and human rights in Britain. The commission supersedes previous separate commissions for gender, race and disability equality, and takes on new commitments to counter discrimination on grounds of sexual orientation, transgender status, age and religion or belief, as well as a central role in protecting human rights. Like its predecessors, the commission is publicly funded but independent from government.

Partly in order to inform the work of the new commission, the government initiated a review of the state of inequality in Britain, chaired by Trevor Phillips. The Equalities Review reported in February 2007, and recommended, among other things, that an equality measurement framework based on the capability approach be adopted by the new commission, and by other public bodies. This recommendation grew out of work by the steering group on measurement, of which the author of this chapter was a member.[1]

Bringing together responsibility for a range of different strands of equality marks a new departure for Britain, although recent European Union (EU) directives make it more likely that this will become the norm, and indeed a number of other European countries already have similar institutions.[2] Although these organisations differ in their scope and in their powers, their common characteristic is bringing together in a single body, at arm's length from government, concerns about equality across a number of different social groups (minority ethnic groups, disabled and non-disabled people, and so on) and across a number of domains of life (employment, housing, family life, and so on).

These developments have been controversial. One concern is that the distinctive histories and character of discrimination associated with each strand, for example, gender and disability, are at risk of being lost in a 'one size fits all' approach to equality (Ben-Galim et al, 2006; Verloo, 2006). How can an account of inequality be given that is sufficiently flexible and sensitive to reflect the particular nature of inequality in each of the different strands, yet comprehensive enough to bring all of them into the same framework? Second, does combining consideration of a range of horizontal inequalities risk marginalising considerations of economic inequality (sometimes referred to as vertical inequality)? Will unified equality bodies advance or hinder the pursuit of broader social justice objectives? Third, and particularly relevant to the institutional form adopted in Britain, is it helpful to bring together the different theoretical foundations and practices associated with equality and human rights advocacy or is this a 'forced marriage' harmful to both parties?

Examining the process of the development and adoption of a capability measurement framework therefore provides an interesting case study in two respects: first, as an example of the application of the capability approach in the context of a developed country, and second, as an example of the kind of framework that could be used to meet the challenges faced by a unified equality commission, in Britain but also potentially elsewhere in Europe.

The chapter assumes a basic degree of familiarity with the capability approach and does not attempt to defend or establish its credentials vis-à-vis other accounts of equality or social justice. Readers who are not familiar with the approach or who are interested in these more fundamental questions are referred to Sen (for example, 1985, 1992, 1999), Nussbaum (2000, 2006) and the growing literature their writing has produced (for a recent collection, see Kaufman, 2006), including critical appraisals (Sugden, 1993; Stewart, 2005; Dowding, 2006), and in-depth analysis of the relationship between the capability approach and human rights (Vizard, 2006).

Instead, the chapter illustrates the definitional, theoretical and methodological challenges that arise in applying the capability approach to a particular policy context. The next section analyses the definition of equality adopted by the Equalities Review. The following section discusses the specification and justification of a list of central and valuable capabilities, while the third section considers the relationship between process and opportunity freedoms. The fourth section examines the limitations of the tools available to detect inequalities in autonomy, choice and control. The chapter concludes with some reflections on the application of the capability approach and the extent to which it can help to meet the challenge of providing an overarching framework for monitoring diverse inequalities in the context of a European country.

A capability-based definition of an equal society

The final report of the Equalities Review (2007, p 6) recommended the adoption of the following definition of an equal society:

> An equal society protects and promotes equal real freedom and substantive opportunity to live in the ways people value and would choose, so that everyone can flourish. An equal society recognises people's different needs, situations and goals, and removes the barriers that limit what people can do and can be.

The definition avoided using the terms 'functioning' and 'capability', despite their central place in the capability lexicon, because public consultation demonstrated that they were easily misinterpreted. Disability groups in particular felt that they implied judgements about personal adequacy.[3]

Nevertheless, the definition has a number of features that illustrate distinctive characteristics of the capability approach, and its potential usefulness for a unified equality commission. First, it focuses on ends rather than means. Equality will be judged on what people are enabled to do and be, not on the resources available to them, or on the 'effort' the state – or anyone else – has made to achieve equality. This sets it apart from traditional equality measures based solely on income, or on welfare expenditure, for example. Concepts like multiple deprivation and social exclusion have also recognised that income poverty is not the only important dimension in thinking about equality, but the capability approach goes one step further in arguing that income is not the right kind of thing to measure at all – it is an input rather than a valuable outcome in its own right. This is especially important in the context of a unified equality commission, because the degree of inequality between different social groups varies on different dimensions. There is significant employment inequality between the majority white population and the Bangladeshi minority in Britain, for example, but rather less – as far as we know – between gay men and straight men. On the other hand, gay men face huge discrimination in support for family life. For disabled children, opportunity to participate in mainstream education may be particularly salient, and so on. A single input, even one that has such far-reaching effects like income, cannot reflect all these different domains of inequality.

Second, the definition recognises people's different needs. This moves it beyond 'first generation' concepts of discrimination, which concentrated on ensuring that everyone was treated identically. This becomes particularly important when making comparisons across some groups, for example across the disabled and non-disabled population, where identical treatment can translate into very different real freedoms. If you cannot read print, being supplied with an identical written job specification to your sighted fellow-applicant does not produce a 'level playing field'. This principle is established in UK law, for example in the 1995 Disability Discrimination Act.

Third, the definition refers to protecting and *promoting* equality, and so removing barriers. These terms signal that there is a role for intervention, on the part of the state and others, to ensure that equality is achieved. This sets it apart from conceptions based on negative liberty, or non-interference, which emphasise freedom *from* rather than freedom *to*. Real freedom, or substantive opportunity, means having the wherewithal to achieve the valuable outcomes in question.

Fourth, the definition recognises the diversity of people's goals. This is important in three ways. First, by focusing on substantive *freedoms*, it avoids the paternalism and cultural imperialism associated with fixing a single 'thick' account of the good life to which everyone must subscribe. An equal society is one in which everyone has the opportunity to participate in a common set of central capabilities, but they need not do so. They might choose to pursue quite other objectives. Second, it gives a central place to individual agency in shaping people's lives, rather than regarding them as victims or pawns. This needs to be balanced, of course, with a recognition of the structural constraints under which people operate. Third, in contrast to utilitarianism and related theories, the definition does not assume that people are interested solely in their own happiness or subjective well-being.[4] Happiness may be one of the goals that people identify for themselves, but it is rarely the sole objective, and is more often a by-product of other valued activities.

Recognising the diversity of people's goals is particularly important for a framework designed to assess inequality across a range of social groups, including different ethnic and religious groups, since cultures and belief systems vary greatly in the emphasis they place on different life objectives. Of course, this also gives rise to potential tensions. In so far as there are conflicts between individual and group freedoms, the definition proposed by the Equalities Review, and in general by the capability approach, resolves in favour of the individual, and in this specific sense is an individualistic framework. This is not to deny that the existence of groups is sometimes instrumentally important for securing individual freedom – indeed, collective action is a powerful mechanism for promoting real freedom – but the significance of groups is seen as instrumental rather than intrinsic.[5]

Specifying and justifying a capability list

One of the respects in which the capability approach is radically – and, in the case of Sen's own work, intentionally – incomplete is the absence of an agreed specification of the capabilities that are to be evaluated. In principle, the range of capabilities is infinite, from the trivial to the profound. A selection is necessary to implement the approach in any given context.

Broadly speaking, there are two approaches to the selection procedure, represented by Nussbaum and Sen respectively.[6] Nussbaum (2000) emphasises the universality of broad components of human flourishing, and warns against inadvertent replication of existing power structures in the course of defining a list of central and valuable capabilities by relying too heavily on subjects' own views. Her list is therefore derived mainly through reasoning from ethical and philosophical first principles, although it is open and revisable in the light of experience and cross-cultural discussion. Sen, by contrast, emphasises the importance of being context-specific from the outset and ensuring that the process is participatory, or at least, open to democratic scrutiny and amendment (for example, Sen 1996; Alkire, 2002). Consequently, he has declined to propose or endorse any specific list of basic capabilities.

Our method aimed to combine these approaches in a two-stage process. In the first stage, we drew up a list of basic capabilities based on international human rights agreements; specifically, the International Covenant on Civil and Political Rights (ICCPR) and the International Covenant on Economic, Social and Cultural Rights (ICESCR). These two covenants can together be seen as codifying the Universal Declaration of Human Rights. Starting from the international human rights framework would, we believed, help to ensure that the list was sufficiently universal and non-arbitrary. Vizard's previous work (2006) had argued that the international human rights framework could be taken to represent a pragmatic consensus on valuable human freedoms. We could have adopted Nussbaum's list as a starting point but its terminology and content seemed remote from contemporary British life (for example, 'having one's bodily boundaries treated as sovereign' or 'being able to live with concern for and in relation to animals, plants, and the world of nature').[7] Moreover, in the specific context in which our evaluation was taking place, drawing on human rights agreements to supply the dimensions of an equality measurement framework was especially attractive, tying together the two parts of the remit of the Equality and Human Rights Commission.

However, in the highly politicised environment of the equalities agenda in the UK, it seemed unlikely that a list generated without specific reference to, or involvement of, the population to which the framework would be applied, stood any chance of being endorsed by policy makers, however fine its philosophical pedigree. In addition, we wanted to ensure that the process was sensitive to issues of particular significance to minorities in Britain today. Accordingly, the second stage of our procedure was a targeted deliberative consultation exercise. The fieldwork was carried out by Ipsos-MORI (see Ipsos-MORI, 2007). Two full-day workshops were conducted, each with 30 participants recruited on the street and by telephone from among the general public, and a series of four smaller-scale workshops and seven in-depth interviews with individuals and groups at high risk of discrimination.[8] In total around 100 people were involved in the consultation.

Participants undertook two exercises. In the first, they were invited to develop and discuss their views about the aspects of people's lives (their own and others') that were most important, and should be protected and promoted for all. What was a really good life like? What would a person need in order to flourish? In the second exercise, participants were presented with our list based on international human rights covenants, and asked to compare it with their own list built up during the first exercise. Were there items on their own list that were missing from the human rights-based list? Were there any on the human rights-based list that should not be there?

This combined method threw up a number of problems of principle and practice, which are discussed below.

Role of deliberative consultation in principle

One of the hazards in combining methods is that they may produce inconsistent results. In our case, how were the lists generated by each part of the process to be combined? What weight should be given to the views of participants in the relatively small-scale and statistically unrepresentative samples that were convened for the consultation, as compared to the 'wisdom of ages' collected in the international covenants? Or, to put it another way, what weight should be given to ideas developed as a political compromise 60 years ago in the shadow of the Second World War, compared to the lived experience of the people at the sharp end of inequality and discrimination in Britain today?

The strictest rule would have been to accept an item only if it appeared explicitly and spontaneously on both lists. In practice this seemed overly restrictive. A number of the most basic human rights did not appear on the spontaneously generated list from the deliberative consultation, because they were taken for granted. For example, the right to life in Article 6 of the ICCPR gives rise to the capability of 'being alive' on the human rights-based capability list, but it was not spontaneously mentioned by participants in the deliberative exercises. When participants were presented with the human rights-based list, they were happy to endorse the inclusion of these very basic freedoms.

On the other hand, a number of items generated through the deliberative exercise, while not explicitly included on the human rights-based list, could be seen as implicit. For example, participants mentioned 'being able to be creative'. A right of 'creativity' is not separately identified in the international human rights framework, but it can be seen as implicit in the combination of freedom of expression (Article 19, ICCPR), right to education (Article 13, ICESCR) and right to cultural life (Article 15, ICESCR). It therefore seemed reasonable to treat some capabilities mentioned by participants, like 'being able to be creative', as refinements of the central capabilities identified in the human rights-based list.

More problematic were cases where items on the human rights-based list were not endorsed by the general public or by particular groups in the deliberative consultation, even when brought to their attention for consideration. In the event, this arose for only one item: being able to form and join a trade union (which is an explicit right in ICESCR).

This is perhaps an interesting example in practice of the distinction Sen makes between valuing and having reason to value (for example, Sen, 1998). Participants in the consultation did not actually value being able to join a trade union. However, it can be argued that they have good reason to value this freedom – bearing in mind that this is a freedom, not an obligation. Were it denied, as it is in Malaysia or Columbia, for example, and the expected deterioration in terms and conditions of employment ensued, the right to form and join a trade union would, one can reasonably assume, be once again highly valued. It is precisely because this freedom has been secured in the past in Britain, that it is not valued in the present.

In principle, there could also have been difficulty over capabilities generated by the deliberative consultation but neither explicit nor implicit in the international human rights framework. In practice, there were no items that fell into this category. This perhaps bears testament to the universality and comprehensiveness of the international human rights framework. There were, however, items mentioned that were not strictly speaking capabilities at all. Several of these described conditions that were considered necessary for living a good or flourishing life, for example, receiving respect from others, and social integration, but which were not activities an individual could engage in or states of being (that is, they were not capabilities). These preconditions were incorporated into the measurement framework as determinants of individual entitlements and as social conversion factors that affected the use to which individuals could put their entitlements, as described in more detail below.

The decision rule we adopted was to include on the final list items generated by *either* the deliberative consultation *or* the international human rights framework (see Figure 10.1: the union of the dotted line and solid line sets). We argued that people had reason to value all elements deriving from the international human rights framework, whether or not they were endorsed by the deliberative consultation, and that they should therefore be included in the final list. Moreover, we recommended that the core list, deriving from the international human rights framework, should be *refined and supplemented* in future through deliberative and other mechanisms, but that the core itself should be regarded as irreducible (Burchardt and Vizard, 2007, p 3).

The issue of inclusion of items spontaneously generated by the deliberative consultation but neither explicit nor implicit in the international human rights framework did not, in practice, arise (empty subset in Figure 10.1). What would have been the appropriate response, had it done so? Given the limited reach of the deliberative exercise it

Figure 10.1: Overlaps between human rights-based capabilities list and list generated through deliberative consultation

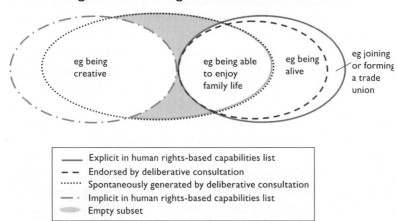

Notes: Final list was union of dotted and solid line sets. Not to scale: size of area does not represent number of elements in set.

would have seemed unbalanced to include an entirely new item on an equal footing to those deriving from the international human rights framework. On the other hand, the history of the identification of human needs and values is a history of struggle. Demands articulated today by a minority may be tomorrow's consensus, so that gaps in the human rights framework identified by members of a deliberative consultation group at particular risk of discrimination and disadvantage should be given particularly close attention. It would perhaps have been appropriate to include such items *provisionally*, subject to endorsement in broader, or deeper, participatory or survey-based research.

Implementing deliberative consultation in practice

Aside from the issues of principle at stake in combining deliberative consultation with a list based on international human rights agreements, there were also practical issues that arose in implementing the combined methods.

First, there was a serious mismatch between political and research timescales. We are, of course, by no means the first researchers to confront this difficulty. The entire process from commissioning to incorporating the results of the deliberative consultation was constrained to a period of less than three months. Large market research or polling companies were the only organisations with the infrastructure in place to recruit the necessary number of participants in the timescale required, and these organisations are relative newcomers to the philosophy and methods of deliberative and participatory approaches. Thus, although the exercises were designed to promote discussion between participants with diverse opinions, with a view to exploring their deeper beliefs and values and observing how attitudes changed through deliberation, there was a tendency in the actual implementation of the consultation towards minimising disagreement (for example, by allocating participants to subgroups according to their political affiliation). In addition, consultation with some groups – older people, for example – was not as extensive (or intensive) as some other groups.[9]

Other difficulties were inherent to the method itself. First, communicating the purpose of the exercise to participants was not straightforward. A number of participants initially felt that equality was impossible to achieve, and therefore there was no point discussing the question, 'equality of what?'. It was necessary to engage participants' imaginations and to give them a licence to be 'unrealistic' before discussion about what everyone *should* be able to enjoy could be got under way.

This difficulty relates to the discussion in the capabilities literature, and more broadly in psychology, on adaptive preferences (Kahneman et al, 1999; Teschl and Comim, 2005). Experiences of life shape beliefs about what is possible, and beliefs about what is possible are a significant influence on expectations and preferences. Given that the participants in our deliberative consultation were living in a society in which economic inequality has been growing for much of the past quarter of a century, and in which progress towards social equality, for example, for gay people, had been frequently halted by resistance from conservative opinion, it was not surprising that many doubted the feasibility of a broad equality agenda. What the general public said they wanted, initially at least, was bounded by what they believed to be possible. Differentiation between conditioned expectations and deeply held beliefs that are robust to changes in information is not easily achieved within a limited period of time. This highlights the danger of basing a normative exercise exclusively on participatory methods, especially if the exercise were to be undertaken without explicit inclusion of minority views.

Finally, we were concerned about the extent to which the outcomes of the consultation were influenced by the stimulus materials provided to participants and by input from the facilitators. These are familiar concerns in this kind of research (Laird et al, 2000; Abelson et al, 2007). Unfortunately we did not have sufficient resources to test the significance of this concern, for example, by providing different stimulus material to different groups, or comparing outcomes for different facilitators, but this would be a useful focus for future methodological research.

Specification of a final list

Despite these reservations, fascinating findings emerged from the deliberative consultation. A full report is given by Ipsos-MORI (2007). From a capability perspective, one revealing outcome was that a number of items from Nussbaum's list, which we had rejected as being too remote from everyday experience in 21st-century Britain, re-emerged through the deliberative process. Participants spontaneously included on their lists: hope, joy and celebration, having goals, and being close to nature. None of these is explicit in the international human rights framework, but each is clearly included in Nussbaum's list (2000, pp 78-80). 'Hope' falls within the major heading of 'Emotions', which Nussbaum explains as including, for example, the capability 'to experience longing' and 'not having one's emotional development blighted by overwhelming fear and anxiety'. 'Joy and celebration' is encompassed by the combination of Nussbaum's 'Affiliation' (which includes being able to 'engage in various forms of social interaction') and 'Play' (which includes 'being able to laugh'). 'Having goals' seems a fairly direct counterpart for Nussbaum's 'Practical Reason: being able to form a conception of the good and to engage in critical reflection about the planning of one's life'. Finally, being 'close to nature' is one element under Nussbaum's heading 'Other species'.

One possible conclusion to draw is that just as 'all roads lead to Rome', so all processes lead to the same list – the conclusion of Qizilbash's (2002) review of the wide range of lists of multidimensional well-being that have been proposed. However, it is more accurate, I think, to see the emphasis in each list as reflecting its origins. Nussbaum's is avowedly Aristotelian, and hence prominently includes capabilities significantly influenced by a person's 'internal capacities', including the senses, reason and emotion. These are not entirely absent from the international human rights-based list, but are implicit rather than explicit, because of its origins in an agreement between states about the human freedoms they will protect and promote. Its focus is therefore more on the activities and states of being directly affected by state action.

Combining the results of the deliberative consultation and the human rights-based list involved judgements about the extent to which elements overlapped or needed to be separately identified, and how they should be grouped into major headings or domains. This process should itself be open to scrutiny and is accordingly reported in detail in Vizard and Burchardt (2007). The question of how to group individual items into broader domains is given little attention in the literature, probably because it is regarded as a merely organisational issue rather than one of principle. In practice, however, the grouping of items into domains can make a significant difference to the prominence given to different elements and how the list is used politically, and there is a need to develop principles to govern this stage of this process.

One approach would be to subject empirical data on the prevalence and distribution of capability-deprivation for all the items on the list to factor or principal component analysis to generate groups or domains. This has two disadvantages. First, it assumes that capabilities that happen to be correlated with each other should be grouped together, and this is not necessarily the case. For example, longevity is in most societies correlated with higher levels of education, but that does not imply that 'Life' should be grouped together with 'Education'. Second, such a procedure requires data on all the elements to be available before a list can be finalised. This falls foul of Robeyns' (2003) criterion, that the selection of capabilities on an (ideal) list should not be data-driven. It may be that compromises have to be made at the level of measurement but the construction of a list should be free of such constraints. Otherwise, data gaps will never be identified and filled.

An alternative approach, and the one which we adopted, is to group items together thematically. Box 10.1 gives the 10 main headings; the full list, which runs to several pages, is given in Burchardt and Vizard (2007). Of course, this does not generate a unique solution. For example, we identified life, physical security and health as three separate domains, but they could equally plausibly have been combined. We judged that being alive was, self-evidently, a precondition for enjoying any of the other capabilities listed and consequently merited a domain to itself. Life expectancy is also extremely unequally distributed across social groups. The distinction between the physical security and health domains was based on the fact that the former includes more negative liberties (freedom from...), while the latter is based more clearly on positive liberties (freedom to...).

Box 10.1: Domains of central and valuable capabilities

Being alive

Living in physical security

Being healthy

Being knowledgeable, being able to understand and reason, and having the skills to participate in society

Enjoying a comfortable standard of living, with independence and security

Engaging in productive and valued activities

Enjoying individual, family and social life

Participating in decision making, having a voice and influence

Being and expressing yourself, and having self-respect

Knowing you will be protected and treated fairly by the law

We grouped capabilities relating to employment and to domestic and care work under a single heading of productive and valued activities. This was partly to signal the value of unpaid work alongside paid work and to recognise the trade-offs that often have to be made between the two kinds of activity. On the other hand, this meant that splitting caring-related capabilities into work aspects and emotional and interpersonal aspects (included under 'individual, family and social life'). Similarly, self-respect (included in 'identity, expression and self-respect') needs to be read with most of the other domains – it is as important in regard to standard of living (being able to go out without shame), as it is to (mental) health, and to voice and influence. In general, the domains need to be treated holistically, rather than giving too much emphasis on artificial divisions between them.

A final issue that arose in specifying the list was whether we needed separate lists for different groups in the population, for example, for women, for disabled people or for children. Given the intended use of the list by a unified equalities commission, with responsibility for monitoring inequality by gender, age, ethnicity, disability, religion/belief, sexual orientation and transgender status, and in particular for examining cross-cutting inequalities, there was a strong presumption in favour of a single list that could be used across the board. Clearly, some items on the list were particularly pertinent for inequality among some groups. For example, freedom from domestic violence is an especially important aspect of gender equality, and being able to access and use public spaces freely (under the domain of identity, expression and self-respect) is of particular significance to gay and bisexual people and, for different reasons, to disabled people. But although inequality in these capabilities is more pronounced and more contentious for some groups than for others, they are nevertheless freedoms which it is important to secure for all.

The exception to this reasoning was a list for children. It did not seem appropriate to include, for example, the capability to participate in free and fair elections in an assessment of inequality either between children, or between children and other age groups. There were a number of other capabilities on the main list that did not seem appropriate for children, for example in relation to reproduction and marriage, and ownership of property and financial products. On the other hand, there were additional capabilities that were important for children but not for other age groups, for example, being protected from (parental) neglect, and being able to access safe, enjoyable and developmental play. We therefore developed a separate list, tailored to the particular interests of children. This list is provisional because, although teenagers were one of the groups that made up the deliberative consultation, we did not have the opportunity to involve children of different ages or to consult in detail with the organisations that represent them. A separate project is now under way to address these issues, including analysis of the UN Convention on the Rights of the Child and consultation with parents and children.

It is interesting to reflect on why, if our reasoning was correct, a separate list is required for children but for no other subgroup of the population. First, childhood is an intense period of capability-formation, unlike any other period of life, and this requires particular support and protection if each child's potential is to be fully developed. This explains why some capabilities need to be added to the main list. Second, the paternalism inherent in restricting someone's freedom in their own interests is more often justifiable in the case of children than for any other group, precisely because their period of capability-formation – including the capabilities of being knowledgeable and engaging in critical reflection – is not yet complete. This explains the need to exclude some capabilities from the list, like participation in elections or freedom in matters of marriage and reproduction.[10]

Developing a measurement framework

The framework

Specifying and justifying a list of central and valuable capabilities is necessary but not sufficient for putting the capability approach to work. How should the list be used to monitor inequality? Drawing on Sen's earlier work on entitlements and conversion factors (for example, Sen, 1981, 1985) and ideas developed by Arndt and Volkert (2007), we recommended the framework illustrated in Figure 10.2.

Figure 10.2: Capability measurement framework

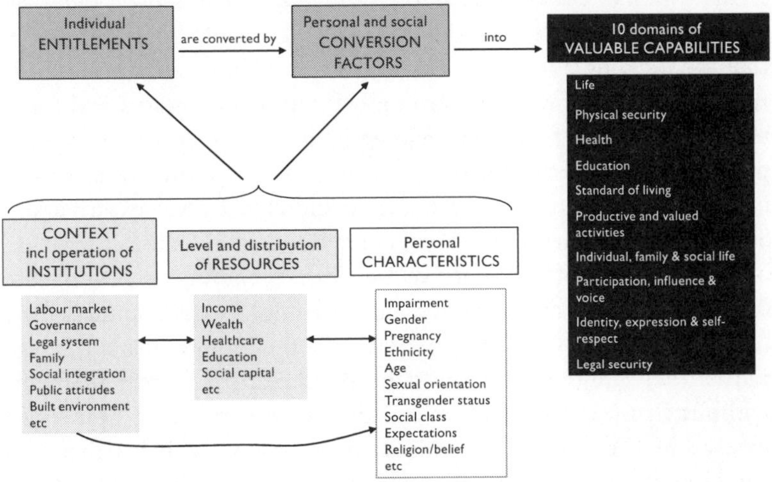

The framework is designed to address three needs: to show how the outcomes that are monitored relate to the determinants of inequality; to assist with the exploration of the causes of inequality; and to identify where policy interventions can be made.

The dark box on the right-hand side of the diagram summarises the 10 domains of central and valuable capabilities on the final list, developed as described in the previous section. The freedom that an individual experiences in each of these domains, and hence also the inequality between individuals' freedom, is determined by the entitlements the individual commands and the rate at which, or extent to which, they can convert these entitlements into valuable beings and doings, as illustrated along the top row of the figure.

Entitlements in this context refer to the formal and informal goods, services and other resources that an individual can actually access and command. The coverage of the term is therefore both narrower and broader than legal rights: narrower, because a legal entitlement to protection from discrimination in employment, for example, that cannot be realised in practice due to the lack of an effective enforcement mechanism would not constitute an entitlement in this sense; and broader, because entitlements here would include the wages an individual was able to command in the labour market and help from a grandparent with childcare, neither of which are legal rights.

Conversion factors may be individual or social. An example of an individual conversion factor is a visual impairment: someone with a visual impairment may convert their entitlement to income, for example, into the valuable outcome of being able to go out safely and securely (under the domain of physical security) at a lower rate than someone without an impairment, because they need a guide dog. In this case, the individual conversion factor interacts with a social conversion factor: the provision (or otherwise) of pavement surfaces and street furniture designed to assist people with visual impairment. In general, public goods give rise to social conversion factors and variations in individuals' characteristics give rise to individual conversion factors. Sen (1992) identifies other sources of heterogeneity in the conversion of entitlements into substantive freedom, including environmental diversities (for example, weather and epidemiology), economic setting (including the existence or otherwise of a functioning market), social norms (determining what must be purchased to 'appear in public without shame', for example) and distribution within a household. Analysing the sources of inequality in terms of inequalities in entitlement and the effect of conversion factors can be a helpful way to understand the causes of inequality.

Individual entitlements and conversion factors are determined by the wider context, the level and distribution of resources and individual characteristics, as illustrated in the bottom row of the diagram. The context includes the operation of economic, political, legal, social and cultural institutions as well as the built and natural environment. The operation of these institutions influences, and is influenced by, the level and distribution of resources within a society. Finally, personal characteristics, including those that are a particular focus of interest for equality commissions like ethnicity and gender, may directly affect the entitlements available to someone, and their conversion of entitlements into valuable outcomes.

Policy interventions can be targeted at either the context or the level and distribution of resources (or both). Policy interventions to alter personal characteristics are either impossible (for example, with respect to ethnicity), undesirable (for example, sexual orientation) or indirect (for example, expectations). This does not of course imply that policy cannot influence the extent to which a given personal characteristic is a determinant of inequality in outcomes. Policies can directly or indirectly change the entitlements available to people with different characteristics and the social conversion factors.

Outcomes and processes

The measurement framework as described relies on differences in capabilities to monitor inequality. The implication is that if two people have the same set of central and valuable capabilities then there is no inequality between them. This, indeed, appears to be part of the definition of the capability approach, which answers the question, 'Equality of what?' with the response, 'Capability'. However, Sen has also written about the distinction between opportunity freedom (capability) and process freedom, and has argued that they are irreducible (Sen, 1999, 2003).

Earlier generations of equality monitoring have tended to emphasise process at the expense of outcomes. For example, 'equal opportunities' is often taken to mean applying the same procedures to everyone. This has led to considerable effort being expended on demonstrating that the procedures have been applied without discrimination, with less effort devoted to ensuring that the result of that procedure offers candidates substantively equal freedom. It therefore seems a step forward to focus attention on what these procedures achieve rather than the procedures themselves. But could the balance tip too far the other way?

A large majority of instances of discrimination lead to substantially unequal freedom. If gay couples are treated with disrespect by the general public, their freedom to use public spaces is curtailed. But it is possible to construct examples in which discrimination would not lead to significantly diminished freedom. A gay man being refused a job purely on the basis of his sexuality is a clear instance of objectionable discrimination. But supposing this man was readily able to secure another job of equal status and pay, the diminution of his freedom in the domain of productive activities barely registers. By construction we can also assume, perhaps unrealistically, that his self-respect is unaffected, and so on. The point of the example is that in theory a *process* may be unjust and unequal, even where the substantive outcome is not.

This issue arose in the development of the measurement framework specifically in relation to self-respect and respect from others. Self-respect is included in the list under the 'identity, expression and self-respect' domain. But participants in the deliberative consultation also wanted to include 'being treated with respect' on the list. Strictly speaking, this is not a capability, since it is something that is done to you rather than by you; it may be instrumental in achieving self-respect but it is not a state of being or an activity. Yet the prevalence of such discriminatory attitudes and behaviour would seem to be an important feature for an equality framework to monitor.

Sen's position is that both process and opportunity freedom matter: he is a committed pluralist in this as in many other matters. For a measurement framework this is an untidy solution, but may nevertheless be necessary. Each of the domains of central and valuable capabilities need to be monitored in terms of outcomes (the extent of freedom enjoyed by different groups in each domain) and processes (the extent of discrimination experienced by different groups).

Measuring choice and control

The picture is not yet complete. Ascertaining the extent of inequality of outcomes in central and valuable domains of life and the prevalence of discriminatory processes does not quite add up to an assessment of the degree of inequality of real freedom. We also need to know about the other outcomes available to each person that they could have secured, had they wished to do so. So we might observe that someone is not in employment, but to know whether 'being employed' is in their capability set, we need an indication of whether they could have been in employment. Various approaches have been suggested, but none is wholly adequate (Robeyns, 2006).

Some have concentrated on the constraints that limit the range of options available to people (Desai and Shah, 1988; Chiappero Martinetti, 1996). Lovell et al (1994) have a theoretical model based on a capability production function, looking at the inputs (entitlements), conversion factors and potential outputs, thereby calculating a capability production frontier. Arndt and Volkert (2007) focus on instrumental freedoms: general purpose capabilities that help to secure a wide capability set. Burchardt (2006) estimates the probability that a functioning is within an individual's capability set by comparing each person's achievements to the range of functionings that others with 'similar' characteristics and circumstances attain, with the definition of 'similar' treated as explicitly normative (to take account of the divergent views on what aspects of their life an individual can reasonably be expected to change). These are attractive approaches but all depend on either knowing, or assuming, which factors are relevant in constraining or facilitating a person's capability.

Anand et al (2005) take a more direct approach, attempting to extract relevant questions from the British Household Panel Survey (BHPS). For example, for the capability of 'being able to move from place to place', they used access to a vehicle, and for the capability of 'being able to have good health', they used, 'does your health in any way limit your daily activities compared to most people of your age?'. Since the BHPS was not designed with the capability approach in mind, the fit is in many cases far from perfect. To overcome this difficulty, Anand and van Hees (2006) implemented their own questionnaire on a smaller sample inviting respondents to indicate, for example, where they feel the 'scope to act with personal integrity in my life' is on a scale of 1 (very good) to 7 (very inadequate). This approach is attractive in its transparency, but without detailed cognitive testing of the way respondents understand the questions, it is difficult to interpret the results.

Alkire (2005) and Ibrahim and Alkire (2007) propose supplementing the measurement of outcomes – being healthy, participating in leisure activities and so forth – with questions on the degree of choice and control that individuals had in reaching those outcomes, based on self-determination theory. This has the advantage of being well validated in psychological research (see Ryan and Deci, 2000; Chirkov et al, 2003). For example, respondents might be asked to rank on a scale of 1 to 6 the significance of each of the following motivations for their health-related activities:

(1) desire to avoid punishment or gain reward;
(2) desire to avoid blame or so that other people speak well of you; and
(3) your own values and/or interests.

A mixture of motivations (1) to (3) is likely to be present in any decision or action; the greater the weight given by respondents to (3), the greater is the degree of autonomy exhibited. Questions of this kind have been tested in a wide range of cultural contexts and found to be reasonably easily understood and to produce reliable responses (Ibrahim and Alkire, 2007). However, as the proponents of this approach recognise, it is not immune from problems of adaptation or the internalisation of oppressive social norms. An individual's perception of their autonomy may not coincide with the degree to which they could in fact exercise other choices, although the individual's own assessment must surely contribute importantly to any overall evaluation of autonomy.

Knowing the health outcome someone has secured, and the extent to which they perceive this outcome reflects their own values and interests, is a good approximation of their health capability, even in the absence of information about the quality and range of alternatives available to the individual. More focused, probably qualitative, research could usefully shed light on groups in the population, or aspects of life, where the range of alternatives is wider, or narrower, than the individual's own sense of autonomy suggests.

Fortunately, although autonomy measurement techniques need further development and testing, the implications for the practice of monitoring inequality are not as serious as one might think. Having good outcomes in each of the 10 domains is a solid foundation for securing a wide capability set, even if the domains themselves are measured in terms of functionings rather than capabilities. Moreover, as Robeyns (2003) suggests, when making comparisons between large social groups, like men and women, with heterogeneous preferences and values *within* each group, it is reasonable to assume for many observed outcomes that any difference is the result of constrained capabilities rather than autonomous choice. For example, although some men and some women may freely choose to be less healthy than they could be, there is no reason to assume that women are systematically more likely to choose to be less healthy than men, or vice versa, given the same capability set. Even where there is more doubt – for example, when comparing cultural practices between ethnic groups – it is reasonable to start from the assumption of no systematic differences in freely endorsed values across groups (and hence attribute observed differences in outcomes to differences in real freedom), and then seek out specific evidence to challenge this assumption.

Conclusion

Maintaining pluralism with respect to the aspects of equality with which one is concerned – outcomes, processes and autonomy – and with respect to the domains of life that are relevant, leads to complexity in measurement and high informational demands. This is often seen as a weakness compared to the elegant efficiency of summarising inequality with a single number, like a Gini coefficient for the income distribution. Although summary statistics of this kind have great appeal to policy makers, they cannot capture the richness of the concepts of equality that are embedded in theories of social justice such as the capability approach. Just as the UN's Human Development Index succeeded in moving development economics away from exclusive concentration on GDP per capita towards consideration of health and education, so one can hope that with careful attention to communication and presentation, governments in the developed world can be persuaded to adopt a genuinely multidimensional interpretation of equality. The fundamental challenges issued by the capability approach to single-valued accounts of human well-being, such as utilitarianism and welfarism, are as relevant in the global North as the global South.

The framework presented in this chapter has advantages in the specific context of unified equality bodies, such as the Equality and Human Rights Commission in Britain and similar organisations elsewhere in Europe. Starting from a general theory of social justice, the framework is comprehensive, but also facilitates strand-specific analysis, by gender, age or other characteristics, singly or in combination. Horizontal and vertical inequalities can be considered jointly: economic inequality can be analysed through standard of living and employment as valuable capabilities, through examining the instrumental role resources have in promoting or inhibiting the achievement of a range of other capabilities, or by including social class as an additional equality characteristic for analysis alongside age and gender and so on. Finally, by adopting international human rights conventions as a starting point for a consensus on central and valuable human capabilities – the domains of life in which equality is to be achieved – the equalities and human rights agendas can become mutually reinforcing, rather than seen as in tension with each other. Although more methodological development and data collection remains to be done, the fears some commentators expressed that the capability approach is unworkable in practice appear to have been much exaggerated.

Notes

[1] The Steering Group was led by Polly Vizard and Tania Burchardt. Other members included Sandra Fredman, Ian Gough, Julie Litchfield, Katherine Rake and Giovanni Razzu, all of whom contributed importantly to the development of the ideas reported in this chapter. Responsibility for the views expressed, and for any errors of fact or judgement, remains with the author alone.

[2] Article 13 of the European Union Treaty of Amsterdam, implemented in the Council Directives 2000/78/EC and 2000/43/EC. Northern Ireland, the Republic of Ireland, Belgium, Hungary, Lithuania, the Netherlands and Norway have officially recognised equality organisations with a broad remit.

[3] Responses to a consultation on the Equalities Review interim report, unpublished.

[4] Some utilitarians recognised that happiness was more likely to be achieved if it was not a conscious aim; nevertheless, happiness remains the underlying object of value for the theory.

[5] This formulation ducks the issue of conflicts between the freedom of one individual and another, for example, my freedom to be openly gay and your freedom to express your views condemning homosexuality. These tensions are inherent in any liberal theory and have been explored thoroughly in the philosophical and legal literatures.

[6] Others have proposed alternatives, including using other theoretical frameworks as a starting point, applying social scientific tools to assess the attitudes and beliefs of a given population, variations on participatory methods and so on. See Vizard and Burchardt (2007) for a fuller discussion.

[7] As we shall see below, our initial assessment proved to be inaccurate in some respects.

[8] Four workshops each with eight participants: lesbian, gay and bisexual people; people with physical impairment; teenagers; and people from minority ethnic groups. Seven in-depth interviews: with a Sikh woman, a Muslim man, a Muslim woman, a Jewish woman, a blind woman, a hearing-impaired man and a dyslexic woman.

[9] Further deliberative consultation has now been commissioned to make good some of these omissions.

[10] This does not preclude other groups, such as disabled people, drawing up lists oriented towards their particular priorities and needs in a given context.

References

Abelson, J., Forest, P. G., Eyles, J., Casebeer, A., Martin, E. and Mackean, G. (2007) 'Examining the role of context in the implementation of a deliberative public participation experiment: results from a Canadian comparative study', *Social Science and Medicine*, vol 64, no 10, pp 2115-28.

Alkire, S. (2002) *Valuing freedoms: Sen's capability approach and poverty reduction*, Oxford: Oxford University Press.

Alkire, S. (2005) 'Subjective quantitative studies of human agency', *Social Indicators Research*, vol 74, no 1, pp 217-60.

Anand, P. and van Hees, M. (2006) 'Capabilities and achievements: a survey', *Journal of Socio-Economics*, vol 35, no 2, pp 268-84.

Anand, P., Hunter, G. and Smith, R. (2005) 'Capabilities and well-being: evidence based on the Sen-Nussbaum approach to welfare', *Social Indicators Research*, vol 74, pp 9-55.

Arndt, C. and Volkert, J. (2007) 'A capability approach for official German poverty and wealth reports: conceptual background and first empirical results', Institut für Angewandte Wirtschaftsforschung (IAW) Discussion Paper 27, Tübingen, www.iaw.edu/pdf/dp2007-27.pdf (accessed 20/09/07).

Ben-Galim, D., Campbell, M. and Lewis, J. (2006) 'Equality and diversity: a new approach to gender equality policy in the UK', *International Journal of Law in Context*, vol 3, no 1, pp 19-33.

Burchardt, T. (2006) *Incomes, functionings and capabilities: The well-being of disabled people in Britain*, PhD thesis, University of London.

Burchardt, T. and Vizard, P. (2007) *Definition of equality and framework for measurement*, Final Recommendations of the Equalities Review Steering Group on Measurement, Paper 1, CASEpaper 120. Also available at www.theequalitiesreview.org.uk/upload/assets/www.theequalitiesreview.org.uk/paper1equality.pdf (accessed 18/05/07).

Chiappero Martinetti, E. (1996) 'Standard of living evaluation based on Sen's approach: some methodological suggestions', *Politeia*, vol 12, no 43/44, pp 37-54.

Chirkov, V., Ryan, R., Kim, Y. and Kaplan, U. (2003) 'Differentiating autonomy from individualism and independence: a self-determination theory perspective on internalization of cultural orientations and well-being', *Journal of Personality and Social Psychology*, vol 84, no 1, pp 97-110.

Desai, M. and Shah, D. (1988) 'An econometric approach to the measurement of poverty', *Oxford Economic Papers*, vol 40, pp 505-22.

Dowding, K. (2006) 'Can capabilities reconcile freedom and equality?', *Journal of political philosophy*, vol 14, no 3, pp 323-36.

Equalities Review (2007) *Fairness and freedom: The final report of the Equalities Review*, London: Equalities Review.

Ibrahim, S. and Alkire, S. (2007) *Agency and empowerment: A proposal for internationally comparable indicators*, Oxford Poverty and Human Development Initiative Working Paper 4, www.ophi.org.uk/pubs/Ibrahim_Empowerment.pdf (accessed 16/10/07).

Ipsos–MORI (2007) *Consulting for a capability list*, www.theequalitiesreview. org.uk/upload/assets/www.theequalitiesreview.org.uk/morireport. pdf (accessed 18/05/07).

Kahneman, D., Diener, E. and Schwarz, N. (eds) (1999) *Well-being: The foundations of hedonic psychology*, New York: Russell Sage Foundation.

Kaufman, A. (ed) (2006) *Capabilities equality: Basic issues and problems*, London: Routledge.

Laird, A., Fawcett, J., Rait, F. and Reid, S. (2000) *Assessment of innovative approaches to testing community opinion*, Edinburgh: Scottish Executive Central Research Unit.

Lovell, C., Richardson, S., Travers, P. and Wood, L. (1994) 'Resources and functionings: a new view of inequality in Australia', in W. Eichorn (ed) *Models a nd measurement of welfare and inequality in Britain*, Berlin: Springer-Verlag.

Nussbaum, M. (2000) *Women and human development: The capabilities approach*, Cambridge: Cambridge University Press.

Nussbaum, M. (2006) *Frontiers of justice: Disability, nationality, species membership*, Cambridge, MA: Harvard University Press.

Qizilbash, M. (2002) 'Development, common foes and shared values', *Review of Political Economy*, vol 14, no 4, pp 463-80.

Robeyns, I. (2003) 'Sen's capability approach and gender inequality: selecting relevant capabilities', *Feminist Economics*, vol 92, nos 2-3, pp 61-92.

Robeyns, I. (2006) 'The capability approach in practice', *Journal of Political Philosophy*, vol 17, no 3, pp 351-76.

Ryan, R. and Deci, E. (2000) 'Self-determination theory and the facilitation of intrinsic motivation, social development and well-being', *American Psychologist*, vol 55, no 1, pp 68-78.

Sen, A. (1981) *Poverty and famines: An essay on entitlement and deprivation*, Oxford: Clarendon Press.

Sen, A. (1985) *Commodities and capabilities*, Oxford: North-Holland.

Sen, A. (1992) *Inequality re-examined*, Oxford: Clarendon Press.

Sen, A. (1996) 'Freedom, capabilities and public action: a response', *Politeia*, vol 12, no 43/44, pp 107-25.

Sen, A. (1998) 'Mortality as an indicator of economic success and failure', *Economic Journal*, vol 108, January, pp 1-25.

Sen, A. (1999) *Development as freedom*, Oxford: Oxford University Press.

Sen, A. (2003) *Rationality and freedom*, Cambridge, MA: Harvard University Press.

Stewart, F. (2005) 'Groups and capabilities', *Journal of Human Development*, vol 6, no 2, pp 185-204.

Sugden, R. (1993) 'Welfare, resources and capabilities: a review of "Inequality Re-examined" by Amartya Sen', *Journal of Economic Literature*, vol 31, December, pp 1947-62.

Teschl, M. and Comim, F. (2005) 'Adaptive preferences and capabilities: some preliminary conceptual explorations', *Review of Social Economy*, vol 63, no 2, pp 229-47.

Verloo, M. (2006) 'Multiple inequalities, intersectionality and the European Union', *European Journal of Women's Studies*, vol 13, no 3, pp 211-28.

Vizard, P. (2006) *Poverty and human rights: Sen's capability perspective examined*, Oxford: Oxford University Press.

Vizard, P. and Burchardt, T. (2007) *Developing a capability list*, Final Recommendations of the Equalities Review Steering Group on Measurement, Paper 2, CASEpaper 121, also available at www.theequalitiesreview.org.uk/upload/assets/www.theequalitiesreview.org.uk/paper2capability.pdf (accessed 18/05/07).

ELEVEN

The limits of compromise? Social justice, 'race' and multiculturalism

Gary Craig

The idea of multiculturalism is now widely under attack. A former UK Home Secretary argues that Muslim women should be unveiled when consulting him as an MP as he wishes to see their face. In France, the wearing of the veil and other religious symbols has been forbidden at public schools; and in Canada, the Province of Ontario, having proposed a degree of autonomy to Muslims in the exercise of sharia law, have backtracked on that position under political pressure. The Dutch government has introduced a series of new policies that spell 'the end of multiculturalism' (Bader, 2005). In some quarters (see, for example, *The Guardian*, 29 January 2007) it has even been argued that multiculturalism has been responsible for the creation of suicide bombers.

This wide-ranging attack raises two important issues. One is that we need to recall that most national polities are now multicultural societies (some having been so for hundreds of years),[1] that is, they have within their populations (a generally increasing number of) people whose national origins lie outside their present country of settlement and who bring differing cultural norms to the latter. A growing proportion of these people, however, have been born and bred in these countries of settlement (43% in the case of the UK) with – in theory at least – the same rights as those of their national majority peers. As Parekh (2000a) reminds us, whether people like it or not (and many politicians, most right-wing media and a body of public opinion apparently do not), multicultural societies are a fact of life and cannot be wished away – other than by the violence of ethnic cleansing. This fact of life, however, has yet to translate into truly multiculturalist policy frameworks.

The second, linked, issue is that the increasing number of those who now argue that multiculturalism has failed demonstrate little understanding of what a multiculturalist policy framework is trying to achieve. Currently, debates in the UK (and elsewhere) increasingly wind the clock back to what was known in the 1950s as an assimilationist policy; those immigrating to the UK were expected to leave their cultural baggage behind them as they arrived at the port of entry and become effectively black or brown Britons. Those arguing against multiculturalism now suggest that there can be little compromise between cultures within specific national political frameworks or, more extravagantly, that the world now witnesses a clash of civilisations (Huntington, 1996). Some (for example, Barry, 2000) set up straw men, requiring of multiculturalism outcomes which it was never intended to achieve. Those arguing in favour of multiculturalist policy, however, generally do so on the basis that it is possible to incorporate people from a range of different cultural origins, respecting the dimensions of difference and diversity in most aspects of culture – dress, food, religion and so on – providing it is done within an overarching acceptance of basic human rights, as, for example, laid out in the United Nations (UN)Charter of Human Rights. If multiculturalism has failed, it does so therefore not in the sense that it has failed to convert those from other countries to the joys of white Anglo-Saxon Protestantism, but because policy and politics have failed to ensure that they have the basic rights enjoyed by their longer-settled co-citizens. The failure lies thus with the British and other settled states and not with those minorities subjected to its policies.

In reality, multiculturalism fails because of the continuing racism within those countries, which, while happy to accept workers from elsewhere (or from aboriginal minorities), to help fill the low-paid, dirty gaps in the labour market that majority (usually) white residents are unwilling to take on, are unwilling to offer the full rights and benefits of citizenship to them (Craig, 2007b). In France, for example, ethnicity is not regarded as a legitimate factor in the determination of citizenship because of the 1789 Republican constitution. Minorities are effectively 'written out' of the French policy process to a large degree and from research that might describe the level and type of disadvantage that they face. The 2005 riots in the Paris *banlieues*, like those in the UK northern cities, are protests by some minorities at their continuing 'hidden' impoverishment, the result of structural racism (Murray, 2006). In Germany, *jus sanguinis*, basing citizenship on the rights of blood ties rather than on *jus solis*, of residence, has meant that the aussiedler returning from Poland or Russia have greater rights to citizenship than, say, migrants of Turkish origin who have worked there for 30 years and have German-born children (Craig, 2002). In Malaysia, whose population is roughly divided equally between people of Malay, Chinese and Indian origin, economically successful

Chinese people and academically successful Indian people find their advancement through many avenues blocked because the Malay constitution explicitly enhances the rights of Malays, discriminating in their favour.[2] In Botswana, the majority Setswana exclude the transient San bushpeople from the political process.

In New Zealand/Aotearoa, despite the Treaty of Waitangi, which provided some legal land rights protection for the Maori, they are still concentrated among the unemployed, in the prison population and in areas of social and economic deprivation. Successive waves of immigration from Europe and from Asia have simply pushed the Maori further up the ladder of disadvantage (Spoonley et al, 1996). The treatment of the aboriginal Koori people of Australia has been even more shameful as their relatively weak land rights are now under threat; indeed, social and economic policy towards them might be regarded as a legacy of 19th-century ethnic cleansing, carried on by other means. Australia, having abandoned its white Australia settlement policy of the early 20th century in the 1970s, has been drifting away from multiculturalist policy and adopting, as are many other 'developed' countries, far more restrictive and focused approaches to immigration (Jakubowicz, 2000). The recent Cronulla 'riots' (properly pogrom), in which the Australian state effectively legitimised racist beatings of people of 'Middle Eastern origin', displays how close such profound racism is to the surface among much of 'white' Australia (Poynting, 2007). The Canadian federal government has at least publicly apologised to the Inuit for its oppressive treatment of them within education policy over the past 100 years although poverty, ill-health and poor social and economic conditions remain strongly racialised to the disadvantage of even long-established minorities (Galabuzi, 2006).[3] The same is true of minorities in the US, although the American constitution regards them not as minorities in a multicultural society but as American citizens created through the 'melting pot' (Kymlicka, 1995; Clarke and Fox-Piven, 2000; Chapter Three, this volume).

Where tensions have arisen in recent years within multicultural societies, it has typically been where the value system of a 'foreign' culture is said to clash with majority values (although these are rarely defined), frequently over relatively low-level issues of dress or food preparation, or, more critically, with values embedded in international human rights conventions (such as the protection of women from forced marriage or from what the 'West' refers to as female genital mutilation). These tensions are not necessarily evidence that multiculturalism has failed but that the process of negotiating multiculturalism is yet to be completed and constitutes work in progress. Most tellingly, multiculturalist policy in the UK (and elsewhere) has not been linked to a framework of social justice. This chapter explores whether social justice has been delivered to the UK's black and minority ethnic (BME) populations in particular (although the arguments resonate with other countries' experience).

Fundamentally, however, the question of achieving social justice is not simply about redistribution. As others demonstrate (Chapters Three, Four and Five, this volume; Young, 1990; Parekh, 2000a, 2000b) multicultural societies worldwide have begun to face the difficulties of incorporating respect and recognition for cultural diversity and difference within a framework of universal rights. Respect and recognition for minorities can be understood as ways in which equality of status, of common citizenship, are operationalised. As we shall see, however, the very modest gains of the past few years in this direction are now unravelling in the context of 'the war on terror'.

Social justice and multiculturalism

Current debates about the meaning of social justice are summarised in our editorial introduction and will not be repeated here. However, there are particular issues within this discourse that relate to multiculturalism. Miller's (1999) argument, for example, about the way in which need may be defined is particularly significant within multicultural societies. If the concept of need is to be validated by all relevant parties, it follows that BME groups should be a party to this process of validation. Currently, they are largely excluded from the political and policy process, a fact that the token co-option of a privileged few into the mechanisms of the state (such as Asian Peers) cannot obscure. Similarly, arguments about the extent to which the market can deliver social justice must acknowledge that the inequities of market economies bear down most heavily on most BME groups (Craig, 2007b; Platt, 2007).

Earlier analyses of social justice also failed to incorporate rights associated with culture and gender, dimensions increasingly recognised in modern policy discourse (Castles, 2000; Fraser, 2001; Lister, 2003) or acknowledge the inequalities associated with geography (JRF, 2004). Social justice has a spatial dimension: we must think carefully about different conceptions of poverty and need in different contexts – and for different groups. The position of medical consultants of Indian origin working in the UK's rural areas provides an interesting illustration. While rural areas are often portrayed as comfortable, higher-income areas, many Indian doctors work in them because they have faced racial barriers in accessing higher-status urban teaching hospital posts, being 'directed' towards lower-status positions, including in rural areas. Their higher profile in such areas – where minority populations are relatively small – then exposes them to further racism (Henderson and Kaur, 1999; Darr et al, 2005).

For Britain's BME groups, the ability to exercise cultural rights should imply the ability to be culturally different within internationally accepted human rights parameters, in a society providing the same social, civil and political rights to all (Hall, 1990). Recently, however, more questions are being asked as to what the parameters of this 'difference' are and, in particular, whether they incorporate a different value system – that is, a different conception of the fundamental meaning of social justice – or whether they are limited to relatively superficial indicators, for example in forms of dress, religious observation or dietary habits (Atkin, 2004). Essentially, the key question is, what room there is for compromise when apparently different value systems compete within a national polity?

Rather than close down the debate by arguing that multiculturalism as a political project is dead, there remains – because multicultural societies exist and will not go away – a critically important theoretical and political agenda, that of exploring the nature of social justice within such societies, particularly those characterised by institutional and individual racism (Kymlicka, 2001; Kelly, 2002; Craig, 2007b). The attacks on the World Trade Center, the so-called 'war on terror' and the growth of Islamophobia have merely heightened this agenda's relevance rather than implying it should be swept away. To blame multiculturalism for increased national or global political tensions – as many now tend to do – is fundamentally to miss the point. As many commentators (and mass demonstrations of British and other populations) suggest, these tensions have their origins elsewhere, notably in the growing imperialist policy of Western economic interests searching for greater control over the world's resources (Chomsky, 2003).

As Miller (1999) suggests, multiculturalism poses a major challenge in widening the notion of the closed political community within which concepts such as need, rights and desert are contested. His is not an argument for 'the elimination of cultural differences, that is, assimilation, but the opening up of national identities so that they become accessible to the members of many (ideally all) cultural groups within existing democratic states' (Miller, 1999, p 263). The political and policy task is thus to ensure that all cultural (BME) groups are recognised and engaged in both determining and acting on the principles of social justice. Miller argues that there is little empirical evidence supporting the view that cultural differences translate into differing conceptions of social justice (an area remaining to be tested) although the multicultural 'settlement' is clearly specific to the historical and political conditions in each nation state (Kymlicka, 1995; Duncan, 2004). For example, in Australia, Canada and New Zealand, the presence of aboriginal populations, with validated legal claims on land, sea shore and natural resources, should be significant in shaping the form of this settlement. Black groups in the UK might partially legitimise their claims by reference to Britain's colonial past: 'we are here because you were there'.

My own wide-ranging definition of social justice, drawing on current political discourse, is of a framework of political objectives, pursued through social, economic, environmental and political policies, based on an acceptance of difference and diversity, and informed by values concerned with:

- achieving fairness, equality of outcomes and treatment;
- recognising the dignity and equal worth and encouraging the self-esteem of all;
- the meeting of basic needs, defined through cross-cultural consensus;
- reducing substantial inequalities in wealth, income and life chances; and
- the participation of all, including the most disadvantaged.

This goes beyond many current definitions by privileging equality of outcomes, and the effective participation of those currently disadvantaged. This is the framework against which evidence outlined below is tested.

'Britishness' and multiculturalism

Since the major growth in immigration from the late 1940s, UK political debates about 'the race relations problem' have been dominated by the question of whether the goal of policy was to assimilate minorities into British culture or integrate them into a multicultural society. Until the 1960s, these debates were dominated by the assimilationist tendency (Law, 1996; Ratcliffe, 2004; Solomos, 2004). Immigration was then explicitly encouraged by government policy for the purposes of economic reconstruction, although political and public opposition rapidly grew (stimulated by hostile media coverage: Craig, 2007b). Currently, political parties compete to present themselves as toughest on immigration policy although the substantial immigration of (white)

Eastern European migrant workers has been treated as a distinct phenomenon, substantially because of the considerable economic benefits (from high levels of labour exploitation) it has brought (Craig, 2007a).

Despite continuing widespread individual and institutional racism (Craig, 2001, 2007b), an acceptance gradually developed from the 1980s that Britain was becoming a multicultural society. There remained, however, considerable disagreement about whether and to what extent cultural diversity should formally be recognised in UK policy frameworks. These debates became increasingly complex as the demography of Britain's minorities moved away from groupings newly immigrating (characteristic of the 1950s and 1960s), to one shaped both by the relative size of minority populations and by a recognition that an increasing proportion of Britain's minority population were UK-born.

Primary immigration was substantially reduced by legislation from the 1970s. Throughout much of the 1980s and the 1990s, debates about the nature of multiculturalism were subdued, emerging intermittently in response to specific incidents, such as urban 'disturbances' – often racialised in popular discourse – or to particular cultural conflicts, such as 'forced marriages' within South Asian communities. By the 1990s, these debates were overshadowed, in terms of immigration policy, by rapidly rising numbers of refugees seeking asylum. Public and political interest in the nature of multiculturalism was, however, stimulated by the report of the Commission on the Future of Multi-Ethnic Britain, characterising Britain as a 'community of communities' (Parekh, 2000b). This was attacked by popular press and government alike, as undermining 'traditional' British values. The report appeared as the extent of continuing racism against Britain's minorities was revealed, partly as a result of high-profile racist incidents (the murder of Steven Lawrence – McPherson, 1999; the asphyxiation of a black psychiatric patient, David Bennett – Blofeld, 2004; and the murder in prison of Zahid Mubarek); and partly through a number of more general enquiries into 'race' relations within the UK (Craig et al, 2005b). Further impetus came from disturbances in several Northern English towns, which, following local and national inquiries (Home Office, 2001a; Ouseley, 2001), led to a national policy focus on community cohesion (Home Office, 2001b).

Government now argues that the major issue facing Britain's minority communities is their failure to 'integrate', and their desire to lead increasingly separate lives, both geographically and culturally, at odds with 'traditional' values of white Britishness. The concept of community cohesion, displacing 'race relations' in political discourse, now challenges recognition of difference as the basis for policy making (Worley, 2005), the question of difference being now perceived as an obstacle to cohesion (LGA, 2002; Home Office, 2004). However, governments are effectively maintaining the janus-faced stance of the post-war period, pursuing increasingly restrictive and punitive immigration policies (with a racist ideological underpinning) while claiming that growing ethnic diversity was a welcome phenomenon (Craig, 2007b). Thus, for example, while promoting assimilationist policies underpinning community cohesion (which ignores the continuing racism characterising British life), the Home Office suggests that 'to be British does not mean assimilation into a common culture so that original identities are lost' (Craig, 2007b, p 6), and that respect for the law, fairness, tolerance and respect for difference were values shared by all Britons, of whatever ethnic origin (Forrest and Kearns, 2000). Meanwhile, UK governments increasingly pick and choose which identities they welcome into the UK.

The *fin de siècle* domestic disturbances were followed by the shocks of the attacks on the World Trade Center and the ensuing 'war on terror'; then by bombings in Madrid, Bali and London, and by Western military intervention in Iraq and Afghanistan. These have been increasingly characterised in both populist and some serious discourse as reflecting a fundamental struggle between the civilisations of 'the West' and Islam (Huntington, 2004). One consequence of inflammatory media and political debate has been increasing numbers of racist attacks, predominantly – but not solely – against Muslims. The far Right has seized the opportunities presented, arguing that some of Britain's minorities have no commitment to integrating within wider society and should be 'encouraged' to return to their countries of origin, despite the fact that many are, as noted, British-born. Cultural tensions are also apparent in responses to government attempts to legislate against religious incitement (Jan-Khan, 2001).

In this contested but confused political and policy context, it is important to establish – on a factual rather than rhetorical basis – whether and to what extent there are significant differences in ideology between the settled white British majority population and minority populations, and the extent to which such differences, if existing, fundamentally impact on values and behaviours. This is a critical task for generating a clearer understanding of the shape of British multiculturalism, responding to what the Royal Society of Arts (RSA, 2006, p 20) argues are the 'fears of an existential crisis within the British/English nation – that there are degrees of ethnic/national diversity which are incompatible with the degree of social cohesion that is a precondition for the existence of a nation.

Social justice, public policy and Britain's minorities

But how has Britain's approach of multiculturalism actually treated its minority populations to date? If we apply the principles of social justice to the position of the UK's BME groups, to what extent can governments' policy frameworks and their outcomes for minorities be said to be fair? There is now fairly extensive research evidence and some pointers to the key findings can be provided. First, let us take the issue of equality of status, and the particular dimensions of respect and recognition. Technically, as noted earlier, all citizens of the UK, of whatever ethnicity, have an equal status as citizens. The UK minority ethnic population is now about 10% of the whole population, but is not uniformly distributed: two London boroughs have a minority population that is now in a majority and many urban areas have minority populations exceeding 15% of the total population. Unlike earlier migration, the minority population has grown recently partly through natural population growth and partly through the growth of refugees (whose numbers are, however, much smaller than claimed by government or hysterical media commentaries). Britain now has a very diverse population – it is not unusual for cities with relatively small minority populations to accommodate more than 50 different languages – and there are settled minorities in every UK local council area.

Individual and institutional racism – that is, abuse and assault by individuals or the maintenance of structures, mechanisms and processes that disadvantage people because of their ethnic origins – are, however, according to official statistics, growing problems.[4] In the last five years, the UK has seen a number of high-level inquiries into aspects of the welfare state pointing to systematic racism and there have been a total of more than 100 racialised murders in the past 10 years.[5] Immigrants detained in government reception centres are now widely known to have been subject to systematic abuse and assault; police in training were recorded (by an undercover journalist) engaging in widespread racist abuse; and other inquiries into structural racism are ongoing.

Despite the fact that legislation was introduced in 2000 to confront racism in public institutions, progress has been very slow. A former UK Home Secretary has called (again) for all public bodies to address racial discrimination within their services, backed by firm action, ethnic monitoring, public service agreements and inspection. Meanwhile, the police service records tens of thousands of incidents of racist abuse and attacks each year (a substantial underestimate of the real extent of the problem according to the British Crime Survey); the number of anti-Semitic attacks has reached a (in recent years) peak; and the fascist British National Party, whose political platform is based in part on repatriating immigrants, fielded record numbers of candidates in recent local and General Elections. A MORI poll for the British Council revealed in 2000 that young people in other countries perceived Britons to be 'arrogant, xenophobic ... racially intolerant ... and frequently drunk' (Craig, 2002, p 154). A second poll found that roughly one third of the UK population admitted that they had racist attitudes and that figure has apparently grown substantially in recent years, in part because of hostile government and media treatment of asylum seekers and refugees and of growing Islamophobia generated by the so-called global 'war on terror'. One consequence of the 9/11 attacks in New York has been the introduction of legislation that has allowed suspected terrorists to be imprisoned for years without trial, and stopping and searching of suspects, which, the Home Office admits, will disproportionately disadvantage people 'of Muslim appearance' (whatever that might be). More recently, in the wake of bombings and attempted bombings in London, people of 'unusual' dress and appearance have been apprehended on – or removed from – cars, buses, trains and aeroplanes, leading one senior police officer of Asian origin to say that a new offence, of 'travelling whilst Asian', had been covertly introduced by the police.

None of this can be regarded as an approach that privileges respect for those who happen to dress, look or speak differently from the majority. At a more modest level, there are a number of struggles being carried forward by minorities over aspects of their culture, which, they argue, should be accepted within a multicultural society in which they also are, in theory at least, full citizens. Examples of this are the right for young women and girls to wear particular forms of clothing – the hijab and the jilbab – at school and at work; for the right for respect for traditional forms of food preparation (for example the current debate about humane ways to kill animals in keeping with the principles of halal food preparation); and for the right to open faith schools. The UK has had Christian schools for hundreds of years but government recently argued that Muslim faith schools undermine community cohesion.

These struggles have occasionally taken a violent form. In 1989, Salman Rushdie's book, *The Satanic Verses*, led to a fatwah, or implied sentence of death, being placed on him by orthodox Islamic clerics although this fatwah was not endorsed by most British Muslims. More recently, tensions between what is described as the British culture of free speech and respect for other religions and cultures was tested when performances of a play, *Bezhti*, portraying murder and abuse within a Sikh Temple, were abandoned as a result of vigorous street protests by some local Sikhs. To date, however, no acts of violence have led to the deaths of UK citizens testing the boundaries between different cultures – as happened in the Netherlands when the filmmaker Theo van Gogh was killed allegedly by a member of an Islamic radical group because he satirised the treatment of women by Muslims. The converse – the racist death of minority people – however, is a frequent occurrence. This is not to argue that there are not tensions in determining the parameters of acceptable behaviour or speech within the UK – events since 9/11 have brought these tensions into sharper focus – and this is precisely what the multicultural project should be negotiating around. The point here is that most minorities feel that their ability to assert their cultural rights are not formally being recognised, particularly in the current climate, and that, for some, resorting to more strident or even violent protest is the only way in which they can have their viewpoint acknowledged (Jan-Khan, 2001).[6] Overall, this evidence suggests that it would be difficult to argue that social justice – in a relational sense – was available to members of UK BME groups and equality of status is thus, clearly, beyond the rhetoric of citizenship, unequally offered.

In terms of equality of opportunity, say of access to goods, services and, in particular, welfare provision, the situation is no better. It is the latter which should provide the basis for the state to compensate for the failure of the market to deliver 'welfare' on a socially just basis. Reviews of both the entire provision of welfare and specific aspects of it within the UK (Modood et al, 1997; Craig, 1999, 2001, 2002, 2005, 2007b; Parekh, 2000b; Platt, 2003) suggest that access to welfare provision is highly unequal, on a basis that is highly racialised. Although this is not an iron law in the sense that some minority groups are now beginning to achieve well despite the obstacles placed in their way, certain minority groups – particularly those of African Caribbean, Bangladeshi and Pakistani origin and more recent arrivals – continue to be concentrated in the most deprived housing neighbourhoods and thus have access only to the schools with the worst conditions, poorest staffing provision and least good records of attainment (Gillborn and Mirza, 2000). Indeed, Gillborn and Mirza argue that BME pupils are disadvantaged systematically by the education system because of its inability to respond flexibly to different cultural contexts. Most strikingly, they conclude that one ethnic group (black young people) actually entered school 20 percentage points in advance of the average but left it 21 points behind the average, a deeply disturbing reflection on racism within the formal educational system. Minorities also have greatest difficulty in accessing appropriate health provision, often because of the failure of health services to respond to specific cultural needs such as for interpretation, to ethnically linked ailments such as sickle cell disorder, or by ethnically or culturally matched provision (Atkin, 2004; Ali et al, 2006). They are obstructed from advancement in the labour market, and often end up in workplaces – if they access the labour market at all – with the poorest working conditions, poorest pay and least security (Britton et al, 2001; Craig, 2002; Cabinet Office, 2003), concentrated among those on the lowest incomes (Craig, 1999; Platt, 2003), a fate also common to recent migrants of Eastern and Central European origins (Craig, 2007a). Increasingly, there is also evidence that BME groups are disproportionately affected by environmental degradation (see Chapter Twelve).

The inability of state welfare to respond to the needs of minority groups is a reflection of its failure to offer them opportunities to participate adequately in important decision-making mechanisms and shape the ways in which services are delivered, another aspect of the definition of social justice given above. BME people have rarely had a formal voice in a wide range of 'community' policy initiatives such as neighbourhood renewal or voluntary sector development. Funding streams to autonomous BME organisations remain marginal within most large-scale mainstream policy initiatives (Craig et al, 2005a; Craig, 2006) and even those flagship initiatives allegedly targeted on BME groups fail to do so effectively (Craig et al, 2007). Where government consults minorities, it deals with what younger minority people now regard as a generation of older 'community leaders', no longer regarded by many as representing them (Jan-Khan, 2001). For example, at a Muslim 'summit' called by (former) Prime Minister Blair after the July 2005 bombings, no one present was under the age of 40.

The definition of social justice set out above is also concerned, most crucially, with equality of outcomes. Looking again across the whole range of welfare provision, outcomes for BME people – with a few notable exceptions – are disproportionately poor compared with the population at large. At the pinnacle of political decision making, the UK House of Commons, there are currently only 19 black and Asian MPs out of a chamber of 630 MPs – barely 3%, compared with a BME population of around 10% – and there has never been an Asian female MP, although Asian women have been settled in the UK for more than 200 years. Educational attainment – in school qualifications, entry to higher education, achievement at the highest level of higher education – is, with some exceptions, far lower for most minority groups than the national average. For example, there are very few (about 2%) black or Asian professors in UK universities and only one black or Asian vice-chancellor or principal in the 110 UK universities. Ironically, for one outcome, young black people score highly – but this was for the number of permanent exclusions from school, the result, it appears, of a complex range of factors but including racist responses from schools that disproportionately label black school pupils (Cooper, 2004).

In the field of health, a recent survey of pay awards in the NHS found them riddled with racism. In terms of mental health, black service users are more likely to be (mis)diagnosed as schizophrenic, contained in psychiatric institutions and treated with electroconvulsive therapy (Rai-Atkins, 2002). Even in those areas where some minorities do well – such as medicine – there is a glass ceiling that stops them achieving the highest honours. Within the police force, barely 2% of the UK force nationally is from BME groups and there is only one black chief constable. There are no black directors of social services in the more than 150 local authority social services departments. While about 5% of social services staff are from minorities, the figure is less than 2% in social services management.

Ironically, as noted, minorities are accused of pursuing a segregationalist approach in relation to housing. This is a classic example of blaming the victim, since for many minorities there is no question of choice, because of limited access to social housing or to affordable mortgage finance: it is only in the poorest-quality housing areas that they have often been able to access accommodation at all. As Smith (1989, p 130) puts it, their concentration in such areas does not explain why minorities 'should pursue this [choice] in the more run-down segments of the housing stock [with poor-quality housing, dangerous neighbourhoods, inadequate health and education provision], rather than in areas where they could secure the symbolic and economic benefits associated with suburban life'.

This summary of a much wider body of evidence demonstrates that, in terms of equality of outcomes, BME groups cannot be said to be treated with social justice. This is not an argument that every person, every structure or every policy in the UK concerned with the provision of welfare is racist; but institutional and individual racism remain prevalent and have a determining effect on the life chances, and of the achievement of full social, economic and political citizenship for most minorities. Faced with this lack of equality of status, of opportunity and of outcome, of second-class citizenship and of a deficit in societal respect and recognition, BME communities have pursued a range of political strategies. The gradualism of parliamentary and political representation

– at every level, from central government to local government, the voluntary sector and so on – has delivered little effective control of the conditions under which most minorities live. Some minorities have pursued a separatist strategy, for example through the creation of autonomous organisations such as faith schools and black housing associations – for which they are again criticised. These might have given a degree of control to such groups but are often situated in a wider context of a lack of resources and struggles to survive.

Over the past 40 years, there have been outbreaks of inter-racial violence in some cities. While some disturbances – 'riots' in the language of the media – were prompted by single events, such as the arrest or death of a black individual, increasingly they may be seen as a political response to the cumulative longstanding disadvantage faced by Britain's minorities (Jan-Khan, 2001). In many parts of Britain, particularly rural areas and areas where there is only a relatively small BME population, there remains a significant level of denial that racism is a problem at all (Darr et al, 2005). This suggests that these disturbances will continue until the UK government, and its population as a whole, acknowledge the claims of social justice for its entire 'citizenry'. It also suggests that the process of negotiation over the way in which social justice can be achieved for Britain's minorities has barely started. The same can be said for the project of multiculturalism. Current political rhetoric, however, suggests that government wishes to abandon the project: minorities will then be left with 'just drumming and dancing', abandoning more fundamental aspects of culture and identity, if they seek the status of full citizens.[7]

Conclusion

Social justice, then, is not a reality for the minorities of the UK – or indeed of other countries that claim the mantle of multiculturalism. The achievement of equally socially just outcomes, in terms of meeting need, or ensuring equality as citizens, in terms of status, opportunity and access, varies from one so-called multicultural country to another, a reflection of the specific structural constraints of each such as the historical development of formal political constitutions or informal political settlements. Every country has, however, a substantial way to go, with poverty and disadvantage having a strongly racialised dimension. A government's preparedness to confront structural and individual racism is thus a critical factor in this process. As Kymlicka shows elsewhere (Chapter Three, this volume), there is no necessary tension between diversity and solidarity yet in the current political climate, the tendency is increasingly to deny minorities effective expression of their cultural and religious rights, allegedly to protect the interests of the majority, with the claims of aboriginal people often effectively rejected altogether. In the UK in particular, New Labour's political project barely scratches the surface of social justice for Britain's minorities who remain strongly represented among the poorest and most marginalised in the UK as a whole (Lister, 2004). Until politics engages effectively with the wider struggle against racism, it is impossible for the demands of social justice to be met.

Notes

[1] Often as a consequence of imperialism or colonialism, followed by economic settlement, as in the case of Canada, Australia, New Zealand, Fiji and Malaysia for example. See, for example, in the case of Canada, Esses and Gardner (2006).

[2] Fenton (2005) argues that political struggle in Malaysia is less about culture and ethnicity than about class and that the task of the government is to create a Malay middle class. Nevertheless, currently, people are prioritised for or excluded from posts because of their ethnic origin.

[3] As this book was going to print, a new Australian government had issued an apology to the Koori for their historic treatment.

[4] See, for example, www.homewoffice.gov.uk/rds/stats, and the outcomes of the UK British Crime Survey

[5] See for example www.irr.org.uk

[6] Martin Luther King argued that 'riots are the language of the unheard'.

[7] A view confirmed by the latest government proposals on immigration, announced on 21 February 2008.

References

Ali, N., Atkin, K. and Craig, G. (2006) *Ethnicity and disability*, London: Royal National Institute for the Blind.

Atkin, K. (2004) 'Primary health care and South Asian populations: institutional racism, policy and practice', in S. Ali and K. Atkin (eds) *South Asian populations and primary health care: Meeting the challenges*, Oxford: Radcliffe.

Bader, V. (2005) 'The Dutch nightmare: the end of multiculturalism?', *Diversite Canadienne*, vol 4, no 1, Winter, pp 9-11.

Barry, B. (2000) *Culture and equality: An egalitarian critique of multiculturalism*, Cambridge: Polity Press.

Blofeld, H. (chair) (2004) *Report into the death of David Bennett*, London: NHS Executive.

Britton, L., Chatrik, B., Coles, R. and Craig, G. (2001) *Missing connexions? Black and Asian excluded young people*, York: Joseph Rowntree Foundation.

Cabinet Office (2003) *Ethnic minorities in the labour market*, London: Cabinet Office.

Castles, S. (2000) *Ethnicity and globalisation*, London: Sage Publications.

Chomsky, N. (2003) 'Chomsky in London', *Red Pepper*, March, pp 22-7.

Clarke, J. and Fox-Piven, F. (2000) 'The USA', in P. Alcock and G. Craig (eds) *International social policy*, Basingstoke: Palgrave.

Cooper, C. (2004) *Understanding school exclusion*, Nottingham: Education Now.

Craig, G. (1999) '"Race", poverty and social security', in J. Ditch (ed) *An introduction to social security*, London: Routledge.

Craig, G. (2001) *'Race' and welfare*, Inaugural lecture, Hull: University of Hull.

Craig, G. (2002) 'Ethnicity, racism and the labour market: a European perspective', in J.-G. Andersen and P. Jensen (eds) *Citizenship, welfare and the labour market*, Bristol: The Policy Press.

Craig, G. (2005) 'Black and minority ethnic children and young people', in G. Preston (ed) *At greatest risk?*, London: Child Poverty Action Group.

Craig, G. (2006) *The engagement and support of Black and minority ethnic voluntary and community organisations in North Yorkshire*, Easingwold: NYFVO.

Craig, G. (2007a) 'They come over here – and benefit our economy', *Regional Review*, Spring, pp 23-5.

Craig, G. (2007b) '"Cunning, unprincipled, loathsome": the racist tail wags the welfare dog', *Journal of Social Policy*, vol 36, no 4, pp 605-24.

Craig, G., Wilkinson, M. D. and Ali, J. (2005b) *A turning point? The state of race relations in Hull*, Kingston upon Hull: Hull City Council/Crown Prosecution Service/Humberside Police.

Craig, G., Adamson, S., Ali, N., Ali, S., Dadze-Arthur, A., Elliott, C., McNamee, S. and Murtuja, B. (2007) *Sure Start and black and minority ethnic populations*, London: DfES.

Craig, G., Taylor, M., Carlton, N., Garbutt, R., Kimberlee, R., Lepine, E. and Syed, A. (2005a) *The paradox of compacts*, London: Home Office.

Darr, A., Atkin, K. and Craig, G. (2005) *Ethnic minorities in a rural labour market*, York: North Yorkshire Learning and Skills Council.

Duncan, C. R. (2004) *Civilising the margins*, Ithaca, NY: Cornell University Press.

Esses, V. and Gardner, R. (2006) 'Multiculturalism in Canada: context and current status', *Canadian Journal of Behavioural Science*, July, pp 1-11.

Fenton, S. (2005) 'Malaysia, capitalist modernity and post-ethnicity', *Diversite Canadienne*, vol 4, no 1, pp 43-5.

Forrest, R. and Kearns, A. (2000) 'Social cohesion, social capital and the neighbourhood', Paper presented to ESRC Cities Programme Neighbourhood Colloqium, Liverpool, 5 June.

Fraser, N. (2001) 'Recognition without ethics?', *Theory, Culture and Society*, vol 18, no 2-3, pp 21-42.

Galabuzi, G.-E. (2006) *Canada's economic apartheid: The social exclusion of racialized groups in the new century*, Toronto: Canadian Scholars Press.

Gillborn, D. and Mirza, H. (2000) *Educational inequality: Mapping race, class and gender*, London: Institute of Education and Middlesex University.

Hall, S. (1990) 'Cultural identity and diaspora', in J. Rutherford (ed) *Identity: Community, culture, difference*, London: Lawrence and Wishart.

Henderson, P. and Kaur, R. (eds) (1999) *Combating rural racism in the UK*, London: Community Development Foundation.

Home Office (2001a) *Community cohesion: A report of the Independent Review Team* (Chair Ted Cantle), London: Home Office.

Home Office (2001b) *Building cohesive communities* (Report of a Ministerial Group, Chair John Denham), London: Home Office.

Home Office (2004) *Strength in diversity: Towards a community cohesion and race equality strategy*, London: Home Office.

Huntington, S. (1996) *The clash of civilisations and the remaking of world order*, New York: Simon and Schuster.

Huntington, S. (2004) *Who are we?*, London: Simon and Schuster.

Jacubowicz, A. (2000) 'White noise: Australia's struggle with multiculturalism', in C. Levine-Rasky (ed) *Working through whiteness*, Toronto: University of Toronto Press.

Jan-Khan, M. (2001) 'The right to riot?', *Community Development Journal*, vol 38, no 1, pp 32-42.

JRF (Joseph Rowntree Foundation) (2004) *Overcoming disadvantage*, York: Joseph Rowntree Foundation.

Kelly, P. (2002) *Multiculturalism reconsidered*, Cambridge: Polity Press.

Kymlicka, W. (1995) *Multicultural citizenship*, Oxford: Oxford University Press.

Kymlicka, W. (2001) *Politics in the vernacular: nationalism, multiculturalism and citizenship*, Oxford: Oxford University Press.

Law, I. (1996) *Racism, ethnicity and social policy*, Hemel Hempstead: Prentice Hall.

LGA (Local Government Association) (2002) *Guidance on community cohesion*, London: LGA.

Lister, R. (2003) *Citizenship: Feminist perspectives* (2nd edition), Basingstoke: Palgrave.

Lister, R. (2004) *Poverty*, Cambridge: Polity Press.

McPherson, W. (1999) *Inquiry into the death of Steven Lawrence*, London: The Stationery Office.

Miller, D. (1999) *Principles of social justice*, Cambridge, MA: Harvard University Press.

Modood, T., Berthoud, R. and Nazroo, J. (1997) *Ethnic minorities in Britain*, London: Policy Studies Institute.

Murray, G. (2006) 'France: the riots and the Republic', *Race and Class*, vol 47, no 4, pp 26–45.

Ouseley, H. (2001) *Community pride not prejudice*, Bradford: Bradford Vision.

Parekh, B. (2000a) *Rethinking multiculturalism*, Harvard: Harvard University Press.

Parekh, B. (2000b) *The future of multi-ethnic Britain*, London: Runnymede Trust.

Platt, L. (2003) *Parallel lives?*, London: Child Poverty Action Group.

Platt, L. (2007) *Ethnicity and poverty*, York: Joseph Rowntree Foundation.

Poynting, S. (2007) 'What caused the Cronulla riot?', *Race and Class*, vol 48, no 1, pp 85–91.

Rai-Atkins, A. (2002) *Best practice in mental health advocacy for Black, Caribbean and South Asian users*, York: Joseph Rowntree Foundation.

Ratcliffe, P. (2004) *'Race', ethnicity and difference*, Maidenhead: Open University Press.

RSA (Royal Society of Arts) (2006) *Migration: A welcome opportunity*, London: RSA.

Smith, S. J. (1989) *The politics of race and residence*, Cambridge: Polity Press.

Solomos, J. (2004) *Race and racism* (3rd edition), Basingstoke: Palgrave.

Spoonley, P., Pearson, D. and McPherson, C. (eds) (1996) *Nga Patai: Racism and ethnic relations in Aotearoa*, Palmerston North: Dunmore Press.

Worley, C. (2005) '"It's not about race. It's about the community": New Labour and "community cohesion"', *Critical Social Policy*, vol 25, no 4, pp 483-96.

Young, I. M. (1990) *Justice and the politics of difference*, Princeton, NJ: Princeton University Press.

TWELVE

Understanding environmental justice: making the connection between sustainable development and social justice

Maria Adebowale[1]

Introduction

Debates on sustainability and the concept of environmental justice reflect a number of macro-arguments on the theory of social justice and distributive justice. There are a number of conundrums within the construct of social justice as it relates to environmental and sustainable development policy. This chapter aims, first, to provide a theoretical understanding of the main issues and second, to illustrate the application of environmental justice theory at UK policy level.

The chapter begins with the concepts of sustainability and environmental justice both at UK and global levels, exploring the constructs of human rights, participation and governance. This discussion leads into a focus on the interpretation of environmental justice at grassroots and policy levels in the UK. It examines the social distribution of the urban and natural environment and its connections to 'race' and income. Finally, it reflects on how theory and interpretation interplay with social policy in relation to government agendas on race relations, social inclusion and regeneration.

Concepts of sustainable development and social justice

> Humanity has the ability to make development sustainable
> – to ensure that it meets the needs of the present without
> compromising the ability of the future to meet their own
> needs. (Brundtland, 1987, p 8)

The United Nations Conference on Human Environment in 1972 is often identified as the watershed for sustainable development discourse. The search for international cooperation on major global issues brought industrialised and 'developing' countries to design a new form of development. This conference stipulated that any agenda for development must include a healthy and productive environment for all humans. More than a decade later, the Brundtland Commission was given the task of framing a new form of equitable development balancing economic, environment and social needs:

> What is needed is a new era of economic growth ... that is forceful and at the same time socially and environmentally responsible ... together we should span the globe, and pull together to formulate an interdisciplinary integrated approach to global concerns. (Brundtland, 1987, p xii)

There seems to be no one uncontested definition of sustainable development, although most agree that its objectives are similar to those proposed by Brundtland. These are to discuss, promote and implement paradigms allowing for the needs of the present generation to be met without compromising the needs of future generations. In practice this means creating benchmarks and indicators giving equal weight to three pillars: economy, environment and society.

The connection between environmental justice and environmental rights with sustainable development is perhaps best expressed within its social and equity principles (see Figure 12.1). Within Brundtland, these principles are based around the need to create development that has at its heart the objective of approaching equity by meeting human needs, particularly the needs of the most poor and vulnerable people. As such, sustainable development is about social issues of distributive equity within and between countries, rich and poor.

Marginalised groups and communities are identified as the poor, indigenous peoples, children, women, minority ethnic groups and those suffering persecution. A sustainable society is a society that seeks to improve quality of life, in particular for people marginalised for reasons of poverty or other forms of social and economic exclusion. At the heart of sustainable development is, then, clearly the rhetoric of social justice as outlined in the Introduction to this book. This is predicated on the belief that all people are equal and that therefore all people have an equal right to having their basic needs met. The sustainable development dialogue also recognises that not all people have equal opportunities or resources required to meet their needs. It

Figure 12.1: Joining up the economy and the environment via the social dimension

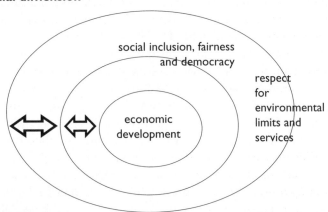

Source: Christie (2001)

also surmises that to achieve sustainable development will require the elimination of unjustified inequalities.

The last two World Summits on Sustainable Development (WSSDs) in 1992 and 2002 sought to steer global action on sustainable development. The 1992 Summit set a prolific number of international standards through laws, policies, guidelines and frameworks. The United Nations Convention on Biological Diversity (UNCBD), its Framework Convention on Climate Change (UNFCC), the Rio Declaration and Agenda 21, among others, all emanated from the 1992 WSSD (Sands, 1997). These helped create an international body of legal treaties, process, guidelines and policy supporting the need to recognise the equity imbalance among, between and within countries. In addition, they facilitated sustainable development benchmarks for equitable environmental, social, civil and political justice.

A closer investigation of the civil and political elements of sustainable development provides an insight into the civil and political paradigm of human rights and environmental justice, offering a framework for understanding the issue of governance at a global level through environmental citizenship and decision making. Legal and political discourse on human rights and environmental justice often discusses the concept of environmental citizenship or environmental democracy. Each is perceived as a fundamental element facilitating the mobilisation of people through political processes of access to environmental information, participation, decision making and justice (see Anderson 1996; Cameron and McKenzie 1996; Mason 1999; ESRC, 2001; Adebowale et al, 2004).

Legal discourse in this area is based around the notions of civil and political rights. International environmental lawyers point to a number of documents from the 1992 WSSD that recognise, implement and protect civil procedural rights. The WSSD documents often highlight tools of democracy as crucial in the strengthening of public power to decide, or be part of, environmental decisions and policy positions at international, regional, national and local levels. Many of the 1992 legal conventions, such as UNCBD, note the particular importance of information gathering, dissemination and decision making with indigenous and local people whose culture and livelihood are reliant on the diversity of biological ecosystems.

When discussing environmental democracy, Agenda 21 and the Rio Declaration are most commonly cited, each dealing directly with the question of environmental citizenship. The quotes below illustrate their stance, that the empowerment of citizens is a central concept in sustainable development and environmental protection:

> The overall objective is to improve or restructure the decision-making process so that consideration of socio-economic and environmental issues is fully integrated and a broader range of public participation assured. (Rio Declaration, Article 8.3, 1992)

> Environmental issues are best handled with the participation of all concerned citizens, at the relevant level. At the national level, each individual shall have appropriate access to information concerning the environment that is held by public authorities, including information on hazardous materials and activities in their communities, and the opportunity to participate in decision-making processes. States shall facilitate and encourage public awareness and participation by making information widely available. Effective access to judicial and administrative proceedings, including redress and remedy, shall be provided. (Rio Declaration, Principle 10, 1992)

The Rio Declaration and Agenda 21 have each now been embedded in environmental and sustainable law and policy around the world, including within the UK. Their principles of participation are used as indicators in sustainable development strategies, forming the basis for new laws. Various legal directives or policy that provide for the practical implementation of participation bind the European Union and its member states. The most obvious examples are the development of Environmental Impact Assessments and the 1998 UNECE Convention on Access to Information, Public Participation in Decision-Making, and Access to Justice on Environmental Matters (The Aarhus Convention), discussed below.

Political discourse, as Mason (1999) suggests, tends to explore the environmental implications of democracy discourse. While also addressing legal norms, its focus is not so much on the process of law-making but rather on how environmental justice can be met with the assent of all citizens (Habermas, 1998). Environmental democracy is thus examined by analysing the present democratic process. Similar to some eco-sociological perspectives, it also seeks to discuss the issue of unequal power structures as part of the environment. The role of environmental justice movements in changing or challenging these unequal power structures is then seen as crucial to the political mobilisation of disenfranchised groups. This is proposed as the opening-up of policy processes to everyone, most importantly to those suffering the greatest impact of environmental degradation – poor and marginalised groups (Janicke, 1997).

Focusing on environmental protection purely for the sake of the environment rather than to improve the human quality of life has hitherto been the predominant ideology of the traditional green or environmental movement. Scott (1990), Redgewell (1996) and Jacobs (1999), among others, suggest that such movements have been concerned with the preservation and conservation of the natural environment and the wilderness. While these movements are obviously shaped by the value given to nature by humans, their priority has been on the environment for the sake of the environment rather than for the sake of human beings. Humans are seen rather as a dominating force causing environmental destruction. The negative impact of human behaviour on the environment is well documented and, to this end, this specific part of the eco-centrists' position is generally not challenged. Much wider political discourse is based on the assumption of the eco-centrists that *all* human beings equally dominate the environment or create similar negative impacts.

Fox (1989) argues, however, that environmental protection needs to understand the social forms of domination within society based on class, 'race' or gender. Social ecologists or eco-sociologists follow Fox's proposition that social exclusion accounts for greater complexity than traditional 'Greens' allow and that the definition of their environment is hence too narrow. They suggest that any definition of the environment should include the concerns of people, such as the inequitable distribution of natural resources, environmental pollution, poverty or inner-city decay. Sustainable development, while recognising the intrinsic value of the environment, also supports a definition of environment broader than just fauna and flora, and is linked to poverty, environmental protection and human rights issues.

Environmental justice: equality and equity

The narrative of equality and justice within the context of environmental justice often refers to the equal or equitable share of the environment (built and natural) of all humans. It predominantly relates to the inequitable impact of environmental 'bads', such as pollution and dirty industries, on socially excluded communities. Environmental equality is thus closely related to discussions on 'ecological debt' or 'ecological footprints'. Each is concerned with who benefits from and who pays the cost for the environment and its degradation (McClaren, 2003).

These considerations are reflected in the sustainable development debate – sustainable development being development that gives equal consideration to social, economic and environmental concerns. Brundtland argues that sustainable development is based on the premise that environmental degradation is based on human activity, but more specifically the activities of the most affluent. Dealing with this inequitable impact is seen as crucial to increasing environmental standards, improving equitable shares of environmental resources, poverty alleviation and strengthening the democratic process.

There are a number of perspectives on how environmental and sustainable development issues are defined within a social justice paradigm. However, the common theme of environmental justice is constructed around the political and legal concepts of substantive civil and political rights. The main components of environmental justice are based most of all on the right of all to a fair environment, a substantive right embedded in natural law, and the right of all human beings to equal resources. The civil and political process then defines the paradigm of empowering participation, access to information and resources (social and political), allowing all human beings to make informed decisions on the environment at micro and macro levels, both between and within generations.

Generally, dialogue around environmental justice has been concerned with evidencing environmental injustice, that is, breaches of the proposed human right to the environment and barriers to environmental decision making. It is generally acknowledged that environmental injustice creates environmental 'bads' impacting disproportionately on marginalised, socially and economically excluded communities and groups. The task of the environmental justice movement, as seen for example in the US, has been to empower the disenfranchised and provide a good example of environmental equality. A detailed analysis of this movement, the actors and resources that created the mobilisation and participation of people, could be used as a model for the mobilisation and resourcing of peoples historically excluded from the UK environment debate.

The US experience centres on the question of environmental distribution and negative impact, building from the general definition of environmental justice as the right for any one group, in particular minority and low-income populations, not to suffer disproportionately high and adverse human health or environmental effects of their programmes, policies and activities. The US Environmental Protection Agency (EPA) environmental justice strategy seems to widen the notion of environmental justice beyond environmental impact to include concepts of environmental governance by the delivery of public-centred decision making. The movement began as part of the civil rights movement by US minority ethnic groups – black, indigenous and Hispanic community groups – culminating in a direct environmental equity movement in the 1980s and 1990s. The main premise of this movement is to achieve equitable distribution of environmental risks across 'racial' and social lines. It has strong support and involvement from the most vulnerable in American society, in particular among 'people of color'. This developed out of concerns, backed by research, that hazardous installations such as toxic waste dumps and polluting factories were mostly sited in areas where most of the population were poor and from minority ethnic groups. Minority neighbourhoods were demonstrably suffering disproportionately from the impacts of industrial and hazardous waste facilities. The movement's call for fair treatment implies that no person or group should shoulder a disproportionate share of the negative environmental impacts resulting from the execution of domestic and foreign policy programmes.

In 1992, as a direct response to calls for laws on environmental equity, the EPA created an Office of Environmental Justice. In February 1994, President Clinton signed Executive Order 12898, 'Federal Actions to Address Environmental Justice in Minority Populations and Low-Income Populations'. However, the complex tangle of political, social and economical issues that environmental justice throws up has meant that while US governments, through the EPA, are developing strategic policy, problems remain. A recent report looking at EJ over the past 10 years in the US by Agyeman and colleagues (2007) shows that black

Americans are still 79% more likely to live in neighbourhoods where industrial pollution is allegedly causing potential health dangers and that residents in these neighbourhoods are poorer, less educated and more often unemployed than those elsewhere. The report bases its discussion on the understanding that environmental justice means that regardless of race, income or culture everyone has the right to be purposefully involved in environmental decision making as it relates to enforcement of environmental laws, policy and development.

The issue of environmental equality and justice can, however, be seen in other global and national social justice agendas in Asia, Africa and Europe. This is illustrated by movements coalescing around access to natural resources and participation in decision making on environmental issues. In Europe there are a number of complex environmental challenges: urban pollution, poor water quality and the locating of hazardous waste sites in residential settlements for Roma in Greece, Hungary and Slovakia, for example (Adebowale and Schwarte, 2007). A perhaps better-known example of environmental justice is the demand for access to oil revenues in the Niger Delta from the Ogoni people. The state execution of Ken Saro-Wiwa, the Ogoni leader, who called for equal access and management of this oil, is a further example of the conflicts around distribution and the interplay between environmental governance and human rights.

Human rights and environmental governance

The use of a human rights approach has increasingly been rooted in the dialogue on environment and sustainable development. The reasoning behind this is the belief that the protection of human rights in relation, to life, health, culture and living standards has essential social, environmental and economic components. The right to life can not be realised without basic rights to clean water, air and land. Many argue that a human rights approach allows the quality of life of people, in particular the most vulnerable, to be a central part of environmental decision making. Simply put, it allows human needs to be included in the quest to protect fauna and flora.

The two main approaches to human rights and the environment involve (a) the use of existing human rights and (b) the need for new human rights to a safe and clean environment. The rights we have already, building on T. H. Marshall and later typologies (see Introduction), are (1) civil and political and (2) economic, social and cultural. The former provide for moral and political order and include the right to life, equality, political participation and association. They are articulated most clearly in the Universal Declaration of Human Rights (1948) and the International Covenant on Civil and Political Rights (1966). When realised, civil and political rights are fundamental to guaranteeing a political order supportive of sustainable development and can protect civil mobilisation around environmental protection and equity.

Economic, social and cultural rights also provide substantive standards for an individual's well-being. The 1966 International Covenant provides one such example stipulating, among others, the right to health, hence recognising the need for environmental improvement. It also provides for self-determination, including the right of all peoples to manage their own natural resources. These so-called 'second generation rights' often have a direct bearing on the human and environmental condition: 'Environmental governance is the exercise of authority over natural resources and the environment' (World Resources Institute, 2003).

Issues around decision making present a good governance perspective on environmental justice. For example, (good) environmental governance is concerned with the distribution of power over decision-making processes in relation to those having the political, economic and administrative authority on environmental issues. This is closely related to the issue of environmental rights and environmental distribution because sharing of power is fundamental to the realisation of human rights and as a balance to the present unequal share of, and to, the environment. Essentially, environmental governance deals with the operation of civil and political rights to realise individual political and civil expression. As such, environmental decision making is central to people's quality of life, particularly aiming at the inclusion of the most vulnerable, excluded by economic or social factors from most forms of decision making. The question of who governs is important because it relates to the development of tools for improving environmental decision-making processes in the UK. The World Resources Institute (2003) report argues that environmental protection and human rights are essentially exercised through good governance, crucial to the 'environmental empowerment of the public'.

Reconciling different perspectives

While there are tensions within and between environmental justice perspectives it is safe to say that the nexus between social and environmental justice includes all of the following:

- a human right to a healthy and safe environment and the responsibility to maintain it;
- a fair share of natural resources and the right not to suffer disproportionately from environmental policies, regulations or laws;
- a civil right to be able to access environmental information and participate in decision making; and
- that the most vulnerable in society should not disproportionately suffer the negative effects of environmental omissions, actions, policy or law.

Which of these is the main focus ultimately depends on the specific issue on which discussion is concentrated but the holistic definition of environmental justice aims to protect basic rights, solve the unequal distribution of environmental 'bads' and provide processes of good governance. Essentially it requires a moving away from the traditional environmental movement's predominant ideology founded on what Dobson (2003) calls the dichotomy of 'environmentalism and ecologism', to a dialogue equally focused on distribution, equality and social justice.

UK perspectives, developments and policy

Environmental justice in the UK: understanding the national perspective

This global perspective on environmental justice provides a framework for analysing environmental justice in the UK. We can provide a brief synthesis around three principal questions. To what extent does the UK recognise environmental justice? Is there a mobilised force of excluded communities around environmental justice? Does UK policy recognise or support an environmental justice agenda?

We shall narrow down the focus of environmental justice to its application to social policy. We do not contend, however, that there is a parallel policy discourse on environmental justice in the context of a human right to a clean and healthy environment and the use of legal systems to protect access to participation and decision making. The Aarhus Convention is a case in point. This Convention, to which the UK government is a signatory, recognises substantive environmental rights in its preamble: '... every person has the right to live in an environment adequate to his or her health and well-being' (Aarhus Convention).

The UK government has to ensure that national legislation is in keeping with the Convention before ratification (which has been persistently postponed). Relevant laws include the Freedom of Information Act and the Directive on Freedom of Access to Environmental Information. Legal challenges have been made against the government under the Convention, for example, as to whether the cost of taking an environmental case to court is prohibitive and therefore not in keeping with the Convention.

Although some policy makers have sought to redefine environmental justice in the UK as having a narrow focus on environmental regulation and enforcement, the overall view is that environmental justice within the sustainable development agenda has far wider social and economic implications.

Environment and social exclusion

> Globally and within the UK, deprived and excluded communities are affected disproportionately by degraded natural resources and their associated risks. (DEFRA, 2005, p 111)

Research and statistics on poverty and social inclusion illustrate that social exclusion and poverty are growing again in the UK (Christie and Warburton, 2001; Palmer et al, 2007), despite the commitment to reducing poverty, social and economic exclusion made by New Labour on taking power in 1997. Creating social inclusion is about constructing processes that recognise economically and socially marginalised groups and bringing them back into mainstream society; the key agency tasked with this role was the Social Exclusion Unit (SEU), established in 1997. The aim of the SEU was to investigate the causes of economic and social exclusion and make recommendations on how it could be remedied. However, the SEU's findings did not seek to find links to environmental issues, despite the fact that a number of its policy papers on transport and neighbourhood renewal, for example, had direct links to environmental issues. The SEU, when asking people living in the 44 most deprived areas in the UK about the things that concerned them, identified air pollution, transport and the appearance of the environment such as litter and graffiti (SEU, 1998). Almost 10 years after this report, a Joseph Rowntree Foundation report suggested that despite the government's rhetorical commitment to social justice, there remain fundamental social and environmental injustices impacting on the poorest (JRF, 2005). Its findings suggested that the poverty gap was increasing and confirmed earlier findings that poor neighbourhoods were likely to receive lower-quality environmental services.

There are a number of reasons why robust policies to tackle environmental justice have not been developed. The first is perhaps the historical culture and political standpoint of the UK environmental movement. This has traditionally dealt with environmental degradation by encouraging conservation, penalising polluters and attempting to change the public pattern of behaviour. The social concerns relating to the unequal impacts of human behaviour identified by eco-sociologists, have rarely been tackled until recently. Mainstream campaigns and environmental programmes by non-governmental organisations (NGOs) have tended to concentrate on ideological debates, such as environmental protection versus economic development. People most affected by the consequences of environmental decision making were not only alienated from an increasingly narrow debate but were insufficiently protected by environmental or economic policy.

However, findings from research on social exclusion and environmental issues support the suggestion that excluded communities are concerned about environmental issues (Burningham and Thrush, 2001; Lucas et al, 2001). The former found that low-income households were concerned about environmental issues and that environmental improvements could enhance the quality of life of disadvantaged people. The authors concluded that, nevertheless, policies were pursued in isolation from their social and economic considerations and certain policies exacerbated existing hardships. Examples included the disproportionate effect of increases in energy and fuel prices, conflict between rural conservation and the need for affordable housing, and the desire to maintain industrial employment while minimising pollution.

Debates around social and economic exclusion and their link to the environment have, however, gathered momentum. Academics, NGOs, community groups, non-departmental public bodies and politicians have begun a dialogue on the links between environment and social exclusion and their integration into a UK environmental justice agenda. The principal concerns taken from this cross-sectoral agenda are the:

- inequitable distribution of environmental 'bads' and goods;
- quality of the built environment such as transport, public space, litter and standard of housing;
- development of a law and policy that facilitates environmental justice through civil and judicial procedures; and

- promotion of the development of resources required for environmental citizenship – access to information, participation and decision making.

Evidence from a number of sources provides strong evidence that in the UK environmental impacts are income-related (see Box 12.1).

Box 12.1: Evidence for the relationship between income and environmental impact

- People living in the most deprived areas have major concerns about pollution, poor public transport and the appearance of their estate.
- Research suggest that families living on incomes of less than £5,000 are twice as likely to live next to a polluting factory than families with incomes of £60,000 or more.
- Pollution is a major factor in poor health and health inequalities, creating or causing cumulative illnesses.
- Child pedestrians from poorer communities are five times more likely to be killed by vehicles than children from the most affluent areas.
- The poorest are disproportionately more likely to spend more than 10% of their income on heating (Scottish Executive, 2002).
- Half of all carcinogenic emissions occur in the 20% most deprived wards, compared to just 9% in the 20% least deprived wards (Environment Agency, 2003).
- River quality is worse in the most deprived areas in England, where up to 50% of watercourses are extensively modified, providing less natural habitat for wildlife (Environment Agency, 2002).
- People of African, Indian, Pakistani or Bangladeshi descent are four times more likely to live in the poorest neighbourhoods in England and much more likely than white people to live in low-income households (National Statistics Online, 2003).

There is little doubt that environmental injustices occur in the UK and there is a clear need for proactive, reflective and robust policy that tackles these issues. However, as in the US and other countries that are facilitating environmental justice policy, there are a number of tensions centring around two key problems:

- The UK is still trying to define what environmental justice means within its own historical, cultural and political context. The lack of adequate research, the continuing ineffective response to racism (see Chapter Eleven) and the unequal distribution of environmental goods and 'bads', despite the government's apparent commitment to social justice, means that environmental justice continues to be overlooked in New Labour's policies. Funding responses to recent floods provide a strong example of this; in wealthy Oxfordshire, the cost of meeting flood damage from Council Tax after government aid was around £6 per household, but in highly deprived Hull, the figure was £1,500 per household.

• The environmental sector is still relatively conservative in its approach to social justice issues. Many environmental NGOs remain rooted in traditional perspectives towards environmental issues, concentrating on traditional fauna and flora conservation. Unfortunately, few community or social sector NGOs recognise, let alone campaign or work on, environmental justice. As a result there is a lack of the kind of leadership or strategic partnership that buoyed environmental justice policy agendas in countries such as the US or South Africa.

Environment, 'race' and community cohesion

The tensions are most clearly illustrated in the UK when considering the lack of integration between environmental and race equality policies. This is not because there are not any connections but rather because the potential connections challenge current implicit notions that social justice can be tackled without significant redistribution of environmental, social and economic resources.

The debate around environmental justice in the UK does not centre on environmental racism, as in the US. Anecdotally, it appears that there is a lack of evidence to support the case for environmental racism in the UK and the absence of sustained debate within black, Asian or minority ethnic communities. There is, however, research that would suggest links between 'race' and environmental inequality. For example, findings from the former Department of the Environment Transport and the Regions suggested that Asian children were more likely to be injured in road accidents (DETR, 2001). The University of Staffordshire also found links between ethnicity and environmental risk exposure. Reminiscent of similar US research, this found a statistically significant bias towards sites being located in wards with a higher proportion of minority ethnic groups (Walker et al, 2001). In addition, transport and health research on the impact on black, Asian or minority ethnic communities find that environmental degradation is an important and disproportionate driver of social exclusion. Brainard and colleagues (2001) and Walker and colleagues (2001) both suggest that 'race' is a factor in the exposure to environmental hazards and health risks. Brainard et al's investigation into the emission levels of carbon monoxide and nitrogen dioxide in the city of Birmingham found that modelled emissions and poverty indicators and race had a strong relationship (Brainard et al, 2001). These biases are also suggested in Walker et al's (2001) research, which suggested a bias in sites on ethnic grounds in relation to the major accident hazard sites and their location. In both studies, researchers state two main caveats in the use of their findings. The first caveat is the preliminary nature of the research and the need to find possibly more appropriate methodology. The second is the lack of a historical context as to the location of hazardous sites and the migration of black communities to those sites.

In general, research findings in the UK do not appear to illustrate direct discrimination as understood by the definition of environmental racism in Chavis (1991). What the evidence to date may suggest is certainly a case of indirect discrimination. That is to say, there may be policy, acts or omissions, which although they do not directly seek to discriminate, nonetheless have the effect of excluding individuals or groups. Overall, however, there seems to be little research that specifically poses questions around ethnicity or 'race' and environmental impacts and the development of evidence-based policy in this area is slow.

Causes for the rarity of environmental research that focuses on issues of 'race' might lie somewhere in the wider polemics of the discourse on 'race' in the UK in general. Gilroy and the Centre for Contemporary Cultural Studies (1982) note a number of tensions within contemporary Britain around the discussion on 'race', suggesting that the discourse on 'race' creates 'racial sensibility'. It is possible that these sensibilities prevent specific research questions and policy development on 'race' and the environment being raised. The result of this could be that ethnicity is made less visible as a valid research area and is subsumed into the wider topic of social exclusion and environment; it is certainly true that ethnicity remains marginal to most social and economic policy development (Craig, 2007).

There are, however, some developments in the area of race relations and social cohesion that may facilitate changes in the way 'race' and environment are discussed in the UK. The (former) Commission for Racial Equality (CRE)[2] began to give an increased focus on the issues of regeneration and housing, which are likely to raise environmental concerns around regeneration and infrastructure. It argued that regeneration programmes, the new neighbourhood renewal schemes and Local Strategic Partnerships (LSPs) are 'important tools in tackling disadvantage and promoting integrated communities' (CRE, 2007, p 6). As such they may have a major impact on minority ethnic groups (CRE, 2007). Concerns have been raised about the ability of the newly created Equality and Human Rights Commission (EHRC) to focus as strongly on the earlier 'race' agendas. Despite this, it is possible that the EHRC may remain committed to the tackling inequality issues uncovered in the CRE's formal investigation into regeneration schemes and the improvement of the physical environment in England, Scotland and Wales under the Race Equality Duty (CRE, 2007). One of this report's conclusions was of the importance of the regeneration of the physical environment and regeneration to racial equality and community cohesion. However, mirroring Gilroy's conclusions of racial sensibility, the report was limited by the lack of adequate data fully to assess the effects of regeneration programmes on race equality and race relations. One potential lever for developing evidence-based policy, however, is the 2000 Race Relations Amendment Act (RRAA), placing a duty on local authorities to promote race equality and to produce a Race Equality Scheme. The report also notes that the production of a council's local development framework has to be the subject of an equality impact assessment to assist the production of action plans, and this should embed race equality into all physical planning decision making. The RRAA also has the potential to create a powerful tool not only for the collation of data previously found lacking but also as a campaign tool by NGOs and community groups seeking to ensure that the duty in the RRAA is made effective and used to eliminate unlawful discrimination and promote equality opportunities in public bodies.

While race equality policy and legislation are potentially powerful tools to tackle environmental justice, their use is limited as they were not established to deal with complex issues of discrimination in relation, for example, to class, economic or social deprivation (Adebowale and Schwarte, 2007). It remains the case that relevant research is limited at present to illustrating the unequal environmental impacts of policy on low-income communities, often regardless of 'race'.

Recent developments suggest that there may be some political will to develop a more holistic approach. For example, there is a memorandum of agreement between the Department of Environment and Rural Affairs (DEFRA) and the Department of Communities and Local Government (DCLG) to work synergistically on environmental justice. There are also a number of partnership agreements and initiatives being developed by some NGOs. Currently, however, the policy response to environmental justice is not tackled strategically across government departments. This said, policy agendas on sustainable development, sustainable communities, regeneration and climate change may turn out to be key drivers for the implementation of robust environmental and social justice policy.

Policy frameworks for environmental and social justice

The sustainable development strategy

Since the government's 1999 strategy, some tentative steps have been made towards integrating the social justice agenda through a new set of indicators and a stronger commitment to a people-centred policy approach. The strategy states that:

> [S]ustainable development must enable people to enjoy a better quality of life, now and in the future. In the words of the Rio Declaration, 'human beings are at the centre of concerns for sustainable development. They are entitled to a healthy and productive life in harmony with nature.' (DETR, 1999)

However, the government's 2005 strategy, *Securing the future* (DEFRA, 2005), makes a specific policy commitment to tackling environmental inequalities. It notes that in the UK, environmental degradation is real for many deprived communities due to historical legacy and the ineffective ways agencies and communities identify key priorities and work together on them.

Environmental justice appears here to be intrinsically linked to the UK's social justice agenda of improving the quality of life of everyone, specifically the most vulnerable. Potentially equally significant is the commitment made by government requiring that minimum standards for a decent and healthy environment are set by adopting and enforcing regulatory frameworks and national policy. It should be noted however, that the strategy does not give any clear steer on how it will tackle the thorny issue of distribution in relation to environmental 'bads' and goods. Indeed, it avoids any radical commitments such as the equal distribution of polluting factories within both poor and wealthy communities. It does, however, commit to a diversity action plan but it is not made clear how that will shape policy over and above improving access to the countryside. Nonetheless, access to green spaces and two further commitments have also provided some indication of evidence-based policy in three main areas:

- access to the natural environment;[3]
- promoting ways in which to help communities improve their environment; and
- safer, greener and clean regeneration and sustainable communities.

The last of these perhaps provides the most scope for environmental justice policy as it also acts as a cornerstone for the first two policy arenas.

Regeneration and sustainable communities

Roberts (2001) states that regeneration in the UK is the connection between the physical condition and the social and political response to it. In practice this has meant that regeneration is concerned with the themes of social improvement, economic growth, housing and health. The evolution of regeneration also shows an environmental approach, which has moved from preservation and conservation to wider concerns about social and environmental synergies. Jacobs and Dutton (2001) comment that the regeneration of urban and rural areas has been an essential tool for tackling social inclusion and the development of the built environment. A number of regeneration schemes have been concerned with the empowerment of communities to take up ownership of programmes and projects.

Neighbourhood renewal was a policy response to the SEU's concern about social exclusion and regeneration issues. The Unit's *National strategy for neighbourhood renewal* (SEU, 1998) set out how the gap between wealthy and poorer neighbourhoods could be reduced. One objective of the strategy was to set up the Neighbourhood Renewal Unit (NRU) whose remit would be to carry out the delivery of the strategy in the 88 most deprived neighbourhoods in England. This was to improve economic prosperity, education standards, health and housing (Lucas et al, 2003). Similarly, Scotland and Wales set up departments or programmes incorporating social justice and renewal strategies. These programmes were all intended to deal with the improvement of environmental standards in areas where the UK's poorest people live, including improvements not only to the built environment but also around access to green or open space.

In Scotland, the Scottish Executive's social justice agenda had social inclusion and regeneration as one central principle. The social justice agenda is to build strong communities and provide equal opportunities and chances to all, most specifically excluded communities and groups. It had a number of targets to close the opportunity gap between the poor and the wealthy. Part of this process was specifically to tackle environmental injustices in Scotland.

To this end the Executive stated that it was tackling environmental injustice primarily in four ways:

- improving air quality in certain urban areas to reduce asthma;
- reducing cardiovascular disease;
- reducing reliance on landfill for waste disposal, many of which are sited near disadvantaged areas; and
- tackling fuel poverty, which impacts disproportionately on the poor, specifically older people.

In England, the former Office of the Deputy Prime Minster's report *Living spaces: Cleaner, greener, safer* (ODPM, 2002), recognised the relationship between environmental equality, social exclusion and economic decline. It noted that while the government is working in these areas the complexity of the relationships needs to be better understood, suggesting that more can be done to understand the relationships and to advocate solutions that are practical.

One such practical solution was to commit the NRU to more work in this area to inform the future work of government departments, local authorities and agencies. The ODPM noted that tackling the specific problems of the poorest communities was a key action point. This included better coordination and resources into these areas and the production of a social and environmental exclusion review with its own set of actions. These commitments to improving public space and neighbourhood environments have been inherited by the DCLG. The environmental justice agenda links closely with the DCLG's remit to support and develop sustainable communities. In addition, the DCLG and DEFRA recognise that the negative impacts of climate change are likely to worsen the already disproportionate environmental and health problems of the poor, despite the fact that they are least likely to have contributed to negative climate change. While NRU research (ODPM, 2002) found that not all deprived areas suffer from a poor-quality environment, and that some affluent areas do suffer from environmental injustice, for example poorer air quality, the DCLG's vision for providing communities with safe, healthy and sustainable environments suggests that they should be a key agency in driving policy that ensures that deprived communities and individuals are protected. There are a number actions that to date may support the DCLG and other policy makers in developing a robust and holistic environmental justice policy framework. For example, the Environment Agency's work in mapping the 50 poorest environments also provides a key research base for developing a more targeted approach and for highlighting where resources within the Agency, across government and within the non-governmental sector may be distributed. Local Strategic Partnerships and Local Area Agreements also provide an opportunity for embedding environmental justice action plans at a local level. Equally important is the challenge of climate change, which requires change in public behaviour and policies that will support this. DEFRA's support of the programme 'Every Action Counts' illustrates the need for action at a community level and at a strategic level within NGOs with social inclusion and/or environmental protection agendas. Capacity Global, a key NGO working to support vulnerable communities on environmental justice issues in the UK, suggests that a policy framework applicable to a sustainable development agenda needs to incorporate participatory rights and processes of community participation (see Box 12.2).

Box 12.2: A sustainable development policy agenda

Access to information

- Create information exchanges between, from and to vulnerable communities on the issues of concern; ensure it is in a format that is best understood by the particular group, for example visual images, gender or 'race'-specific formats.
- Create dialogue forums in which vulnerable communities feel confident to speak and be heard.
- Assess regularly, with vulnerable groups, specific impacts of environmental degradation and environmental management systems in use.
- Develop and amend environmental management, local community plans, strategic partnerships and management processes in accordance with information and concerns from dialogue with vulnerable communities.

Access to participation and decision making

- Ask what might be acting as a barrier to participating in environmental management.
- Work with the community or group to find ways of tackling these barriers.

- Offer resources, travel, accommodation, tools, childcare and literacy classes where possible.
- Provide user-friendly management methods – and ask if they are user-friendly!
- Allow for self-management based on a framework agreed to by the group or community.

Access to justice
- Work with groups or communities to tackle decisions or omissions that create or have the potential to create environmental injustice.
- Provide access to legal and scientific resources.
- Campaign to stop discriminatory practice or behaviour.

Essentially, Capacity Global suggests that while policy drivers are required at a government level, these must be informed by the communities and individuals most likely to be impacted by environmental inequalities. This will provide a crucial foundation for effective policy that supports participatory practice.

Conclusion

The predominant ideology of the environmental debate has been concerned with the preservation and conservation of the natural environment or wilderness. As poverty reduction is linked to environmental protection and vice versa the integrated relationship between society and environment has become increasingly important in order to represent 'environment' beyond the constructs of biological ecosystems. Alarming patterns of environmental degradation are linked globally to multiple deprivation and there is an accepted and growing evidence base for recognising and developing environmental justice in the UK and elsewhere, building on earlier experience in the US.

The sustainable development perspective facilitates the move from a traditional environmental perspective of nature conservation to a modern environmental perspective concerned with the negative impacts on the poorest and historically socially excluded groups. The usefulness of this perspective lies in its ability to foreground the social perspective on the environment, how it is defined, studied and acknowledged specifically in relation to human rights, 'race' and regeneration. However, while there is an emerging evidence base for delivering environmental justice policy there is as yet no strategic approach to deliver this policy across government or within major NGOs in the UK. The key reasons for this are, in summary, as follows:

- the failure of the environmental movement until recently to address social justice and equality issues;
- the scarcity of well-resourced and politicised black *environmental* organisations;[4]
- the domination of the civil and political element of environmental justice over environmental equality;
- a common perception of community concern as focusing only on specific social and economic issues;
- a continuing resistance to action from government hidden behind demands for further scientific authority and validation of claims;
- little or low media attention; and
- a lack of leadership or sponsorship to underpin the vision and legitimacy of the environmental justice approach.

Despite this, there are now a number of policy frameworks recognised as giving an important basis for integrating environmental justice into social justice policy. These include environmental law enforcement, a focus on sustainable communities, and the demands of 'race' equality and community cohesion. A truly comprehensive and robust policy that can in practice deal with environmental injustices will require an understanding of the tensions existing within a policy area, which requires the equal distribution of environmental 'bads' and goods.

Notes

[1] The author would like to thank her colleague Philip, and Gary Craig for help in completing this chapter.

[2] In October 2007 the CRE merged with the Equal Opportunities Commission and the Disability Rights Commission into the Equality and Human Rights Commission.

[3] The Diversity Review conducted by the former Countryside Agency (which has since merged with English Nature to form Natural England) provides an important evidence base on barriers to the countryside for black and minority ethnic groups.

[4] A recent national consultation by DEFRA on its relationship with the Third Sector identified only one black environmental group among hundreds of consultees.

References

Adebowale, M. and Schwarte, P. (2007) *Environmental justice and race equality in the European Union*, London: Capacity Global.

Adebowale, M., Church, C. and Shepard, P. (2004) *Environmental justice in London: Linking the equalities and environmental policy agenda*, London: London Sustainability Exchange.

Agyeman, J., Bullard, R. and Evans, B. (eds) (2003) *Just sustainabilities: Development in an unequal world*, London: Earthscan.

Anderson, M. (1996) 'Human rights approaches to environmental protection an overview', in A. E. Boyle and M. Anderson (eds) (1996) *Human rights approaches to environmental protection*, Oxford: Clarendon Press.

Brainard, J.S., Jones, A.P., Bateman, I.J., Lovett, A.A. and Fallon, P.J. (2002) 'Modelling environmental equity: access to air quality in Birmingham, UK', *Environment and Planning A*, vol 34, pp 695-716

Brundtland, G.H. (1987) *Our common future: World Commission on Environment and Development*, Oxford: Oxford University Press.

Bullard, R., Mohai, P., Saha, R. and Wright, B. (eds) (2007) *Toxic wastes and race at twenty: 1987-2007*, Cleveland, OH: United Church of Christ (www.ucc.org/assets/pdfs/toxic20.pdf).

Burningham, K. and Thrush, D. (2001) *Rainforests are a long way from here*, York: Joseph Rowntree Foundation.

Cameron, J. and McKenzie, R. (1996) 'Access to environmental justice and procedural rights in international institutions', in A. E. Boyle and M. Anderson (eds) *Human rights approaches to environmental protection*, Oxford: Clarendon Press.

Chavis, B. (1991) *The historical significance and challenges of the First National People of Color Environmental Leadership Summit*, Proceedings of the First National People of Color Environmental Leadership Summit, Washington DC: United Church of Christ Commission for Racial Equality.

Christie, I. (2001) 'Mapping the "values agenda"', Presentation for The Environment Foundation, 31 May-1 June.

Christie, I. (2001) Joining up economy and empowerment via social dimensions,

Christie, I. and Warburton, D. (2001) *From here to sustainability: Politics in the real world*, London: Earthscan.

Craig, G. (2007) 'Cunning, unprincipled, loathsome: the racist tail wags the welfare dog', *Journal of Social Policy*, vol 36, no 4, pp 339-56.

CRE (Commission for Racial Equality) (2007) *Regeneration and the Race Equality Duty*, London: CRE.

DEFRA (Department of Environment, Food and Rural Affairs) (1999) 'Guiding principles and approaches', in *A better quality of life: Strategy for sustainable development for the United Kingdom*, Cm 4345, London: The Stationery Office (www.sustainable-development.gov. uk/publications/uk-strategy99/04.htm).

DEFRA (2005) *Securing the future: Delivering UK sustainable development strategy*, Cm 6467, London: DEFRA.

DETR (Department of the Environment Transport and the Regions) (2001) 'Asian kids at risk on the roads', *News Release 196*, 30 March, London: DETR.

Dobson, A (2003) 'Social justice and environmental sustainability: ne'er the twain shall meet', in J. Agyeman, R. Bullard and B. Evans (eds) *Just sustainabilities: Development in an unequal world*, London: Earthscan.

Environment Agency (2002) *The urban environment in England and Wales: A detailed assessment*, Bristol: Environment Agency.

Environment Agency (2003) 'Environmental equality and socially excluded groups', Unpublished, The Environment Agency, Bristol.

ESRC (Economic and Social Research Council) (2001) *'Environmental justice – rights and means to a healthy environment for all'*, ESRC Global Change Programme, Special Briefing No. 7, Swindon: ESRC.

Fox, W. (1989) 'The deep ecology–ecofeminism debate and its parallels', *Environmental Ethics*, vol 11, pp 2-25.

Gilroy, P. and Centre for Contemporary Cultural Studies (1982) *The empire strikes back: Race and racism in 70s Britain*, London: Routledge.

Habermas, J. (1998) *The inclusion of the other: Studies in political theory*, Cambridge, MA: MIT Press.

Jacobs, B. and Dutton, C. (2001) 'Social and community issues', in P. Roberts and H. Sykes (eds) *Urban regeneration: A handbook*, London: Sage Publications.

Jacobs, M (1999) *Environmental modernisation: The New Labour agenda*, London: Fabian Society.

Janicke, M. (1997) 'The political system's capacity of environmental policy', in M. Janicke and H. Weidener (eds) *National environmental policies: A comparative study of capacity building*, Stuttgart: Springer Verlag.

JRF (Joseph Rowntree Foundation) (2005) *Environmental problems and service provision in deprived and more affluent neighbourhoods*, York: JRF.

Lucas, K., Grosvenor, T. and Simpson, R. (2001) *Transport, the environment and social exclusion*, York: York Publishing Services for JRF.

Lucas, K., Ross, A. and Fuller, S. (2003) *What's in a name?: Local Agenda 21, community planning and neighbourhood renewal*, York: JRF.

McClaren, D (2003) 'Environmental space and ecological debt', in J. Agyeman, R. Bullard and B. Evans (eds) *Just sustainabilities: Development in an unequal world*, London: Earthscan.

Mason, M. (1999) *Environmental democracy*, London: Earthscan.

National Statistics Online (2003) www.ons.gov.uk

ODPM (Office of the Deputy Prime Minister) (2002) *Living spaces: Cleaner, greener, safer*, London: ODPM.

Palmer, G., MacInnes, T. and Kenway, P. (2007) *Monitoring poverty and social exclusion*, London: New Policy Institute/JRF.

Redgewell, C. (1996) 'Life, the universe and everything: a critique of anthropogenic rights', in A. E. Boyle and M. Anderson (eds) *Human rights approaches to environmental protection*, Oxford: Clarendon Press.

Roberts, P. (2001) 'The Evolution, definition and purpose of urban regeneration', in P. Roberts and H. Sykes (eds) *Urban regeneration: A handbook*, London: Sage Publications.

Sands, P. (1997) *Principles of international environmental law*, Manchester: Manchester University Press.

Scott, A. (1990) *Ideology and the new social movements*, London: Unwin Hyman.

Scottish Executive (2002) *Social justice: A Scotland where everyone matters*, Edinburgh: Scottish Executive.

SEU (Social Exclusion Unit) (1998) *Bringing Britain together: A national strategy for neighbourhood renewal*, Cm 4045, London: SEU.

Walker, G., Fairburn, F. and Bickerstaff, K. (2001) *Ethnicity and risk: The characteristics of populations in census wards containing major accident hazards in England and Wales*, Occasional Papers, Series A: Geographical Research, Stoke on Trent: Department of Geography Stoke on Trent, University of Staffordshire.

World Resources Institute (2003) *World resources report: Decisions for the earth*, Washington, DC: World Resources Institute.

Index

Page references for notes are followed by n